GIANTS

THE GLOBAL POWER ELITE

PETER PHILLIPS

Introduction by
William I. Robinson

SEVEN STORIES PRESS
New York • Oakland • London

Copyright © 2018 by Peter Phillips

A SEVEN STORIES PRESS FIRST EDITION

All rights reserved. No part of this book may be reproduced, stored in a retrieval system, or transmitted in any form or by any means, including mechanical, electronic, photocopying, recording, or otherwise, without the prior written permission of the publisher.

Seven Stories Press
140 Watts Street
New York, NY 10013
sevenstories.com

College professors and high school and middle school teachers may order free examination copies of Seven Stories Press titles. To order, visit www.sevenstories.com or send a fax on school letterhead to (212) 226-1411.

Library of Congress Cataloging in Publication

Names: Phillips, Peter, 1947- author.
Title: Giants : the global power elite / Peter Phillips.
Description: New York : Seven Stories Press, [2018]
Identifiers: LCCN 2018017493| ISBN 9781609808716 (pbk.) | ISBN 9781609808723
  (ebook)
Subjects: LCSH: Wealth--Political aspects. | Elite (Social sciences) |
  Capitalism--Political aspects.
Classification: LCC HC79.W4 .P495 2018 | DDC 330.92/2--dc23
LC record available at https://lccn.loc.gov/2018017493

Printed in the USA.

9 8 7 6 5 4 3 2 1

"In this important book, Peter Phillips has advanced progressive thinking about power in several ways. He has expanded sociologist C. Wright Mills's model of social structure from the national power elite to the Transnational Capitalist Class. He identifies key power holders within that class, thus highlighting an ethic of individual as well as institutional accountability. And he does so within a consistent human rights framework that is much required in today's political climate. *Giants: The Global Power Elite* is a crucial map for desperately needed social change."
—ROBERT HACKETT, professor, School of Communication, Simon Fraser University

"The unabated global concentration of capital and deepening inequality is putting humanity on the brink of extinction. The financial behemoths running this oppressive and violent economic order have largely operated in the shadows, but Peter Phillips names the names in his latest work. *Giants* answers, in great detail, the commonly asked but rarely answered question: Who really pulls the strings? This book outlines the handful of individuals who manage the most powerful think tanks, investment firms, and corporate boards, and who make society's decisions at the expense of the planet. **Giants is an essential tool to understand those at the reins of empire and capitalist hegemony, so we can be empowered to fight for our survival.**"
—ABBY MARTIN, host of the investigative news program *The Empire Files*

"Following decades of research on power elites, Peter Phillips's book *Giants* exposes the power networks that link the world's wealthiest individuals and organizations and the ideological justifications that sustain their power. Impeccable original research provides the foundation for an impassioned call to action that reflects Phillips's abiding commitments to social justice and human rights. **This book is essential reading for anyone who wants to understand socioeconomic inequality in the twenty-first century, and it is vital inspiration for those committed to creating a better world.**"
—ANDY LEE ROTH, associate director of Project Censored

"Peter Phillips challenges us to re-evaluate the role of powerful financial interests in shaping American life. More than a discussion about an abstract elite, *Giants* enumerates key players by names, interests, and roles. Valuable material for people who like critical thinking."
—LOAN K. LE, PHD, president and CEO of the Institute for Good Government and Inclusion (IGGI)

"**This book is a fearless exposé of the ascendancy of a class of global elites and the power they wield around the world. Brilliantly argued and meticulously documented. . . .** Phillips writes with compassion and humanity, and also tells us that unveiling mechanisms of power is a necessary first step in reshaping a global economic system to address the current crises of democracy, equality, and environmental destruction."
—ROBIN ANDERSEN, professor of communication and media studies, Fordham University

"*Giants: The Global Power Elite* is an admirably accessible outing of the global oligarchy. The graphics work well and the writing is very clear and engaging. Peter Phillips has collected an awesome range of data and presents it really well. I salute his efforts here and hope the book finds many readers."
—WILLIAM CARROLL, professor of sociology, University of Victoria

"Dr. Phillips does an incredible job of detailing the seventeen global financial giants that carry most of the power and control in our world, those that contribute to many of the social problems we are struggling with worldwide, but that often remain hidden from accountability. **As a radical sociologist whose work is reminiscent of the great C. Wright Mills, Dr. Phillips names these giants and gives the reader a useful primer for social activism. He details how these groups stay protected by private security firms and the ways in which media spin keeps them looking clean. Speaking truth to power, Dr. Phillips ends his work with an open letter to these global giants, which I proudly signed, inviting them to reimagine a more just society.**"
—SUSAN RAHMAN, PHD

"***Giants: The Global Power Elite* is a must-read for anyone concerned with how the concentration of wealth in the hands of a small number of global political elites affects the well-being of humanity and the ultimate sustainability of life on earth.** In the best tradition of political sociology, with a strong, data-driven analysis, Peter Phillips demonstrates that a small Global Power Elite has 'rigged' a global economy to serve its own interests at the expense of the well-being—even the longevity—of humankind."
—anthropologist DONNA BRASSET, PHD

"The global elite, with their associated armies and police forces, are, at an accelerating rate, destroying the planet based on their bottom line. . . . Indeed, the planet, our children, and our grandchildren are facing a very bleak future if these titans of global control continue to have their way. Their policies have already carried us to the brink. *Giants: The Global Power Elite* is a field guide to what these greedy destroyers are up to in the name of profit and global control of planetary resources. Read it and weep, and then act to resist it however you can. As Joe Hill said: 'Don't mourn, organize!'"
—DENNIS J. BERNSTEIN, executive producer of the radio news program *Flashpoints*

"If you want to know who is actually ruling the world—read this book. If you want to know the organizations they use and the networks that create them—read this book. If you want to know 'what needs to be done' to stop them from destroying the planet—read this book and then take action."
—DAVID COBB, 2004 Green Party presidential nominee, co-founder of Cooperation Humboldt

DEDICATION

Mary M. Lia

Thank you, loving wife, for twenty years of caring,
friendship, and support.

CONTENTS

PREFACE

Giants: The Global Power Elite follows in the tradition of C. Wright Mills's 1956 book, *The Power Elite*. Like Mills, we seek to raise awareness of power networks affecting our lives and the state of society. Mills described the power elite as those "who decide whatever is decided" of major consequence. Sixty-two years later, power elites have globalized and built institutions that facilitate the preservation and protection of capital investments everywhere in the world.

Central to the idea of a globalized power elite is the concept of a Transnational Capitalist Class, theorized in academic literature for some twenty years. Chapter 1 of this book reviews the transition from the nation state power elites described by Mills to a transnational power elite centralized on the control of global capital around the world. The Global Power Elite function as a nongovernmental network of similarly educated wealthy people with common interests of managing, facilitating, and protecting concentrated global wealth and insuring the continued growth of capital. Global Power Elites influence and use international institutions controlled by governmental authorities—namely, the World Bank, International Monetary Fund (IMF), NATO, World Trade Organization (WTO), G7, G20, and many others. These world governmental institutions receive instructions and recommendations for policy determinations from networks of nongovernmental Global Power Elite organizations and associations.

Our effort is to identify the most important networks of the Global Power Elite and the individuals therein. We name some 389 individuals in this book as the core of the policy planning nongovernmental networks that manage, facilitate, and protect the continued concentration of global capital. The Global Power Elites are the activist core of the Transnational Capitalist Class—1 percent of the world's wealthy people—who serve the uniting function of providing ideological justifications for their shared interests and establishing the parameters of needed actions for implementation by transnational governmental organizations.

This concentration of protected wealth leads to a crisis of humanity, whereby poverty, war, starvation, mass alienation, media propaganda, and environmental devastation are reaching a species-level threat. We realize that humankind is in danger of possible extinction and recognize that the Global Power Elites are probably the only ones capable of correcting this condition without major civil unrest, war, and chaos. This book is an effort to bring awareness of the importance of systemic change and redistribution of wealth, to readers as well as to the Global Power Elites themselves, in the hope that they can begin the process of saving humanity.

We also think that democratic, nonviolent social movements of resistance and non-cooperation that use the Universal Declaration of Human Rights as a moral code can accelerate the process of redistribution of wealth, pressuring the Global Power Elite into actions they are not yet comfortable taking.

In Chapter 2, we identify the seventeen global financial Giants, those money management firms controlling more than one trillion dollars in capital. These Giants collectively manage more than $41.1 trillion in a self-invested network of interlocking capital that spans the globe. The Giants in turn invest not only in each other, but in many hundreds of investment management firms, many of which are near-Giants, resulting in tens of trillions of dollars coordinated in a single vast network of global capital controlled by a very small number of people. Their constant objective is to find enough safe investment opportunities for a return on capital that allows for continued growth. Inadequate capital-placement opportunities lead to dangerous speculative investments, buying up of public assets, and permanent war spending.

We identify the 199 directors of the global financial Giants by name, with short biographies and public information on their individual net wealth. Information on these Global Power Elite managers of the Giants forms the essential part of Chapter 3. The biographies give us a sense of the common interests and backgrounds these 199 people reflect. We also go into greater biographical depth on three of the most important managers of the global Giants.

These 199 managers of global capital are closely interconnected through numerous networks of association, which include the World Economic Forum, the International Monetary Conference, university affiliations, various policy councils, social clubs, and cultural enterprises. It is certainly safe to conclude they all know each other personally or know of each other in the shared context of their positions of power.

In Chapter 4, we examine the membership of two very important nongovernmental Global Elite policy-planning organizations. Both are nonprofit corporations, with research and support staff who set instructions and policies for implementation by transnational governmental institutions like the

G7, G20, IMF, WTO, and World Bank. The 32 members of the Group of Thirty and the 55 people on the extended executive committee of the Trilateral Commission comprise a central group of 85 (two overlap) facilitators of global capitalism. These individuals work to insure that global capital remains safe, secure, and growing.

Wealth concentrated traditionally requires a system of laws and police power to protect itself. This is certainly true for the global concentration of capital. In Chapter 5, we examine the power of the US/NATO military empire. This transnational military police state operates in nearly every country in the world, and threatens nations that do not fully cooperate with global capital with covert activities, regime change, and heavy negative propaganda. We also examine how the global Giants invest in war making as a method of using surplus capital for a guaranteed return, with an increasing use of private military/security companies for protection of Global Power Elites and their wealth.

The Global Power Elite are well aware of their existence as a very small wealthy 1 percent minority in a vast sea of impoverished humanity. The Atlantic Council, for example, serves as a nonprofit, nongovernmental policymaking group to protect the security of concentrated wealth, a goal often described as part of our national "vital interests." We identify the 35 key Global Power Elite individuals on the executive committee of the Atlantic Council. These people are the essential protectors of concentrated global capital. The Pentagon, NATO, and intelligence agencies pay close attention to their recommendations and research reports.

Networks of power and concentrated capital require continued ideological justification. In Chapter 6 we examine the degree of investment by the Giants in corporate media and the expanding use of public relations propaganda companies in the news systems of the world. The six major global media organizations offer a continuing ideological justification for corporate capitalism and diminish or censor information that questions the ongoing concentration of wealth and increasing inequality. We have a media system that seeks to control all aspects of human thinking and promotes continued consumption and compliance. The dominant ideological message from corporate media today is that the continued growth of the economy will offer trickle-down benefits to all humans and save the planet.

Chapter 7 is a summary and what-needs-to-be-done statement that emphasizes the continuing crisis of humanity and the need for corrective action in the near future. Activists involved with social movements challenging the juggernaut of concentrated wealth should be aware that their continued actions are vital to the survival of humankind. Pressure must be maintained for the Global Power Elite to take measures that protect not only themselves but all of humanity. We must turn the trickle-down into a river of resources that reaches every human being on the planet. Recognizing the importance of the Universal Declaration of Human Rights will be vital in this process.

The postscript of this book is a letter to the Global Power Elite asking them to consider future generations when making decisions regarding global capital, and urging them to take corrective action before more serious and inevitable unrest and environmental devastation take effect.

Peter M. Phillips
Professor of Political Sociology
Sonoma State University

WHO RULES THE WORLD?

We are living through times of dire global crisis. Social polarization worldwide has reached unprecedented levels. The figures compiled by the international development agency Oxfam are now well known: the richest 1 percent of humanity in 2017 controlled more than half of the world's wealth; the top 30 percent of the population controlled more than 95 percent of global wealth, while the remaining 70 percent of the population had to make do with less than 5 percent of the world's resources. In January 2018, shortly after US president Donald Trump boasted that his hand was on a "bigger nuclear button" than that of North Korea, the Bulletin of Atomic Scientists pushed the doomsday clock forward to just two minutes to midnight. In that same month, the *Economist* (Jan. 27) ran a cover story warning of "the growing threat of great-power conflict." Climate change and ecological degradation around the world are wreaking havoc. In California, where I live, prolonged drought induced by climate change[1] unleashed wildfires in 2017 that left several hundred dead or injured, only to be followed in early 2018 by flash floods and mudslides that took several dozen more lives and forced the university where I teach to shut down for several weeks. If we do not annihilate ourselves in a nuclear holocaust or descend into the barbarism of a global police state, we will have to confront the threat of a human-induced sixth mass extinction that scientists say has already begun.

The obscene inequalities of global capitalism are not sustainable. They are fueling right-wing populist insurgencies and neo-fascist movements among the downwardly mobile sectors of the global working and middle classes, incited by demagogic politicians who promise to halt the decline and restore some semblance of stability, often through racist and nativist appeals, as the rise of Trumpism in the United States so well illustrates. The relationship between rising inequality, social conflict, and political crises has long been demonstrated in the sociological literature. As inequality escalates and wealth concentrates among an ever-smaller portion of the world's population, demand contracts and the global market cannot absorb the output of the global economy. The Transnational Capitalist Class, or TCC, cannot find outlets to profitably reinvest the trillions of dollars that it has accumulated. In recent years it has turned to wild financial speculation in the global casino, raiding and sacking of public budgets, war making, and the extension of systems of social control and repression to sustain accumulation and contain the real or potential rebellion of the poor and the marginalized.

It is clear that humanity's survival depends now more than ever on the radical reform, if not the outright overthrow, of the system of global capitalism. Systems based on coercive domination are unstable. Yet there is simply no basis for consensual rule under the current conditions of global capitalism. The most urgent political question of our time is how to bring about a worldwide redistribution of wealth and power, restoring resources for the poor majority, to offset the explosive—indeed, suicidal—contradictions of the system. If we are to achieve such a redistribution, we must gain an understanding of the global power structure. This is the task that Professor Phillips has set out to accomplish in the present study. And accomplish it he does! Using the tools of social science research and documentation, he identifies the vast networks of transnational corporate power that shape the lives of everyone on our planet. This timely and critically important study gives us an answer to the question, "Who rules the world?"

In the finest tradition of power elite studies first introduced by C. Wright Mills in his classic 1956 book, *The Power Elite*, Professor Phillips exposes an inner core of 389 individuals drawn from the upper echelons of the Transnational Capitalist Class who stand at the very apex of this global power structure. An earlier generation of power elite studies focused on the corporate and political networks that rule at the national level. But this earlier generation of studies has become outdated in the wake of capitalist globalization. What once were national capitalist classes have developed through the transnational integration of their capital into a transnational capitalist class. In *Giants: The Global Power Elite*, Professor Phillips builds on a spate of recent studies that show how globalization has resulted in the transnational interpenetration of national power networks. We see a cementing now at the global level of political and economic power in this transnational elite through an unprecedented concentration of financial capital and through the political influence that this economic control wields over states as well as intergovernmental and transnational state institutions.

I have been studying global capitalism for three decades and researching the TCC for the past twenty years. I was nonetheless shocked to learn in reading this study both the extent to which global economic power is concentrated in a tiny financial elite and the magnitude of that power. A stunningly small group exercises control over the fate of humanity. In short, seventeen global financial conglomerates collectively manage $41.1 trillion "in a self-invested network of interlocking capital that spans the globe." Moreover, these seventeen are cross-invested in each other to such an extent that it appears as simply a mass of interlocking global financial capital. The figure of $41 trillion is actually misleadingly low because, as the study shows, it does not include the value of capital stock that these conglomerates hold in all branches of the global corporate structure. This amalgamated mass of transnational finance capital is deeply invested in media, industry, commerce, and the global military–industrial complex.

The Global Power Elite works out policies to advance their interests with regard to the management and protection of global capital and the enforcement of debt collection worldwide in such private policymaking forums as the World Economic Forum, Trilateral Commission, Group of 30, Atlantic Council, and Bilderberg Group, and in such transnational state institutions as the World Bank, International Monetary Fund, G20, and Bank for International Settlements. At the same time they are strategically placed to then impose these policies through their members' positions within individual states and transnational state institutions. Simply put, the enormous concentrations of economic power translate into enormous influence over global policymaking. This relationship of economic (class) power to state power is one in which the TCC issues commands to government officials. As one member of the global elite, whom Professor Phillips cites, put it, these officials are "pilots flying our airplane." In Professor Phillips's words, the Global Power Elite "doesn't produce recommendations, but rather instructions which they expect to be followed."

The study before the reader does not pretend to show us *how* we can confront the Global Power Elite—to force it to change course, if not overthrow it outright. This is not a political manifesto. For much of the twentieth century, mass struggles of the working and popular classes, the colonized, racially oppressed, and the poor, forced on the system a redistribution of wealth that offset the polarization inherent in capitalism. Elites responded to the upsurge from below by launching a counter-offensive in the latter decades of the twentieth century that came to be known as neoliberal globalization. By going global, capitalists were able to break free of the constraints to unbridled profit-making and wealth accumulation at the nation-state level. The result was the unprecedented concentration of wealth among the TCC. But Professor Phillips also alludes to the upsurge of resistance struggles and social change movements that are contesting the Global Power Elite and their decadent system. Indeed, if a global police state is emerging as itself a profit-making enterprise, its paramount political purpose is to suppress the global revolt. As this revolt advances, it needs to understand the global power structure it is up against. This study makes an indispensable contribution to that understanding.

There is growing concern among reformist elements of the transnational elite that unchecked inequality threatens the stability of global capitalism and that there must be some sort of redistribution. These elites have been scrambling to find ways to reform the system in order to save capitalism from itself and to undercut more radical challenges from below. On the one hand, the crisis of global capitalism and the increasing concern among the reformist elements of the transnational elite are leading to sharp divisions within the global ruling bloc. On the other hand, the widening splits in the bloc and the urgency of reform open up new possibilities for those from below struggling for more far-reaching change to seek strategic political alliances. History has shown us that the major reforms of capitalism have come at times of acute crisis, when the ruling groups are divided, and when there are powerful mass social movements from below. The major reform movements—for instance, of the 1930s and the 1960s—came out of militant mass struggles placing demands on the state and elites for radical change. The major reforms of capitalism came less from enlightened elites than from mass struggles from below that forced elites to reform. In my view, the best way to achieve a reform of capitalism is through struggle against it.

William I. Robinson
Professor of Sociology
University of California, Santa Barbara

CHAPTER 1

TRANSNATIONAL CAPITALIST CLASS POWER ELITE
A SEVENTY-YEAR HISTORY[2]

TRANSNATIONAL RULING ELITES

Oxfam International reported in January 2016 that 62 people hold as much wealth as half the world, and one year later Oxfam reported that half the world's wealth was now owned by only eight men.[3] Wealth concentration is happening so rapidly that it is feasible that someday soon one man will hold more wealth than half the humans in the world. The top six billionaires in 2017, with their country of citizenship and estimated net worth, were Bill Gates (US, $88.8 billion), Amancio Ortega (Spain, $84.6 billion), Jeff Bezos (US, $82.2 billion), Warren Buffett (US, $76.2 billion), Mark Zuckerberg (US, $56 billion), and Carlos Slim Helú (Mexico, $54.5 billion). *Forbes*'s billionaire list contained 2,047 names in 2017.[4] These global capitalist elites are fully aware of these vast inequalities and their rapidly growing concentration of wealth. The billionaires are similar to colonial plantation owners. They know they are a small minority with vast resources and power, yet they must continually worry about the unruly, exploited masses rising in rebellion. In an effort to promote greater democracy and equality, this book is an attempt to explain how these vast wealth differences continue to grow and what mechanisms of power protect and maintain these giants of capitalism. How can it be that the US Congress has recently passed a massive tax reduction for the richest elites in the country, giving them added billions of concentrated wealth? Understanding how power and inequality is sustained can perhaps offer us opportunities to fight for and win democracy and equality in today's world.

A long tradition of sociological research documents the existence of a dominant ruling class in the United States. These elites set policy and determine national political priorities. The American ruling class is complex and competitive. It perpetuates itself through interacting families of high social standing with similar lifestyles, corporate affiliations, and memberships in elite social clubs and private schools.[5]

The American ruling class has long been determined to be mostly self-perpetuating,[6] maintaining its influence through policymaking institutions such as the National Association of Manufacturers, US Chamber of Commerce, Business Council, Business Roundtable, Conference Board, American Enterprise Institute for Public Policy Research, Council on Foreign Relations, and other business-centered policy groups.[7] These associations have long dominated policy decisions within the US government.

In his 1956 book *The Power Elite*, C. Wright Mills documented how World War II solidified a trinity of power in the United States that comprised corporate, military, and government elites in a centralized power structure motivated by class interests and working in unison through "higher circles" of contact and agreement. Mills described how the power elite were those "who decide whatever is decided" of major consequence.[8] These higher-circle decision makers tended to be more concerned with inter-organizational relationships and the functioning of the economy as a whole rather than just advancing their particular corporate interests.[9] Mills is careful to observe that the conception of a power elite does not rest solely on personal friendship, but rather relies on a broader ideology of shared corporate system goals.[10]

The higher-circle policy elites as a segment of the American upper class are the principal decision makers in society. Although these elites display some sense of "we-ness," they also tend to have continuing disagreements on specific policies and necessary actions in various sociopolitical circumstances.[11] These disagreements can block aggressive reactionary responses to social movements and civil unrest, as in the case of the labor movement in the 1930s and the civil rights movement in the 1960s. During these two periods, the more liberal elements of policy elites tended to dominate the decision-making process and supported passing the National Labor Relations and Social Security Acts in 1935, as well as the Civil Rights and Economic Opportunity Acts in 1964. These pieces of national legislation were seen as concessions to the ongoing social movements and civil unrest, and were implemented instead of instituting more repressive policies.[12]

In the past few decades, and especially since the events of 9/11, the policy elites in the United States have been mostly united in support of an American empire of military power that maintains a repressive war against resisting groups—typically labeled "terrorists"—around the world. This war on terror is really much more about protecting transnational globalization, the worldwide free flow of financial capital, dollar hegemony, and access to oil, than it is about repressing terrorism. The United States has a long history of interventions around the globe for the purpose of protecting our "national interests." Increasingly, the North Atlantic Treaty Organization (NATO) is a partner with the US global dominance agenda, reflecting the broadening transnational economic nature of our national interests.

THE TRANSNATIONAL CAPITALIST CLASS

Capitalist power elites exist around the world. The globalization of trade and capital brings the world's elites into increasingly interconnected relationships—to the point that scholars, over the past few decades, have begun to theorize the development of a Transnational Capitalist Class (TCC).

In one of the early works on the TCC, *The Transnational Capitalist Class* (2000), author Leslie Sklair argued that globalization has elevated transnational corporations to more influential international roles, with the result that nation-states became less significant than international agreements developed through the World Trade Organization (WTO) and other international institutions.[13] Emerging from these multinational corporations is a transnational capitalist class, whose loyalties and interests, while still rooted in their corporations, are increasingly international in scope.

Sklair writes that "a new class is emerging that pursues people and resources all over the world in its insatiable desire for private profit and eternal accumulation. This new class is the Transnational Capitalist Class (TCC), composed of corporate executives, globalizing bureaucrats and politicians, globalizing professionals and consumerist elites." Sklair further discusses how the TCC is the emerging control mechanism of globalization, and that the TCC is showing class-like solidarity in its actions. This united class action reproduces itself through a shared belief that continued growth through profit-driven consumerism will by itself eventually solve global poverty, mass inequality, and environmental collapse.[14]

William I. Robinson followed in 2004 with his book *A Theory of Global Capitalism: Production, Class, and State in a Transnational World*.[15] Robinson claimed that five hundred years of capitalism had led to a global epochal shift in which all human activity is transformed into capital. In this view, the world had become a single market, which privatized social relationships. Robinson saw the TCC as increasingly sharing similar lifestyles, patterns of higher education, and consumption. The global circulation of capital is at the core of an international bourgeoisie, who operate in oligopolistic clusters around the world. These clusters of elites form strategic transnational alliances through mergers and acquisitions with the goal of increased concentration of wealth and capital. The process creates a polyarchy of hegemonic elites.

The concentration of wealth and power at this level tends to over-accumulate in the hands of increasingly fewer elites to the point where capital has limited safe investment opportunities, leading to pressures for speculative/risky investments. The Global Power Elites of the TCC make efforts to correct and protect their interests through global organizations like the World Bank, World Trade Organization, International Monetary Fund, the G20, G7, World Economic Forum, Trilateral Commission, Bilderberg Group, Bank for International Settlements, and other transnational associations. Robinson claimed that, within this system, nation-states become little more than population containment zones, and the real power lies with the decision makers who control global capital.[16]

A more recent work on the TCC is William K. Carroll's *The Making of a Transnational Capitalist Class* (2010). Carroll's work focused on the consolidation of the transnational corporate-policy networks between 1996 and 2006. He used a database of the boards of directors of the five hundred largest global corporations, showing the concentrated interconnectedness of key corporations and a decreasing number of people involved. According to this analysis, the average number of members on corporate boards has dropped from 20.2 to 14.0 in the ten years of his study. Furthermore, financial organizations are increasingly the center of these networks. Carroll argued that the TCC at the centers of these networks benefit from extensive ties to each other, thus providing both the structural capacity and class-consciousness necessary for effective political solidarity.[17]

The Handbook of Transnational Governance (2011) lists 52 trans-governmental networks, arbitration bodies, multi-stakeholder initiatives (with internet cooperation), and voluntary regulation groups (fair labor/trade associations).[18] These TCC bodies, among the 52 cited, include the Basel Committee on Banking Supervision; the Financial Action Task Force, established in 1989 to address money laundering and terrorist financing; the Financial Stability Board, created in 1997 after the Asian financial crisis to provide financial ministers with a communications platform on an international level, conveying recommendations to the G7 and G20; the International Accounting Standards Board; and the International Association of Insurance Supervisors.

Deeper inside the Transnational Capitalist Class is what David Rothkopf calls the "superclass." In his 2008 book *Superclass: The Global Power Elite and the World They are Making*, Rothkopf argued that the superclass constitutes 6,000 to 7,000 people, or 0.0001 percent of the world's population.[19] They are the Davos-attending, Gulfstream/private jet–flying, megacorporation-interlocked, policy-building elites of the world—people at the absolute peak of the global power pyramid. They are 94 percent male, predominantly white, and mostly from North America and Europe. Rothkopf claims that these are the people setting the agendas at the G8, (now the G7 after the exclusion of Russia), G20, NATO, the World Bank, and the WTO. They are from the highest levels of finance capital, transnational corporations, the government, the military, the academy, nongovernmental organizations, spiritual leaders, and even shadow elites. (Shadow elites include, for instance, the deep politics of national security organizations in connection with international drug cartels, that extract 8,000 tons of opium from US war zones annually, then launder $500 billion through transnational banks, half of which are based in the United States.)[20]

The TCC/Global Power Elite represent the interests of several hundred thousand millionaires and billionaires who comprise the richest people in the top 1 percent of the world's wealth hierarchy. Ironically, this extreme accumulation of concentrated capital at the top creates a continuing problem for the global money managers, who must scour the world for new investment opportunities that will yield adequate returns on capital.

Rothkopf's definition of the superclass emphasizes its influence and power. The 2,043 world billionaires in 2017 collectively hold $7.67 trillion in wealth. Bill Gates remains the richest person in the world, with his fortune growing by $11 billion from 2016 to 2017 to a total of $88.8 billion.[21] Billionaires are part of the superclass, but not all billionaires are part of the Global Power Elite in terms of directly influencing global policies. However, almost all billionaires would agree that protecting their own wealth and its continued growth is a good idea for nation states, police forces, and policy makers to try to insure.[22]

The annual World Economic Forum meeting at Davos hosting personnel from the top one thousand global corporations has, since 1971, highlighted the continuing problem of global inequality and other major world issues. The January 2017 meeting promoted a report entitled "'It's too easy to insulate yourself'—Davos leaders reflect on social divides." The report declared that elites must not isolate themselves from the rest of the world. Philip Jennings of UNI Global Union stated that "if we want to create a society that works for all, everyone must have a seat at the decision-making table, in some capacity." Unique to the 2017 meeting was its inclusion of Xi Jinping, president of the People's Republic of China. Xi's message was that many of the problems in the world today are the result of economic globalization. A 2017 panel addressed the question "Is basic income for all just a dream?"

It is safe to say that overall the World Economic Forum continues as a celebration of wealth, globalization, and capitalism. Even while discussing world problems, the participants avoid really addressing specific solutions to global poverty and permanent war other than promoting continued economic growth.

Our view of the World Economic Forum is that it is similar to the annual summer encampment of the San Francisco Bohemian Club.[24] Both events host thousands of elites (exclusively men in the latter club) to hear selected keynotes/panels from famous, important individuals on the major socioeconomic topics of the day. Time for discussion and "meet and greet" is offered in both settings. However, neither event makes formal policy recommendations or sets specific agendas for global governance consideration. In this book, we are going to present information that shows how transnational elites interact as a class of people and function as managers of global capital. We identify 389 Global Power Elites as the key managers of concentrated capital, the facilitators of capital growth, and the system's protectors. These people are at the power elite core of the Transnational Capitalist Class. They generally know or know of each other—often personally—do business together, hold significant personal wealth, share similar educational and lifestyle backgrounds, and retain common global interests. Nearly all serve on the boards of directors of major capital investment firms or other major corporations and banks. They meet in nongovernmental policy organizations and form new ones as needs arise to privately make decisions for governments, security forces, and world institutions to implement. Transnational power elites hold a common ideological identity of being the engineers of global capitalism, with a firm belief that their way of life and continuing capital growth is best for all humankind.

CRISIS OF HUMANITY

We have University of California, Santa Barbara, sociologist William I. Robinson to thank for his book *Global Capitalism and the Crisis of Humanity* (2014), which helps frame this section of our introductory chapter.[25] Robinson claims that the world faces an unprecedented crisis of social inequality, environmental degradation, global violence, and economic destabilization. He says the world system has centralized and over-accumulated capital to the point that investment opportunities are limited and that there are only three mechanisms of investing excess capital: risky financial speculation, wars and war preparation, and the privatization of public institutions. The use of these mechanisms tends to result in a government legitimation problem, in which democratic structures are continually undermined and militarized police states are emerging around the world.

If national police/military are unable to effectively contain internal resistance movements in nations favorable to the TCC's capital interests, then selected international forces, from the United States, NATO, United Nations, or private military, will be brought in for control/support. These military interventions are ideologically justified as peacekeeping or humanitarian missions. However, if governments/regimes are viewed as unfavorable to the TCC's capital interests, then resistance forces will be supported and encouraged toward regime change, as in the cases of Libya, Syria, Iraq, Yemen, Somalia, Ukraine, Venezuela, and Yugoslavia. These interventions, both in support of regimes and against them, have terrible human consequences, including civilian casualities, increased starvation and disease, and massive numbers of displaced refugees.

The world's total wealth is estimated to be close to $255 trillion, with the United States and Europe holding approximately two thirds of that total; meanwhile, 80 percent of the world's people live on less than $10 per day, the poorest half of the global population lives on less than $2.50 per day, and more than 1.3 billion people live on only $1.25 per day.[26]

William I. Robinson writes about the trifurcation of humanity into the 1 percent, 20 percent, and 80 percent, whereby wealth continues to concentrate in the upper one fifth of humanity.[27] TCC elites take pride in pointing out that the world currently has the largest middle class ever.[28] However, that standard of living does not extend down into the vast majority of humanity, and it likely never will under global capitalism as it is organized in the world today.

The *Los Angeles Times* reports that "1 in 9 people go to bed hungry each night. This 1/9th is 795 million people on the planet who are suffering from chronic hunger, according to the United Nations World Food Program. The UN forecasts that an additional 2 billion people will be lacking food by 2050. In addition, 1 in 3 people suffer from some form of malnutrition, which means they lack sufficient vitamins and minerals in their diet, which can lead to health issues such as stunted growth in children. . . . Each year, poor nutrition kills 3.1 million children under the age of 5."[29] Twenty-five thousand per day, more than 9 million people per year, die from starvation and malnutrition.[30] This slaughter is occurring around the world every day. Starvation is mostly the result of people having too little money to purchase food for their families. These families lack the resources to acquire the nutrition needed to keep their children alive and healthy. Chronic hunger is mostly a problem of distribution, as one third of all food produced in the world is wasted and lost.[31]

So while millions suffer, the TCC financial elites focus on seeking returns on trillions of dollars, which can and does include speculation on the rising cost of food and land. They do this in cooperation with each other in a global capitalist system of TCC power and control that structurally entraps them in cycles of economic growth and contraction, with continuing mass humanitarian consequences.

Capital speculation includes global agricultural lands on

which indigenous farmers are replaced by power elite investors. In the last ten years, more than $90 billion has been invested in 78 countries for buying up more than 74 million acres of farmland. The result is mass corporate farming, usually for export, and the removal of these lands as a local food source.[32]

While many TCC elites are aware of global poverty, real solutions to hunger and death get lost to the continuing frantic rush for return on capital. Governmental systems for saving wasted food could significantly reduce hunger in the world. Perhaps an even more simple solution to hunger would be a 25 percent wealth tax on the world's 2,000 billionaires, which, if evenly distributed, would likely eliminate hunger in the world permanently.

War and war preparation is another area in which the TCC invests excess capital. Stockholm International Peace Research Institute reports world military spending at $1.69 trillion in 2016, or 2.2 percent of global GDP.[33] In 2016 the top military spenders (spending more than $10 billion each) were the United States ($611 billion), China ($215 billion), Russia ($69 billion), Saudi Arabia ($63 billion), India ($55 billion), France ($55 billion), the United Kingdom ($54 billion), Japan ($46 billion), Germany ($41 billion), South Korea ($36 billion), Italy ($28 billion), Australia ($24 billion), Brazil ($23 billion), Israel ($18 billion), Canada ($15 billion), Spain ($14 billion), United Arab Emirates ($14 billion), Turkey ($14 billion), Iran ($12 billion), Algeria ($10 billion), and Pakistan ($10 billion).[34] Still timely are Dwight Eisenhower's 1953 words, "Every gun that is made, every warship launched, every rocket fired signifies, in the final sense, a theft from those who hunger and are not fed, those who are cold and are not clothed."[35]

The post-9/11 wars continue to wreak havoc, chaos, and death in the Middle East, Africa, and other regions. More than

180,000 people died in world conflicts in 2014.[36] In 2017 more than 65.6 million people were displaced refugees fleeing war and famine.[37] These wars are not just the results of military adventurism and political conflicts, but are motivated both by propagandized ideological fears and the desire for profit on military capital investments. Lockheed Martin takes the leads in profitmaking from war, with sales of $36.4 billion in 2015.[38] The perpetual war on terrorism is good for business and TCC capital investment.[39] War becomes an institutionalized mechanism for continued TCC capital concentration and growth that brings above average returns with little risk.

For many the ultimate crisis of humanity, short of a global nuclear war, is environmental degradation. Religious scholar David Ray Griffin asks, in his book *Unprecedented*, can civilization survive the CO_2 crisis?[40] Since pre-industrial times the temperature has risen 1.4 degrees Fahrenheit, causing significant changes in the world's weather. Just one hundred companies have been the source of more than 70 percent of the world's greenhouse gas emissions since 1988.[41] There is at least a ten-year lag between CO_2 emissions and temperature changes. So even if CO_2 emissions are drastically cut now, we will continue to see rising temperatures for decades ahead.[42] These rising temperatures will lead to increasingly severe weather events: extreme storms, record-breaking heat and cold, floods, fires, tidal surges, high death rates, and financial losses.[43] We will see massive fresh water and food shortages.[44] These disruptions and shortages will lead to climate wars and civil unrest.[45] Indeed, diseases caused by pollution cause nine million premature deaths annually.[46] All of this will, in the near future, if left unchecked, result in ecosystem collapse and massive extinctions of life on earth, perhaps even including human extinction.[47]

Amazingly, TCC/Global Power Elite money managers study the transforming environment for new investment opportunities. Climate change investing can be profitable, according to *Forbes*, and getting in on low-carbon investments, and sectors that will benefit should climate stress increase—such as defense, health care, and property insurances—can prove lucrative.[48] Increasing interest in new mining opportunities available due to global warming is an important issue in Greenland.[49] Private investment in the control of water sources is seen as an increasingly attractive opportunity for power elite speculation.[50]

The Global Power Elite identified in this book are the world's central capitalist money managers. Each year they accumulate greater concentration of wealth and are embedded in an unrelenting quest for more. The most important concern for the TCC/power elite is protecting capital investment, insuring debt collection, and building opportunities for further returns. If protecting the environment is profitable, then green investments are acceptable. What remains unacceptable is the spending of money on people, the environment, and services that do not benefit capitalism. This lack of concern for human betterment, intended or not, is the core contradiction of the Transnational Capitalist Class and the true crisis of capitalism. Reversing this madness is the duty of all humanitarian-oriented people, which we believe can collectively and nonviolently be achieved in the near future.

We believe also that by naming the Global Power Elite and their systems of hegemony we can encourage enough of them to recognize their own humanitarian impulses, whereby they will collectively, in cooperation with civil societies, encourage an organized reshaping of our global economic system and face the reality of our environmental crisis.

CHAPTER 2

THE GLOBAL
FINANCIAL GIANTS
THE CENTRAL CORE OF
GLOBAL CAPITALISM[51]

In this chapter, we identify the world's top seventeen asset management firms. Each of these firms each has in excess of one trillion dollars of investment capital under management. The total capital under management by all seventeen companies is in excess of $41.1 trillion. These firms are the Giants of international capitalism. The wealth they manage comes from many thousands of millionaires, billionaires, and corporations, who allow asset management firms to invest their money in the market with the expectation of above-average returns on their capital.

These seventeen Giants of capitalism that collectively manage this concentration of more than $41.1 trillion in funds operate in nearly every country. They are the central institutions of the financial capital that powers the global economic system. Western governments and international policy bodies tend to work in the interests of these financial Giants to protect the free flow of capital investment and insure debt collection everywhere in the world.

A 2011 University of Zurich study completed by Stefania Vitali, James B. Glattfelder, and Stefano Battiston at the Swiss

Federal Institute of Technology, reported that a small group of companies—mainly banks and financial institutions—wields huge power over the global economy.[52] Applying mathematical models—usually used to model natural systems—to the top 43,060 transnational corporations in the world economy, the study found that 147 companies controlled some 40 percent of the world's wealth.[53] Fifteen of our seventeen top asset management companies are listed as the most superconnected firms in the world.

The Zurich study is very significant to our understanding of centralized transnational corporations. The study certainly supports the concept of a highly centralized structure of capital managed by an increasingly smaller number of institutions with vast power. This implies that the directors/managers of these Giants are an emerging power elite inside the Transnational Capitalist Class (TCC) with high levels of internal connections and interactive capabilities. The Zurich study's authors were careful in 2011 to not claim that a high concentration of wealth in the hands of a few top executives necessarily determines a structure of power. To properly understand the power of an emerging Global Power Elite, a sociological network analysis and qualitative interpretations of the key actors in this highly concentrated system is essential.

GIANTS: TOP ASSET MANAGEMENT FIRMS WITH MORE THAN $1 TRILLION IN EARLY 2017

Name	Country	Assets in Mgmnt (in Trillions)	Superconnected Global Rank (2010)
1. BlackRock*	US	$5.4	—
2. Vanguard Group	US	$4.4	8
3. JP Morgan Chase	US	$3.8	6
4. Allianz SE (PIMCO)	Germany/ US	$3.3	27
5. UBS	Switzerland	$2.8	9
6. Bank of America Merrill Lynch	US	$2.5	10
7. Barclays plc	Great Britain	$2.5	1
8. State Street Global Advisors	US	$2.4	5
9. Fidelity Investments (FMR)	US	$2.1	3
10. Bank of New York Mellon	US	$1.7	16
11. AXA Group	France	$1.5	4
12. Capital Group	US	$1.4	2
13. Goldman Sachs Group	US	$1.4	18
14. Credit Suisse	Switzerland	$1.3	14
15. Prudential Financial	US	$1.3	—
16. Morgan Stanley & Co.	US	$1.3	21
17. Amundi/Crédit Agricole	France	$1.1	24
TOTAL 17 Firms (199 Directors)		**$41.1**	

*Note: BlackRock acquired Barclay's Global Investors's assets management business in 2009. likely putting them into a current ranking of the most interconnected firms. In 2017 BlackRock increased assets under management by 22 percent to $6.29 trillion and reported a $1.2 billion tax benefit in the fourth quarter from Trump's tax cut package.[54]

We think that the world needs to know which companies comprise the core of global capitalism, and thus who makes the financial decisions regarding the use of the world's wealth. This is actually a fairly straightforward—labor-intensive—research effort: most of the information is not only publicly available but it is also online. We started with the top 50 most centralized companies from the previously cited 2011 Swiss study.[55] This identified the world's most centralized and interconnected corporations. We also wanted to consider those groups managing the largest volumes of financial capital, so we used as our core data set the top asset management firms with more than one trillion dollars in assets in 2017.[56]

Fifteen of the top seventeen asset management firms were among the top 27 most centralized firms identified in the Swiss study, and nine are among the top ten superconnected firms. In Chapter 3 we identify the 199 people on the boards of directors of these top seventeen asset management firms. Collectively, they manage more than $41.1 trillion in funds and operate in nearly every country in the world. This $41.1 trillion does not include the equity balances—which number in the billions of dollars—that each of these firms holds in company assets, nor the massive increases in assets resulting from the Trump tax cuts in 2017.

The top asset management firms tend to invest in each other, making this network a solid core of interlinked companies with shared investments worldwide. JPMorgan Chase and fourteen other trillion-dollar Giants are invested directly in BlackRock.[57] The seventeen Giants collectively invest $403.4 billion in each other. This interlocked capital is likely much higher than estimated here, more in the $1 trillion–2 trillion range, given that the Giants' NASDAQ data set of $9.8 trillion only gives us investment information on about 24 percent of the total $41.1 trillion. But these estimates are enough to clearly show that the Giants are significantly invested in each other. The result of this cross-investment is an interlocked global capital structure amassing greater and greater wealth to the continuing detriment of billions of people worldwide.

GLOBAL FINANCIAL GIANTS

Direct Capital Investments in Other Giants:
Total $403.4 Billion
2017[58]

JPMORGAN CHASE ($3.8 TRILLION UNDER MANAGEMENT)
NASDAQ DATA SET $439 BILLION
TOTAL $15.57 BILLION INVESTED IN OTHER GIANTS

Vanguard Group	$3.56 billion	BlackRock	$1.19 billion
State Street	$282 million	Bank of America	$5.2 billion
Bank of NY Mellon	$535 million	Morgan Stanley & Co.	$2.5 billion
Goldman Sachs Grp	$658 million	UBS	$618 million
Prudential Financial	$663 million	Barclays plc	$354 million

JPMorgan Chase top major holdings: S&P 500 Exchange Traded Funds (ETF) ($43.7 billion), Apple ($8.9 billion), Microsoft ($7.1 billion), United Health Group ($5 billion), Alphabet (Google) ($8.4 billion), Pfizer ($5 billion), Amazon ($4.1 billion), Facebook ($3.8 billion), Philip Morris ($1.7 billion), Berkshire Hathaway ($1 billion).

VANGUARD GROUP ($4.4 TRILLION UNDER MANAGEMENT)
NASDAQ DATA SET $2.2 TRILLION
TOTAL $72.1 BILLION INVESTED IN OTHER GIANTS

JPMorgan Chase	$26.9 billion	Bank of America	$19.2 billion
Goldman Sachs Grp	$6 billion	Morgan Stanley & Co.	$4.9 billion
BlackRock	$4.3 billion	Bank of NY Mellon	$3.7 billion
Prudential Financial	$3.5 billion	UBS	$1.5 billion
FMR	$2.1 billion		

Vanguard Group top major holdings: Apple ($58.5 billion), Microsoft ($46.3 billion), Alphabet (Google) ($42 billion), Amazon ($31 billion), Facebook ($28.4 billion), Johnson & Johnson ($28 billion), Berkshire Hathaway ($24 billion), Citigroup ($14.1 billion), Philip Morris ($11.8 billion)

BANK OF AMERICA MERRILL LYNCH
($2.5 TRILLION UNDER MANAGEMENT)
NASDAQ DATA SET $594 BILLION
TOTAL $70.14 BILLION INVESTED IN OTHER GIANTS

BlackRock	$2.7 billion	Vanguard Group	$55.6 billion
State Street	$264 million	FMR	$1.6 billion
JPMorgan Chase	$6.3 billion	Bank of NY Mellon	$301 million
Goldman Sachs Grp	$1.5 billion	Morgan Stanley & Co.	$869 million
UBS	$143 million	Allianz SE (PIMCO)	$153 million
Prudential Financial	$518 million	Credit Suisse	$123 million

Bank of America Merrill Lynch top major holdings: S&P 500 ETF ($35.5 billion), Ishares (Global ETF) ($47.7+ billion), Apple ($7.1 billion), Philip Morris ($3.1 billion), Alphabet ($6 billion), Facebook ($3.5 billion)

BLACKROCK ($5.4 TRILLION UNDER MANAGEMENT)
NASDAQ DATA SET $2.04 TRILLION
TOTAL $66.1 BILLION INVESTED IN OTHER GIANTS

JPMorgan Chase	$24.4 billion	Bank of America	$19.3 billion
Goldman Sachs Grp	$6 billion	Morgan Stanley & Co.	$5.5 billion
Prudential Financial	$3.7 billion	Bank of NY Mellon	$3.1 billion
State Street	$2 billion	FMR	$2 billion

BlackRock top major holdings: Apple ($53.24 billion), Microsoft ($40.1 billion), Ishares ($40.1 billion), Amazon ($27.4 billion), Facebook ($24.1 billion), Berkshire Hathaway ($20.2 billion), Alphabet ($37.4 billion), Citigroup ($14.5 billion), Philip Morris ($9.7 billion)

PRUDENTIAL FINANCIAL
(1.3 TRILLION UNDER MANAGEMENT)
NASDAQ DATA SET $72 BILLION
PRUDENTIAL PLC NASDAQ DATA SET $32 BILLION
TOTAL $4.1 BILLION INVESTED IN OTHER GIANTS

BlackRock	$87 million	Goldman Sachs Grp	$315 million
Vanguard Group	$113 million	State Street	$94 million
JPMorgan Chase	$1 billion	Bank of NY Mellon	$259 million
Bank of America	$1.14 billion	Morgan Stanley & Co.	$915 million
UBS	$166 million	FMR	$28 million

Prudential Financial top major holdings: Apple ($2.4 billion), Microsoft ($2.3 billion), Alphabet ($2 billion), Amazon ($810 million), Berkshire Hathaway ($735 million), S&P 500 ETF ($500 million), Ishares ($930 million), Philip Morris ($267 million)

GOLDMAN SACHS GROUP
($1.4 TRILLION UNDER MANAGEMENT)
NASDAQ DATA SET $321 BILLION
TOTAL $9.4 BILLION INVESTED IN OTHER GIANTS

BlackRock	$362 million	Vanguard Group	$2.8 billion
State Street	$191 billion	FMR	$237 million
Bank of America	$2.1 billion	Bank of NY Mellon	$297 million
Morgan Stanley & Co.	$447 million	JPMorgan Chase	$2.4 billion
UBS	$236 million	Prudential Financial	$398 million

Goldman Sachs Group top major holdings: S&P 500 ETF ($11.5 billion), Ishares ($11.8 billion), Apple ($5.2 billion), Amazon ($4.1 billion), Microsoft ($3.4 billion), Alphabet ($4.1 billion), Berkshire Hathaway ($1.4 billion), Philip Morris ($768 million)

UBS ($2.8 TRILLION UNDER MANAGEMENT)
NASDAQ DATA SET $170 BILLION
TOTAL $16.17 BILLION INVESTED IN OTHER GIANTS

Vanguard Group	$12.3 billion	JPMorgan Chase	$1.39 billion
Allianz SE (PIMCO)	$179 million	Goldman Sachs Grp	$210 million
Bank of America	$656 million	Morgan Stanley & Co.	$145 million
Barclays plc	$192 million (Ishares)	BlackRock	$1.05 billion

UBS top major holdings: S&P 500 ETF ($9.5 billion), Apple ($2.4 billion), Microsoft ($2.4 billion), Ishares ($19 billion), Alphabet ($2.42 billion), Facebook ($1.3 billion), Philip Morris ($317 million)

CREDIT SUISSE ($1.3 TRILLION UNDER MANAGEMENT)
NASDAQ DATA SET $79.9 BILLION
TOTAL $2.89 BILLION INVESTED IN OTHER GIANTS

Bank of America	$415 million	Morgan Stanley & Co.	$124 million
FMR	$80 million	UBS	$1.6 billion
Goldman Sachs Grp	$197 million	Bank of NY Mellon	$72 million
State Street	$53 million	Prudential Financial	$87 million
BlackRock	$97 million	Allianz SE (PIMCO)	$72 million
Vanguard Group	$123 million		

Credit Suisse top major holdings: United Health Group ($2.2 billion), Apple ($1.7 billion), Microsoft ($1.2 billion), Amazon ($870 million), Facebook ($732 million), Alphabet ($1.38 billion), S&P 500 ETF ($458 million), Ishares ($1.9 billion), Berkshire Hathaway ($456 million), Philip Morris ($305 million)

BARCLAYS PLC ($2.5 TRILLION UNDER MANAGEMENT)
NASDAQ DATA SET $43 BILLION
TOTAL $883 MILLION INVESTED IN OTHER GIANTS

JPMorgan Chase	$231 million	Bank of America	$230 million
Goldman Sachs Grp	$167 million	Vanguard Group	$83 million
Morgan Stanley & Co.	$51 million	Prudential Financial	$44 million
State Street	$43 million	BlackRock	$34 million

Barclays top major holdings: S&P 500 ETF ($1.3 billion), Apple ($779 million), Amazon ($771 million), Ishares ($1.3 billion), Facebook ($415 million), Microsoft ($391 million), Alphabet ($532 million), Berkshire Hathaway ($318 million), Philip Morris ($197 million). Barclays, once the most centralized corporation in the world, sold their global asset management division to BlackRock in 2009. Barclays Capital remains in the top ten asset management firms, having acquired the core business of Lehman Brothers in 2008.

MORGAN STANLEY & CO.

($1.3 TRILLION UNDER MANAGEMENT)

NASDAQ DATA SET $344 BILLION

TOTAL $23 BILLION INVESTED IN OTHER GIANTS

JPMorgan Chase	$3.6 billion	Bank of America	$1.7 billion
Vanguard Group	$14.6 billion	Goldman Sachs Grp	$843 million
BlackRock	$824 million	Allianz SE (PIMCO)	$416 million
Prudential	$412 million	Bank of NY Mellon	$101 million

Morgan Stanley & Co. top major holdings: S&P 500 ETF ($10 billion), Ishares ($21.2 billion), Apple ($6 billion), Microsoft ($5 billion), Amazon ($4.9 billion), Facebook ($4.3 billion), Alphabet ($5.1 billion), Berkshire Hathaway ($2.5 billion), Philip Morris ($1.8 billion)

STATE STREET GLOBAL ADVISORS

($2.4 TRILLION UNDER MANAGEMENT)

NASDAQ DATA SET $1.2 TRILLION

STATE STREET CORPORATE

NASDAQ DATA SET $32 BILLION

TOTAL $59.7 BILLION INVESTED IN OTHER GIANTS

JPMorgan Chase	$17.9 billion	Bank of America	$12.8 billion
Morgan Stanley & Co.	$8 billion	Goldman Sachs Grp	$5.8 billion
BlackRock	$4.7 billion	Bank of NY Mellon	$3 billion
Prudential Financial	$2.3 billion	FMR	$1.2 billion
Vanguard Group	$2.4 billion	Capital Group	$706 million
UBS	$170 million	Amundi	$67 million
Credit Suisse	$53 million	Barclays plc	$43 million
Crédit Agricole	$48 million		

State Street Global Advisors top major holdings: Apple ($35 billion), Microsoft ($24.4 billion), Johnson & Johnson ($21.5 billion), Amazon ($17.8 billion), Facebook ($15.4 billion), Alphabet ($23.2 billion), Citigroup ($93 billion), Philip Morris ($6 billion), Ishares ($748 million)

AXA GROUP ($1.5 TRILLION UNDER MANAGEMENT)
NASDAQ DATA SET $23.5 BILLION
$867 MILLION INVESTED IN OTHER GIANTS

State Street	$13 million	JPMorgan Chase	$113 million
Vanguard Group	$358 million	Prudential Financial	$15 million
BlackRock	$46 million	Goldman Sachs Group	$26 million
Morgan Stanley & Co.	$22 million	Bank of NY Mellon	$44 million
UBS	$122 million	Bank of America	$108 million

AXA Group top major holdings: Apple ($610 million), Microsoft ($310 million), Amazon ($275 million), Alphabet ($510 million), Facebook ($210 million), Citigroup ($78 million), Ishares ($739 million), Philip Morris ($51 million), S&P 500 ETF ($11.9 million)

BANK OF NY MELLON
($1.7 TRILLION UNDER MANAGEMENT)
NASDAQ DATA SET $378 BILLION
TOTAL $11 BILLION INVESTED IN OTHER GIANTS

JPMorgan Chase	$4 billion	Bank of America	$2.8 billion
Goldman Sachs Grp	$907 million	BlackRock	$635 million
Prudential Financial	$601 million	Morgan Stanley & Co.	$583 million
State Street	$422 million	FMR	$252 million
Vanguard Group	$672 million	UBS	$176 million

Bank of NY Mellon top major holdings: Microsoft ($9.1 billion), Apple ($8.9 billion), Johnson & Johnson ($5 billion), Amazon ($4.5 billion), Facebook ($4 billion), Alphabet ($7.6 billion), Citigroup ($3.5 billion), Berkshire Hathaway ($3.6 billion), Philip Morris ($1.8 billion), Ishares ($3.4 billion)

FIDELITY INVESTMENTS (FMR)
($2.1 TRILLION UNDER MANAGEMENT)
NASDAQ DATA SET $855 BILLION
TOTAL $29.1 BILLION INVESTED IN OTHER GIANTS

JPMorgan Chase	$9.6 billion	Bank of America	$9.2 billion
Goldman Sachs Grp	$1.9 billion	Morgan Stanley & Co.	$1.96 billion
State Street	$1.65 billion	BlackRock	$1.68 billion
Vanguard Group	$1.96 billion	UBS	$596 million
Allianz SE (PIMCO)	$402 million	Prudential Financial	$201 million

Fidelity Investments (FMR) top major holdings: Apple ($24 billion), Facebook ($22 billion), Amazon ($37 billion), Alphabet ($31 billion), Microsoft ($41 billion), Berkshire Hathaway ($11.2 billion), Citigroup ($8.3 billion), Ishares ($15.8 billion), Philip Morris ($2.2 billion)

CAPITAL GROUP ($1.4 TRILLION UNDER MANAGEMENT)
CAPITAL GROUP NASDAQ DATA SET $354 BILLION
CAPITAL WORLD GROUP NASDAQ DATA SET $467 BILLION
CAPITAL INTERNATIONAL INVESTORS $87 BILLION
TOTAL $18.5 BILLION INVESTED IN OTHER GIANTS

JPMorgan Chase	$5.2 billion	Prudential Financial	$1.59 billion
UBS	$1.55 billion	Goldman Sachs Grp	$3.7 billion
State Street	$635 million	Bank of America	$1.083 billion
BlackRock	$3.4 billion	Bank of NY Mellon	$1.3 billion

Capital Group top major holdings: Amazon ($12.5 billion), Microsoft ($9 billion), Verizon ($6.2 billion), Philip Morris ($5.4 billion), Alphabet ($13.3 billion), Apple ($11.8 billion), United Health Care ($5.4 billion), Berkshire Hathaway ($8.9 billion), Citigroup ($1.1 billion), Facebook ($10.2 billion), S&P 500 ETF ($11 million)

ALLIANZ SE (PIMCO)
($3.3 TRILLION UNDER MANAGEMENT)
NASDAQ DATA SET $80.6 BILLION
TOTAL $3.7 BILLION INVESTED IN OTHER GIANTS

JPMorgan Chase	$1 billion	Bank of America	$1.03 billion
UBS	$361 million	Morgan Stanley & Co.	$291 million
Prudential Financial	$282 million	Vanguard Group	$371 million
Bank of NY Mellon	$110 million	Goldman Sachs Grp	$89 million
BlackRock	$64 million	Credit Suisse	$60 million
FMR	$52 million		

Allianz SE (PIMCO) top major holdings: S&P 500 ETF ($3.7 billion), Apple ($2 billion), Microsoft ($1.4 billion), Amazon ($1.26 billion), Facebook ($1.26 billion), United Health Care ($1.1 billion), Alphabet ($1.15 billion), Ishares ($1.98 billion), Philip Morris ($87 million)

AMUNDI/CRÉDIT AGRICOLE
($1.1 TRILLION UNDER MANAGEMENT)
NASDAQ DATA SET $32.3 BILLION
TOTAL $1.27 BILLION INVESTED IN OTHER GIANTS

JPMorgan Chase	$633 million	BlackRock	$172 million
Bank of America	$244 million	Bank of NY Mellon	$62.5 million
Morgan Stanley & Co.	$50 million	State Street	$67.5 million
FMR	$24.5 million	Goldman Sach Grp	$22.9 million

Amundi/Crédit Agricole top major holdings: Apple ($1.49 billion), Microsoft ($1.4 billion), Alphabet ($1.3 billion), Citigroup ($446 million), Amazon ($440 million), Ishares ($31 million)

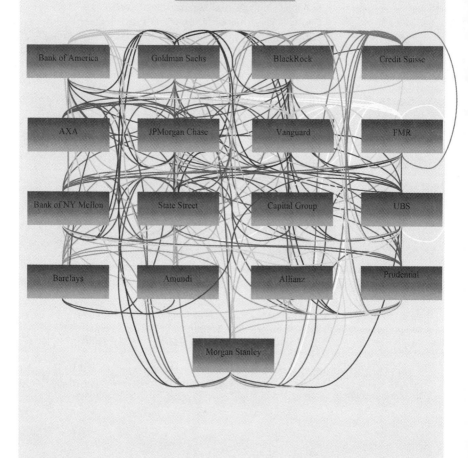

Global Giants
Investment
Connections

Capital concentration is continuing at an accelerated rate. In 2017, during the course of writing this book, three asset management firms acquired Giant status by holding more than one trillion dollars of investment capital. The New Giants are BNP Paribas from France (with $1.2 trillion under management), Northern Trust of Chicago (with $1.1 trillion), and Wellington Management Company of Boston (with $1 trillion). The three new Giants are each cross-invested in the other Giants.

The next nine largest money management firms, each holding in excess of $800 billion, are Near Giants. Near Giants include Aegon from the Netherlands (with $962.9 billion under management), Natixis Global Asset Management from France (with $961 billion), Deutsche Asset Management from Germany (with $838 billion), HSBC from the United Kingdom (with $831 billion), and six US firms—Nuveen (with $948 billion), T. Rowe Price (with $948 billion), TIAA (with $938 billion), Invesco Ltd. (with $917 billion), and Affiliated Managers Group (AMG) (with $803 billion). Collectively the seventeen Giants, along with the three New Giants and the nine Near Giants, manage in excess of $53 trillion of the world's wealth. This concentrated wealth management figure is pushed even higher if you add in the next 39 largest asset management firms, reaching in excess of $74 trillion of inter-invested centralized capital controlled by 69 cross-invested firms.

A NASDAQ review of investors and portfolios for the thirteen New Giants and Near Giants shows multiple co-investments between them and the Giants.

BNP Paribas (France, $1.2 trillion under management). Co-investors: JPMorgan Chase, Bank of America

Global Giants, New Giants, & Near Giants Investment Connections

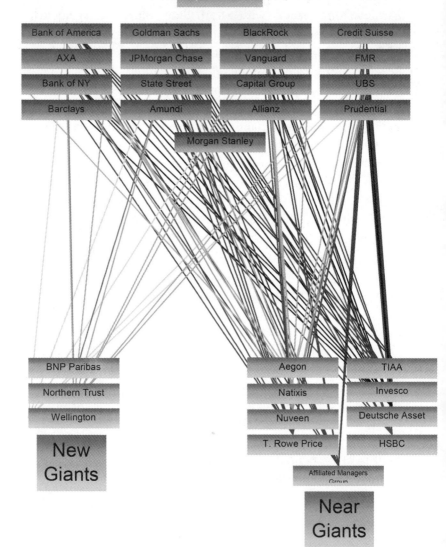

Giants

Bank of America	Goldman Sachs	BlackRock	Credit Suisse
AXA	JPMorgan Chase	Vanguard	FMR
Bank of NY	State Street	Capital Group	UBS
Barclays	Amundi	Allianz	Prudential

Morgan Stanley

BNP Paribas	Aegon	TIAA
Northern Trust	Natixis	Invesco
Wellington	Nuveen	Deutsche Asset
	T. Rowe Price	HSBC

New Giants

Affiliated Managers Group

Near Giants

Northern Trust (US, $1.1 trillion under management). Co-investors: Vanguard Group, BlackRock, Fidelity Investments (FMR), State Street, JPMorgan Chase, Goldman Sachs Group, Bank of NY Mellon, Bank of America, UBS

Wellington Management Company (US, $1 trillion under management). Co-investors: JPMorgan Chase, Bank of America, BlackRock, Prudential Financial, UBS

Near Giants

Aegon (Netherlands, $962.9 billion under management). Co-investors: Bank of America, Goldman Sachs Group, BlackRock, Credit Suisse, UBS, Vanguard Group, Bank of NY Mellon

Natixis Global Assets Management (France, $961 billion under management). Co-investors: JPMorgan Chase, Bank of America, BlackRock

Nuveen (US, $948 billion under management). Co-investors: Bank of America, Prudential Financial, Bank of NY Mellon, BlackRock, UBS

T. Rowe Price (US, $948 billion under management). Co-investors: Vanguard Group, BlackRock, State Street, Capital Group, JPMorgan Chase, Bank of America, Bank of NY Mellon, Goldman Sachs Group, UBS, Amundi, Fidelity Investments (FMR), Prudential Financial, Barclays plc

TIAA (US, $938 billion under management). Co-investors: JPMorgan Chase, Bank of America

Invesco Ltd. (US, $917 billion under management). Co-investors: Vanguard Group, BlackRock, UBS, State Street, JPMorgan Chase, Bank of NY Mellon, Amundi, Fidelity Investments (FMR), Goldman Sachs Group, Bank of America, Prudential Financial

Deutsche Asset Management (Germany, $839 billion under management). Co-investors: JPMorgan Chase, Bank of America, Vanguard Group, Goldman Sachs Group, Amundi, Bank of NY Mellon, Credit Suisse, UBS, Prudential Financial, Allianz SE (PIMCO), Capital Group, AXA Group, Barclays plc

HSBC (UK, $831 billion under management). Co-investors: JPMorgan Chase, Bank of America, Goldman Sachs Group, Prudential Financial, BlackRock, Fidelity Investments (FMR), Capital Group, UBS, Credit Suisse, Bank of NY Mellon

Affiliated Managers Group (AMG) (US, $803 billion under management). Co-investors: Vanguard Group, BlackRock, State Street, Bank of America, Goldman Sachs Group, Fidelity Investments (FMR), Amundi, JPMorgan Chase, Bank of NY Mellon, UBS, Prudential Financial, Credit Suisse

It is interesting to note that most of the Giants and Near Giants are heavily invested in Silicon Valley technology companies. Apple, Microsoft, Alphabet, and Facebook take the lead, with hundreds of billions of dollars invested in their shares. Also of note is the degree to which several Giants have invested in Ishares, the S&P 500 Exchange-Traded Fund (ETF), and various national and international index funds. These investments are similar to mutual funds, but offer easy buy-ins and exits. Black-

Rock offers many hundreds of ETF fund groups, as do most of the other financial Giants. In a sense, Ishares and ETFs are market stability investments, with firms investing collectively in each other based on the stability of capital growth overall in the world. The seventeen Giants collectively have a NASDAQ-listed investment level of $261.7 billion in Ishares and ETF.

Some collaboration may be inferred here, in that, if these co-investments were simply based on decisions seeking a good return, there would seemingly be a greater difference in the types of investments made by the various financial Giants. Whatever the rationale for the similarities of investment strategies, the fact that the seventeen Giants are highly inter-invested is very clear. This interpenetration of financial investments creates a vast consolidation of centralized global capital with a commonality of interests.

The Giants and key power elite individuals are directly supportive of the worldwide negative environmental and health effects of Coca-Cola. Coke is a major contributor to obesity, type 2 diabetes, and tooth decay. More than ten teaspoons of sugar are in a single bottle of Coke. Some 184,000 deaths annually are linked to drinking Coke and similar sugary beverages.

Blood sugar levels increase dramatically within 20 minutes of drinking the Cola, explains [British pharmacist Niraj] Naik, causing a burst of insulin. The liver then turns the high amounts of sugar circulating our body into fat.

Within 40 minutes, the body has absorbed all of the caffeine from the Cola, causing a dilation of pupils and an increase in blood pressure. By this point, the adenosine receptors in the brain have been blocked, preventing fatigue.

Five minutes later, production of dopamine has increased—a neurotransmitter that helps control the pleasure and reward centers of the brain. . . . [T]he way Coca-Cola stimulates these centers is comparable to the effects of heroin, making us want another can."[59]

Coca-Cola, the world's largest soft drink company, released more than 110 billion single-use plastic bottles into the environment in 2017, some 59 percent of its global packaging. Only a tiny fraction of these bottles will ever be recycled.[60] It takes 450 years for a plastic Coke bottle to degrade in the environment.[61]

Global Giants invested in Coca-Cola include Vanguard Group ($12.8 billion), BlackRock ($11.1 billion), Capital Group ($10.4 billion), State Street ($7.6 billion), Bank of America ($3.1 billion), Fidelity Investments (FMR) ($2.8 billion), Bank of NY Mellon ($2 billion), Morgan Stanley ($1.59 billion), UBS ($1.5 billion), JPMorgan Chase ($865 million), Goldman Sachs Group ($756 million), Prudential Financial ($375 million), Credit Suisse ($358 million), and Amundi/Crédit Agricole ($303 million).

Other Practices in Common

Authorities have deemed the largest banks "too big to fail," and generally respond to the banks' criminal activities with weak reforms and very few prosecutions.[62] The American government has refused to prosecute any top officials from the multitude of banks that have laundered billions of dollars for illegal drug cartels. Powerful banking corporations, such as JPMorgan Chase, have continually refused to comply with American anti–money laundering (AML) laws.[63]

This refusal to prosecute is often hailed as an honorable move that serves to protect all individuals from devastation. US Assistant Attorney General Lanny A. Breuer explained the refusal to prosecute the bank HSBC in 2013: "Had the US authorities decided to press criminal charges, HSBC would almost certainly have lost its banking license in the US, the future of the institution would have been under threat and the entire banking system would have been destabilized."[64]

Not only are these powerful corporations considered "too big to fail," they appear to have become too big to tell apart. In 2012, the six largest US banks, JPMorgan Chase, Bank of America, Wells Fargo, Citigroup, Goldman Sachs Group, and US Bancorp, had $9.3 trillion of assets, an amount equivalent to some 65 percent of the US GDP and 93 percent of the total trading revenue of all US banks.[65] Traditionally, banks and assets management firms have been understood as separate entities, competing against one another in order to entice consumers to deposit funds and invest. Such competition theoretically forces each bank to offer its best rates. However, in reality these banks found that competing against one another was less profitable than working together. Realizing that their interests lie side by side, the managers of the global Giants have been highly motivated to join forces—legally or not—to manipulate laws, policies, and governments to their advantage.

The global Giants' corporate boards meet on a regular basis to encourage the maximization of profit and the long-term viability of their firm's business plans. If they arrange for payments to government officials, conduct activities that undermine labor organizations, seek to manipulate the price of commodities or engage in insider trading in some capacity, they are in fact forming conspiratorial alliances inside those boards of directors. The ramifications of this lack of competition in the banking industry can be devastating for the general public. Consider, for example, the Libor price-fixing scandal. JPMorgan Chase, UBS, and Barclays plc (among thirteen other Giants) were implicated in the Libor scandal, falsifying the data that was used to create benchmark rates beginning in 2003.[66] Based on faked data, those rates affected the prices of everything from auto, home, and student loans to credit cards and mortgage and commercial loans, and even the price of currencies themselves. The Financial Services Authority in the United Kingdom fined Barclays $450 million.[67] A number of other Libor prosecutions by US and European regulatory bodies have led to several major settlements. In 2012 UBS paid European regulators fines of $1.5 billion. JPMorgan Chase and Citigroup each paid a significant penalty as well. Citigroup paid $425 million in 2016 after findings by US officials showed that senior managers at the bank knew about the Libor manipulations. In 2015 Deutsche Bank agreed to a $2.5 billion fine for manipulations by its London-based branch.

In addition, these same banks pleaded guilty in 2015 to manipulating global currency exchange markets. Citigroup, JPMorgan Chase, Barclays plc, Royal Bank of Scotland, and UBS paid more than $5 billion in fines to the US Justice Department and other regulators. The Justice Department did not indict any individuals for the crimes.[68]

The International Swaps and Derivatives Association's ISDAfix scandal also looks a lot like the Libor case. The same superpower banks were investigated to determine whether or not they manipulated ISDAfix, a benchmark number used to calculate the prices of global interest rate swaps.[69] Because cities and sovereign governments use interest rate swaps to help manage their debts, manipulation of those rates has far-reaching impacts, particularly for the poor and working classes, as economic safety nets are subject to "austerity" measures—i.e., budget cuts—that favor protection of financial capital. In 2017 Royal Bank of Scotland, Barclays, Citigroup, and Goldman Sachs Group paid settlements on ISDAfix collusion for a total of $570 million.[70]

Not only were rates illegally fixed and data falsified, but the offending banks also used individual consumers' investments to engage in criminal activity. The Vanguard Group was accused of investing its clients' money into illegal offshore gambling sites, prompting a class-action lawsuit under the Racketeer Influenced and Corrupt Organizations (RICO) Act. Vanguard did not deny such wrongdoing, but a judge determined that when the plaintiffs (Vanguard's clients) were harmed, they lost their money due to the government's crackdown on such illegal gambling, rather than due to Vanguard's investing in such sites.[71] However, it is clear that if Vanguard had not invested client money in illegal ventures, there would have been no negative repercussions from such a government crackdown. As journalist Matt Taibbi declared, "Everything is rigged."[72] Indeed, it seems that the corporate elite will never be made to pay for their crimes against consumers—we are unlikely to see such prosecutions. After six months in office the Trump administration has cut penalties levied by federal agencies on financial firms by two thirds. Fines against banks for the first six months of 2016 were $1.4 billion, while fines for the same period in 2017 were down to $489 million.[73]

Interestingly, there is a trial pending in Southwark Crown Court in London against four prior Barclay's executives. Former Barclays CEO John Silvester Varley, and key executives Roger Jenkins, Tom Kalaris, and Richard Boath are charged with conspiracy to commit fraud. Their trial is scheduled for January 2019. The charges stem from the illegal borrowing of billions of dollars from Qatar to cover deficits during the 2008 economic crisis. They are the first senior bankers to face criminal charges stemming from the 2008 economic crisis. It remains to be seen if tradition will prevail and the four are let off lightly.[74]

We do not claim that any single person identified in this study has done anything illegal. We only point out that the institutional, structural arrangements within the money management systems of global capital relentlessly seek ways to achieve maximum return on investment, and that the conditions for manipulations—legal or not—are always present. As these institutions become "too big to fail," their scope and interconnectedness pressure government regulators to shy away from criminal investigations, much less prosecutions. The result is a semi-protected class of people with increasingly vast amounts of money, seeking unlimited growth and returns, with little concern for the consequences of their economic pursuits on other people, societies, cultures, and environments.

With money comes power, influence, and propaganda. Black-Rock and numerous other banks and Wall Street institutions are financially backing groups like the Parent Revolution and StudentsFirst, whose agendas are to privatize and subsequently corporatize our public school system.[75] The global financial Giants are laying the foundation for the privatization of the world. If public, democratic institutions—including schools, post offices, universities, militaries, and even churches—become privately owned entities, then corporate interests will truly dominate. As that happens, we become a neo-feudal society in which the reign of kings is replaced by private corporate ownership and the people are cast in the feudal role of powerless peasants.

The financial Giants are supposedly in competition, but given the concentrated wealth they share they are essentially required by the system to cooperate together for their greater good. This includes finding and supporting commonalities of investment opportunities and shared risk agreements, and working collectively for political arrangements that create advantages for their system as a whole.

This tight group of seventeen financial Giants are the central core of global financial capitalism. It is these firms that set the priorities for monetary investments in businesses, industry, and governments. Their number-one priority is to bring in average returns on investment of 3 percent to 10 percent or more. Where the investments occur is less important than a continious return that supports growth in the overall market. Therefore investments in war weapons, tobacco, fossil fuels, farm land, pesticides, vaccines, private prisons, charter schools, fast foods, security companies, spyware, cruise ships, vacation resorts, or nuclear power are all just investments requiring adequate returns.

Our main point here is that these firms need to maintain the investment of more than $41.1 trillion somewhere in order to insure the continued growth of global capitalism. Failure to have growth results in the stagnation of investment returns and the possible collapse of the entire global financial system. The Giants have few options for investing all of their resources. Safe, risk-free investments that offer solid returns are their first choice option, and as a result they all invest in each other to varing degrees. After that, their surplus capital needs to be invested, and they are faced with investing in highly speculative bubbles like the home loan packages that led to the crisis of 2008, or having governments spend increasingly more money on wars and security, or the buying up of public resources such as water systems, schools, highways, utilities, and parks.

It is not just these seventeen firms alone that support this system of capital investment and continuing growth. They are the central core of thousands of capitalist investments firms and banks that are collectively embedded in this system of mandatory growth. Their interests are fully recognized by the major institutions in society. Governments, intelligence services, policymakers, universities, police forces, militaries, and corporate media all work in support of their vital interests.

Capitalism is an economic system that inevitibly adjusts itself via contractions, recessions, and depressions. Yet we are entrapped in a web of enforced growth and profitmaking that has huge humanitarian consequences for billions of people. An honest, open look at real human options is vitally needed.

MANAGERS
THE GLOBAL POWER ELITE OF
THE FINANCIAL GIANTS

In Chapter 3 we identify the people on the boards of directors of the top seventeen assets management Giants. Each of these firms has in excess of one trillion dollars of assets under management. The collective total assets under management by all seventeen companies is in excess of $41.1 trillion.

These seventeen Giants have 199 directors on their boards. This group of 199 individuals represents the financial management core of global capitalism. They collectively manage this concentration of $41.1 trillion in funds and operate in nearly every country in the world. They are the central decision makers regarding the financial capital that powers the global economic system. Western governments and international policy bodies tend to work in the interests of this power elite financial core to protect the free flow of capital investment and debt collection everywhere in the world.

The specific names of the power elites running the financial centers of the world are rarely identified in the context of a world class-structure. Corporate media and mainstream academics often choose to leave undisclosed the names of the most powerful people in the world at the financial management core of the Transnational Capitalist Class.

The world's corporate media pay absolutely no attention to such academic concepts as the "Transnational Capitalist Class." A ProQuest search of news coverage, completed on June 6, 2017, using the term "Transnational Capitalist Class," returned only sixteen news stories in the past decade—most from foreign media, and a letter to the editor by this author in Santa Rosa's *Press Democrat* on June 21, 2015. An earlier letter to the editor was in the *Las Cruces Sun-News* on October 3, 2013, citing our 2013[76] research, and Leslie Sklair has a letter in the London Guardian January 22, 2013. The idea of the emergence of a transnational capitalist class in China was reported by Targeted News Service on June 27, 2013. However, the concept of a global transnational capitalist class is essentially completely absent from corporate news coverage in the United States and Europe. It is clear that, given the numerous books and published research on the TCC discussed in Chapter 1, corporate media censor the topic and generally refuse to address who constitutes this most elite group of powerful people in the world.

We think that the world needs to know who comprises the power elite core of the TCC, and thus who makes the financial decisions regarding the investment management of global capital. Thankfully, this is actually a fairly straightforward, if labor-intensive, research effort, as most of the information is not only publicly available but also online.

One hundred thirty-six of the 199 power elite managers (70 percent) are male. Eighty-four percent are whites of European descent. The 199 power elite managers hold 147 graduate degrees, including 59 MBAs, 22 JDs, 23 PhDs, and 35 MA/MS degrees. Almost all have attended elite private colleges, with 28 attending Harvard or Stanford.

People from twenty nations make up this central financial

power elite core. One hundred seventeen (59 percent) are from the United States; 22 each are from Britain and France; thirteen each are from Germany and Switzerland; three each are from Italy, Singapore, India, Austria, and Australia; two each are from Japan and Brazil; and one each are from South Africa, the Netherlands, Zambia, Kuwait, Belgium, Canada, Mexico, Qatar, and Colombia. They live in or interact regularly in a number of the world's great cities: New York City, Chicago, London, Paris, Munich, Tokyo, and Singapore. (Note: From the available information, we counted about two dozen power elite managers who hold dual citizenship.)

The power elite managers take active part in global policy groups and governments. They serve as advisors to the IMF, World Trade Organization, World Bank, Bank for International Settlements, Federal Reserve Board, G7, and G20. Many have attended the World Economic Forum. Many of the US directors are members of the Council on Foreign Relations and the Business Roundtable in the United States.

These 199 directors are an important part of Rothkopf's "superclass." They control the investment decisions for the Giants with more than $41.1 trillion of investment capital. In addition, these 199 power elite managers also serve on 202 smaller investment management firms and banks, controlling hundreds of billions of dollars of investment capital through these smaller (often private) investment management firms. These smaller firms are included in the managers' individual listings in this chapter. People's lives depend on these managers' decisions. Speculation on global food that raises prices may mean profits for investors, but it can also result in starvation for tens of thousands. Shifts in investment strategies can bring unemployment to millions.

Western governments and international policy bodies seek to serve the interests of this financial core of the TCC. Wars are initiated to protect their interests. Uncooperative regimes are undermined and overthrown in support of the free flow of global capital for investments anywhere that returns are possible. We think that identifying the people with such power and influence is an important part of a democracy that seeks to protect a commons in which all humans might share and prosper.

TRILLION-DOLLAR ASSET MANAGEMENT FIRMS: BOARD OF DIRECTORS BY COUNTRY OF CITIZENSHIP

Allianz SE (owners of PIMCO [Pacific Investment Management Company]) Assets under management: $3.3 trillion

Sergio Balbinot (Italy), Oliver Bäte (Germany), Jacqueline Hunt (South Africa), Helga Jung (Germany), Christof Mascher (Austria), Günther Thallinger (Austria), Axel Theis (Germany), Dieter Wemmer (Switzerland & Germany), Werner Zedelius (Germany)

Amundi/Crédit Agricole Assets under management: $1.1 trillion

Virginie Cayatte (France), Laurence Danon Arnaud (France), Rémi Garuz (France), Laurent Goutard (France), Robert LeBlanc (France), Michel Mathieu (France), Hélène Molinari (France), Xavier Musca (France), Yves Perrier (France), Christian Rouchon

(France), Andrée Samat (France), Renée Talamona (France), Eric Tazé-Bernard (France)

AXA Investment Managers Assets under management: $1.5 trillion

Thomas Buberl (Germany), Jean-Pierre Clamadieu (France), Ramon de Oliveira (France), Irene Dorner (UK), Denis Duverne (France), Jean-Martin Folz (France), André François-Poncet (France), Angelien Kemna (Netherlands), Isabelle Kocher (France), Suet Fern Lee (Singapore), Stefan Lippe (Switzerland & Germany), François Martineau (France), Deanna Oppenheimer (US & UK), Doina Palici-Chehab (Germany & France)

Bank of America Merrill Lynch Assets under management: $2.5 trillion

Sharon L. Allen (US), Susan S. Bies (US), Jack O. Bovender Jr. (US), Frank P. Bramble Sr. (US), Pierre J.P. de Weck (Switzerland), Arnold W. Donald (US), Linda Parker Hudson (US), Monica C. Lozano (US), Thomas J. May (US), Brian T. Moynihan (US), Lionel L. Nowell III (US), Michael D. White (US), Thomas D. Woods (Canada), Robert David Yost (US)

Bank of New York Mellon Assets under management: $1.7 trillion

Linda Z. Cook (US), Nicholas M. Donofrio (US), Joseph J. Echevarria (US), Edward P. Garden (US), Jeffrey A. Goldstein (US), Gerald L. Hassell (US), John M. Hinshaw (US), Edmund F. "Ted" Kelly (US & Ireland), John A. Luke Jr. (US), Jennifer B. Morgan

(US), Mark A. Nordenberg (US), Elizabeth B. Robinson (US), Charles W. Scharf (US)

Barclays plc Assets under management: $2.5 trillion

Michael Ashley (UK), Tim Breedon (UK), Sir Ian Cheshire (UK), Mary Francis (UK), Crawford Gillies (UK), Sir Gerry Grimstone (UK), Reuben Jeffery III (US), John McFarlane (UK), Tushar Morzaria (UK), Dambisa Moyo (Zambia), Diane Schueneman (US), James (Jes) Staley (US), Ashok Vaswani (India)

BlackRock plc Assets under management: $5.1 trillion

Abdlatif Al-Hamad (Kuwait), Mathis Cabiallavetta (Switzerland), Pamela Daley (US), William S. Demchak (US), Jessica P. Einhorn (US), Laurence (Larry) D. Fink (US), Fabrizio Freda (Italy), Murry S. Gerber (US), James Grosfeld (US), Robert S. Kapito (US), Sir Deryck Charles Maughan (UK), Cheryl Mills (US), Gordon M. Nixon (Canada), Charles H. Robbins (US), Ivan Seidenberg (US), Marco Antonio Slim Domit (Mexico), John Silvester Varley (UK), Susan Lynne Wagner (US)

Capital Group Companies Assets under management: $1.4 trillion

Tim D. Armour (US), Noriko H. Chen (US), Kevin G. Clifford (US), Phil de Toledo (US), Mike C. Gitlin (US), Darcy Kopcho (US), Rob W. Lovelace (US), Martin A. Romo (US), Brad Vogt (US)

Credit Suisse Group AG Assets under management: $1.3 trillion

Iris Bohnet (Switzerland), Andreas Gottschling (Germany), Alexander Gut (UK & Switzerland), Andreas N. Koopmann (Switzerland), Seraina (Maag) Macia (Australia & Switzerland), Kaikhushru (Kai) S. Nargolwala (Singapore), Joaquin J. Ribeiro (US), Urs Rohner (Switzerland), Severin Schwan (Austria & Germany), Jassim Bin Hamad J.J. Al Thani (Qatar), Richard E. Thornburgh (US), John Tiner (UK), Alexandre Zeller (Switzerland)

FMR Corporation [Fidelity Investments] (Johnson Family controlled)Assets under management: $2.1 trillion

Marc Robert Bryant (US), Abigail Pierrepont Johnson (US), Edward Johnson III (US), C. Bruce Johnstone (US), Charles Sumner Morrison (US)

Goldman Sachs Group Assets under management: $1.4 trillion

Lloyd C. Blankfein (US), M. Michele Burns (US), Mark A. Flaherty (US), William W. George (US), James A. Johnson (US), Ellen J. Kullman (US), Lakshmi N. Mittal (India), Adebayo O. Ogunlesi (Nigeria), Peter Oppenheimer (US), David A. Viniar (US), Mark O. Winkelman (Netherlands)

JPMorgan Chase & Co. Assets under management: $3.8 trillion

Linda B. Bammann (US), James A. Bell (US), Crandall C. Bowles (US), Stephen B. Burke (US), Todd A. Combs (US), James S. Crown (US), James (Jamie) Dimon (US), Timothy P. Flynn (US), Laban P. Jackson Jr. (US), Michael A. Neal (US), Lee R. Raymond (US), William C. Weldon (US)

Morgan Stanley & Co. Assets under management: $1.3 trillion

Erskine B. Bowles (US), Alistair Darling (UK), Thomas H. Glocer (US), James P. Gorman (Australia & US), Robert H. Herz (UK & US), Nobuyuki Hirano (Japan), Judith A. (Jami) Miscik (US), Dennis M. Nally (US), Hutham S. Olayan (Saudi Arabia & US), James W. Owens (US), Ryosuke Tamakoshi (Japan), Perry M. Traquina (US), Rayford Wilkins Jr. (US)

Prudential Financial Assets under management: $1.3 trillion

Thomas J. Baltimore Jr. (US), Gilbert F. Casellas (US), Mark B. Grier (US), Martina Hund-Mejean (Germany), Karl J. Krapek (US), Peter R. Lighte (US), George Paz (US), Sandra Pianalto (Italy & US), Christine A. Poon (US), Douglas A. Scovanner (US), John R. Strangfeld (US), Michael A. Todman (US)

State Street Corporation Assets under management: $1.3 trillion

Kennett F. Burnes (US), Patrick de Saint-Aignan (US & France), Lynn A. Dugle (US), Dame Amelia C. Fawcett (US & UK), William C. Freda (US), Linda A. Hill (US), Joseph (Jay) L. Hooley (US), Sean O'Sullivan (Canada & UK), Richard P. Sergel (US), Gregory L. Summe (US)

UBS AG Assets under management: $2.8 trillion

Michel Demaré (Belgium & Switzerland), Reto Francioni (Switzerland), Ann F. Godbehere (UK & Canada), William G. Parrett (US), Julie G. Richardson (US), Isabelle Romy (Switzerland), Robert W. Scully (US), David Sidwell (US & UK), Axel A. Weber (Germany), Beatrice Weder di Mauro (Switzerland & Italy), Dieter Wemmer (Switzerland & Germany)

Vanguard Group Assets under management: $4 trillion

Mortimer (Tim) J. Buckley (US), Emerson U. Fullwood (US), Rajiv L. Gupta (India & US), Amy Gutmann (US), JoAnn Heffernan Heisen (US), F. Joseph Loughrey (US), Mark Loughridge (US), Scott C. Malpass (US), F. William McNabb III (US), André F. Perold (US & South Africa), Peter F. Volanakis (US)

We have examined some of the key individuals among the top ranks of the Global Power Elite's financial managers. Looking at a few individually can deepen our understanding of the nature of the TCC as a class and the roles of the managers of the seventeen Giants.

Laurence D. Fink: Chairman and CEO of BlackRock plc

Larry Fink (age 65) grew up in a middle-class Jewish family from Van Nuys, California. He attended UCLA, earning a BA in Political Science and an MBA from the UCLA Anderson Graduate School of Management. In 1976 he was hired at First Boston's bond department, where over the next several years he added close to one billion dollars to First Boston's bottom line and became the youngest member of the management team at age 31. He was active in helping arrange the securitization of GMAC auto loans, and was one of the first to create mortgage-backed securities. He was part of the emerging debt-securitization market that transformed global finance in the 1990s and helped lead to the international financial collapse of 2008.

In 1986, Larry Fink misjudged the interest market, leading to a $100 million loss for First Boston. This loss undermined his early successes and led to his being pushed out of the company two years later.[77]

The experience of being forced out of First Boston seems to have stayed with him his entire life, resulting in a personal drive to build BlackRock into the largest money management firm in the world. The firm currently manages $5.4 trillion in funds under direct investment, with another $10 trillion for which BlackRock provides investment advising. Fink founded BlackRock under the umbrella of Blackstone Group in 1988. His primary focus was to increase the ability of firms to determine risk on investments. He created the Asset Liability and Debt and Derivatives Investment Network (Aladdin, for short), which today employs 2,300 analysts using thousands of computers to monitor and test all aspects of the global financial market, which includes stress-testing securities against sudden interest rate changes, political events, and market surprises. More than seventy firms, including Deutsche Bank and Freddie Mac, use Aladdin services for market decisions.[78]

In 2006, Fink acquired Merrill Lynch's investment management business, which raised BlackRock's assets to more than $1 trillion and doubled its size. And in 2009 BlackRock bought Barclays Global Investors from the British banking giant Barclays plc for about $13.5 billion in one of the largest deals in the money management industry.[79]

BlackRock came though the 2008 global economic crisis relatively unscathed compared to many other firms; they did lose some $8–10 billion overall, but made money off the collapse by contracting with the US government to manage various aspects of the Troubled Asset Relief Program (TARP).

Larry Fink has been married to his high school sweetheart since the mid-1970s. They own three homes—an Upper East Side apartment in New York City, a 26-acre farm in North Salem, and a house in Aspen. Fink enjoys fly-fishing, skiing, folk art, and wine. He hardly uses e-mail or Twitter, preferring the phone and face-to-face conversations. He is often seen at Ristorante San Pietro, just around the corner from his office on East 52nd Street. Fink wears a gold Rolodex, but refuses to own a company jet, and instead flies commercial. He is aware of the prejudices of Wall Street's WASP investment bankers, whom he thinks look down on Jewish and Italian traders.[80] A lifelong Democrat, Fink was a top contender for Secretary of the Treasury had Hillary Clinton been elected president, and he has been a leader in advocating for the privatization of Social Security.[81]

In 1988, BlackRock Realty Advisors took over management

of Stuyvesant Town–Peter Cooper Village's 20,000 apartments. In 2006, BlackRock bought the Manhattan complex for a top-of-the-market price of $5.4 billion with the idea that they could push out rent-controlled tenets and increase revenue to market prices. The plan failed, forcing a co-investor, California Public Employees' Retirement System (CalPERS), to take a $500 million loss and drop BlackRock as manager of their apartment portfolio.[82] When asked about the CalPERS loss, Fink responded, "We're not perfect and I've never said to anyone that we were going to be perfect. Our investors had all the information we did and they did their own due diligence.... My mom gets her pension from CalPERS."[83]

Larry Fink directly influences investment strategy for some $15 trillion of global capital. For this he received more than $25 million in compensation in 2016. Fink's Aladdin research system continues to allow BlackRock to generally exceed returns on investment above the market average. His Exchange-Traded Fund (ETF) allows investors to easily buy and sell as though they are purchasing stock. For the first quarter of 2017, BlackRock posted earnings of $4.89 per share, up from $4.25 the year before, and boosted their portfolio to $5.4 trillion.[84] Twenty-eight thousand investors are currently with BlackRock, including Donald Trump.[85]

Increasingly, Larry Fink is invited to offer policy recommendations on economic issues. He has been on several panels at the annual World Economic Forum. He was invited, along with a few other Wall Street executives, to an Obama White House dinner hosting Chinese President Xi Jinping.[86] He is a director of the Council on Foreign Relations (CFR) and the Business Roundtable, a trustee of New York University and the Museum of Modern Art, and has been named one of the world's most respected leaders by *Fortune* magazine in 2016, "CEO of the Decade" by Financial News in 2011, and one of the "World's Best CEOs" by *Barron's* for eleven consecutive years.[87]

Fink seems not to be highly involved in direct transnational global governance, having little to say publicly about the IMF, World Bank, Bank for International Settlements, NATO, or the US military empire other than being concerned with government interference in the market. He does speak about his concern for the "retirement crisis," whereby older people are retiring in poverty, and he wants legislation requiring retirement investment by all working people and the privatization of the Social Security fund.[88] In two interviews he was asked about the environment, and in both cases he gave only brief responses. In his January 2017 letter to his investors, he wrote, "I remain a firm believer that the overall benefits of globalization have been significant, and that global companies play a leading role in driving growth and prosperity for all. However, there is little doubt that globalization's benefits have been shared unequally, disproportionately benefitting more highly skilled workers, especially those in urban areas."

Larry Fink is a powerful member of the TCC Global Power Elite, given the huge slice of global capital he controls. His net worth was estimated at $340 million in 2012, and grew to probably twice as much in 2017.[89] He is also highly interconnected inside the Global Power Elite financial core of the TCC. Certainly, he is one of the leading global financial elites. He and his associates are capable of making policy adjustments that could significantly address the needs of the billions of people living on a few dollars a day, and the life-threatening global environmental crisis. While aware of these global issues, Fink firmly believes that expanding market capitalism is best overall for the world.

James (Jamie) Dimon: President and CEO of JPMorgan Chase

Jamie Dimon has been the CEO of JPMorgan Chase since 2005. JPMorgan Chase is the largest bank in the United States and third largest in the world by total assets. JPMorgan Chase earned $24.8 billion in 2016 and has control of $3.8 trillion in deposits and client assets.[90] Jamie Dimon was born in 1956 and raised in New York City as the son and grandson of stockbrokers. His grandfather Panos Papademetriou left Greece in 1921 and changed his last name to Dimon. Both Jamie's father and grandfather worked for Shearson, Hammill & Company, an investment banking and retail brokerage firm.[91] Dimon attended the Browning School, a New York City private all-boys college preparatory academy.

Dimon went to Tufts University in Massachusetts, earning a BA degree in Psychology and Economics. After two years working with a management consultant firm, he enrolled at Harvard Business School, earning an MBA as a Baker Scholar in 1982.[92] A Baker Scholar is the highest honor for graduating MBAs at Harvard, awarded only to the top 5 percent of students. In 1982 Dimon started working at American Express under the personal guidance of Sandy Weill, a family friend. Dimon stayed with Weill as his immediate assistant through several mergers and acquisitions. In 1996 Dimon became CEO of Smith Barney (Smith Barney became part of Morgan Stanley in 2012). In 1998, Dimon and Weill engineered a merger between Travelers and Citicorp, creating a giant investment banking group called Citigroup. Dimon was named president of Citigroup and co-headed the investment bank and brokerage unit Salomon Smith Barney.

In a surprise move in November 1998, Sandy Weill fired Dimon—officially he was asked to resign. The resignation was completed after a $30 million severance deal was negotiated. Dimon's net worth at this time was estimated at $100 million. He was immediately courted by numerous other firms, but remained out of the work force for eighteen months. During these eighteen months, he took up boxing for physical fitness, and used the time to read and contemplate his best options. He and his family toured Europe for six weeks, and he visited his brother in Denmark.[93]

A week after Weill formed Citigroup, a midwest bank merger between Columbus, Ohio–based Banc One and First Chicago NBD created Bank One. The merger made Bank One the fifth largest bank in the United States. The post-merger bank had numerous difficulties due to the two banks' different operating systems and cultures, and in December 1999—more than a year after Dimon was fired from Citigroup—the CEO of Bank One retired under pressure, and the board of directors began a search for a new CEO.

Bank One was a large financial institution in need of strong leadership, and Dimon saw the job as an opportunity to get back into the game. On March 27, 2000, Bank One announced the appointment of Dimon as the new chairman and CEO. Dimon moved his family to Chicago, buying a 15,000 square-foot mansion, and jumped into Bank One management. More than 10,000 of the 80,000 employees were let go. High salaries were cut and the board of directors was pared down from 22 to 14. Several of Dimon's friends from Citigroup came over to Bank One to work with him. He standardized the operating systems, increased the rules for risk, limited unsafe investments, cut dividends by 50 percent, and increased the bank's capital reserves. His goal was to build a "fortress balance sheet" that would allow

Bank One to weather market downturns.[94] To show his commitment to his new job, Dimon invested $60 million of his own money into Bank One stock. Bank One posted profits of $2.6 billion in 2001, $3.3 billion in 2002, and $3.5 billion in 2003. These profits set up the opportunity for a Bank One merger with JPMorgan Chase in 2004.

After the merger in 2004, Dimon became the president and chief operating officer of JPMorgan Chase & Co. Dimon was named chairman of the board in 2006.[95] In the next several years under Dimon's control, JPMorgan Chase became the top investment bank in the United States and the number-one credit card provider, and grew to $3.1 trillion in assets management in 2017. Dimon was named on *Time* magazine's list of the world's most influential people in 2008, 2009, and 2011. Dimon's net worth is $1.3 billion and his current salary at JPMorgan Chase is $27.5 million.[96] Dimon obtained billionaire status in 2015 despite some ups and downs over the years at JPMorgan Chase. President Obama's financial disclosures for 2011 show he had $500,000–1 million in a JPMorgan Chase private client asset management checking account.[97]

Under Dimon's tenure JPMorgan Chase was fined $2 billion for violations of the Bank Secrecy Act, due to its failure to report suspicious activities by Bernie Madoff.[98] In 2017 JPMorgan Chase paid a $55 million fine after being accused of charging at least 53,000 African American and Hispanic borrowers inflated rates and fees on home mortgage loans between 2006 and at least 2009.[99] In September 2011 the Federal Housing Finance Agency sued JPMorgan Chase and other firms for abuses in the sale of mortgage-backed securities to Fannie Mae and Freddie Mac. JPMorgan Chase was one of five large mortgage servicers that in February 2012 consented to a $25 billion settlement to resolve allegations of loan servicing and foreclosure abuses.[100] In November 2013 JPMorgan Chase paid $4.5 billion to settle claims by a group of institutional investors that the bank had sold them faulty mortgage-backed securities between 2005 and 2008.[101]

Dimon is active in policymaking, using his position of influence on Wall Street to promote and serve on numerous organizations. He holds a seat on the Federal Reserve Bank of New York, serves on the United Negro College Fund (UNCF) board, serves as a trustee of the New York University School of Medicine, and is active on the Business Roundtable Executive Committee as chairman. He annually attends the World Economic Forum, giving keynote talks. In an interview at Davos in 2017 he advocated for bank deregulation and US tax reform.[102] Dimon is a member of the Council on Foreign Relations (CFR) and was a speaker in the CFR CEO Speakers Series in 2012. He remains a member of the Trilateral Commission[103] and attends the annual Bilderberg Group meetings.[104]

Dimon and his former boss Sandy Weill played a critical role in pushing for the elimination of the 1933 Glass–Steagall Act, which prohibited commercial banks from direct involvement in investment banking. In 1999, under the Clinton administration, the law was changed to allow commercial banks to invest in derivatives and securities, leading to massive bank investments into the US home mortgage market. The 2008 global credit crisis was directly related to credit practices that, due to escalating home values, allowed people, even those with poor credit, to borrow without proving their income.[105] Anticipating a downturn, JPMorgan Chase used hedge funds to bet against the housing market, making money on the downturn while at the same time still selling housing investment securities. As a result, JPMorgan Chase was fined by the Securities and Exchange Commission $153 million in 2011 for securities fraud.[106]

The burst of the housing bubble almost caused a collapse of the global financial system. By 2010, after massive government bailouts, new banking rules were enacted by the Obama administration. The Dodd–Frank Wall Street Reform and Consumer Protection Act was passed, with a key component, the Volcker Rule (Title VI of the Act), that restricts the ways banks can invest, limiting speculative trading.[107] Dimon was one of the Wall Street leaders firmly opposed to the Volcker rule. This opposition didn't go unnoticed at the White House, and Dimon, who was once called "Obama's Favorite Banker," was left uninvited to State dinners for a while.[108] In 2012 Dimon was asked by Huffington Post why he was such a consistent defender of Wall Street and critic of government finance rules. His response was, "This is not the Soviet Union. . . . This is the United States of America. . . . Guess what. . . . It's a free fucking country."[109]

Dimon's Letter to Shareholders for 2017 includes a significant section on public policy where he acknowledges concerns with decline in US productivity growth, higher cost health care than most developed countries, twenty million felons in the United States, a decline in the labor force participation rate, high drop-out rates for schools, and low wages. However, in answer to these problems, he writes, "The United States needs to ensure that we maintain a healthy and vibrant economy. This is what fuels job creation, raises the standard of living for those who are hurting, and positions us to invest in education, technology and infrastructure in a programmatic and sustainable way to build a better and safer future for our country and its people. America's military will be the best in the world only as long as we have the best economy in the world."[110]

John McFarlane: Chairman of Barclays Bank

The 2011 Zurich study reporting the most superconnected firms in the world ranks Barclays Bank as the number-one most connected firm. Barclays is a 300-year-old banking company founded in 1690 in London. Barclays grew with the expansion of the British Empire and now offers services in more than 50 countries and territories, serving some 49 million clients. As a multinational global bank, Barclays offers retail, wholesale, and investment banking, wealth management, mortgage lending, and credit cards. Barclays offered the United Kingdom's first credit cards in 1966.[111] Barclay's shares have ranged in price from a high of $55.70 in 2007 to $16.50 in 2010 and $7.80 in 2016.[112] The decline in share value and the continuing impacts of the Libor and exchange rates scandals has resulted in the replacement of two CEOs in the last decade and the hiring of John McFarlane in January 2015 as non-executive director. McFarlane quickly became chair of the board and acting CEO.

John McFarlane was born in Dumfries, Scotland, in 1947. He attended Dumfries Academy, founded in 1804 for the most gifted students in the area. Students were required to wear uniform blazers and ties over white shirts. The school teaches a college preparatory curriculum with an emphasis on "Respect, Ambition, Compassion, Fairness, and Responsibility."[113] McFarlane attended the University of Edinburgh, earning an MA degree in 1969, and an MBA from the Cranfield University School of Management in 1975. While in his MBA program, McFarlane also worked for Ford Motor Company. In 1975 he joined Citibank, where he eventually became head of Citibank UK and Ireland, and head of Citicorp Investment Bank Ltd.

From 1997 to 2007 McFarlane worked as CEO of Australia and New Zealand Banking Group Ltd., also serving as chairman of the board for the Australian Bankers' Association. Returning to Great Britain, McFarlane served on the board of several banks and investment firms, including the Royal Bank of Scotland Group plc, London Stock Exchange, Aviva plc (an international insurance and investment firm),[114] FirstGroup plc (a major transportation company including railroads and buses in Great Britain, Ireland, and the United States [FirstGroup owns Greyhound]),[115] and Westfield Corporation, which owns 35 shopping centers in Britain and the United States.[116] He also serves on the European Financial Services Round Table, regularly attends the World Economic Forum,[117] and was president of the International Monetary Conference.

John McFarlane is married with three daughters, makes sculptures, plays acoustic guitar in a skiffle band, and grows olives in Provence. He plays golf, paints, and loves singing. He is known to sing "House of the Rising Sun" at charity events. McFarlane promised to bring ethical standards to Barclays, and tightened up the company dress code by requiring business dress and no flip-flops, T-shirts, or jeans at work.[118] He believed that Barclays needed stronger customer service and lower salaries. He spoke at the annual conference of the British Bankers' Association, attacking the bonus culture of banking by arguing that bankers earn too much.[119]

McFarlane's plans for Barclays were to streamline the operations globally, keeping core profitable sections and cutting back in other areas. Several thousand people were laid off over the first few years, and the goal was to double pre-tax profits. McFarlane's compensation was set at a little over $1 million for his work.[120] When he arrived at Barclays, McFarlane complained about the bureaucracy, saying that "they have 375 management committees and that is 370 too many."[121] He has committed to stay on as chair until 2019.[122] Part of his chair duties include serving on the Brexit negotiating committee. McFarlane is reported to have said that "much of the finance industry's lobbying remains focused on convincing European officials that they should give financial services a special deal to continue to operate unrestricted across the single market."[123]

Under McFarlane's lead, Barclays quickly hired James (Jes) Staley as CEO in October 2015. Staley was managing partner of BlueMountain Capital, a $22 billion hedge fund, and had spent more than 30 years at JPMorgan Chase, where he was the CEO of the Corporate Investment Bank under Jamie Dimon's supervision. Staley's total compensation from Barclays for 2016 was $3.6 million.[124] Staley served on the Investor Advisory Committee on Financial Markets of the Federal Reserve Bank of New York, and he was a member of the Council on Foreign Relations.[125]

Jamie Dimon, Larry Fink, and John McFarlane share similar lifestyles and ideological orientations. They believe in the importance of global capitalism as a system that is beneficial for the world. They recognize that inequality and poverty are important issues, but believe that capital growth will eventually solve these problems. They justify this belief by claiming that there are now more middle-class people in the world than ever before. They remain relatively non-expressive about environmental issues, but certainly recognize that investment opportunities may change due to climate modifications. As millionaires they own multiple homes, and each is married with three children. They attended elite universities, rose quickly in international finance, and have become top leaders in the Global

Power Elite financial core of the TCC. The institutions they manage have been shown to engage in illegal collusions with others, but the regulatory fines by governments are essentially seen as just part of doing business. They belong to numerous national and transnational policy organizations, and participate in service to nonprofit institutions, universities, medical facilities, and cultural institutions.

We invite you to read the names, backgrounds, and public financial information of these 199 power elites listed below to develop a full understanding of the magnitude of the concentration of power and wealth in so few hands. As you read this list, watch for special titles like "Former Deputy Director of the CIA," "Secretary General of France," "Chief of Staff" for a US President, "Chancellor of the Exchequer at Her Majesty's Treasury," "Dame Commander of the Order of the British Empire," "Minister of Finance," "Minister of Defense," "son of the former richest person in the world," "member of the National Security Council," "Chief of Staff" to a Secretary of State, "House of Lords," "House of Commons," "Federal Reserve," "CyberPatriot," "Monetary Authority," and various other government cabinet-level positions.

GLOBAL POWER ELITE MANAGERS OF THE FINANCIAL GIANTS: CAPITAL CORE OF THE TRANSNATIONAL CAPITALIST CLASS (AS OF 2017)

All 199 alphabetical listings appear in the following format:

Name, Country of Citizenship **CB-** Corporate Boards/Current Corporate Employment **PE-** Prior Corporate Employment/

Boards **PC**- Policy Councils, Philanthropic Organizations, Government **E**- Education **F**- Public Financials.[126] In almost every case the financials cited are only a portion of income and net worth.

Abdlatif Al-Hamad, Kuwait **CB**- Director: BlackRock, Director General/Chairman of the Board of Directors: Arab Fund for Economic and Social Development **PE**- Minister of Finance and Minister of Planning of Kuwait, Morgan Stanley, Marsh & McLennan Companies, American International Group, National Bank of Kuwait **PC**- Kuwait Investment Authority, Arab Planning Institute, IFC Banking Advisory Group (World Bank), United Nations Committee for Development Planning, Commission on Global Governance, World Economic Forum, Trustee: International Institute for Strategic Studies – London **E**- Claremont College, Harvard International Affairs Program **F**- BlackRock compensation $255,500 (2017), BlackRock shares 4,767—$2.26 million (2016)

Sharon L. Allen, US **CB**- Director: Bank of America Merrill Lynch **PE**- Deloitte Touche Tohmatsu Ltd., Catalyst **PC**- Chair: National Board of the YMCA, President's Export Council, Women's Leadership Board at the John F. Kennedy School of Government at Harvard, World Economic Forum **E**- University of Idaho **F**- Bank of America compensation $345,000 (2016), Bank of America shares 63,468—$1.7 million (2016); on *Forbes*'s list of "The 100 Most Powerful Women in the World" for four consecutive years

Tim D. Armour, US **CB**- Equity Portfolio Manager and Chairman: Capital Group Companies **PE**- Various positions at Capital Group Companies **E**- Middlebury College (BA in Economics) **F**- Capital Group compensation N/A (private company), though in a 2010 divorce trial the value of Tim Armour's Capital Group stock was projected to be $97.8 million

Michael Ashley, UK **CB**- Director: Barclays plc, KPMG Europe llp ("ELLP"), Deloitte Touche Tohmatsu Ltd., The Financial Reporting Council Ltd. **PC**- Institute of Chartered Accountants in England and Wales, HM Treasury's Audit Committee, European Financial Reporting Advisory Group **E**- Burnham Grammar School Academy **F**- Barclays compensation $271,170 (2016), Barclays shares 62,250—$604,446 (2016)

Sergio Balbinot, Italy **CB**- Allianz SE, UniCredit SpA, La Centrale Finanziaria Generale SpA, Bajaj Allianz General Insurance Co. Ltd., Participatie Maatschappij Graafschap Holland NV, Generali (Schweiz) Holding AG, Deutsche Vermögensberatung AG **PE**- Assicurazioni Generali SpA, Trieste & Deutscher Lloyd **PC**- Europ Assistance Holding SA, World Economic Forum **E**- University of Bologna (BA in Business Management, MBA) **F**- Allianz annual compensation $2.5 million (2016)

Thomas J. Baltimore Jr., US **CB**- Director: Prudential Insurance Company of America, Park Hotels & Resorts, Hilton Worldwide Holdings **PE**- MedStar Health, The RLJ Companies, PricewaterhouseCoopers llp, Integra LifeSciences Holdings Corp., Duke Realty Corp. **PC**- National Association of Real Estate Investment Trusts, American Hotel & Lodging Association, Industry Real Estate Finance Advisory Council, Trustee: University of Virginia Darden School Foundation, Director: Thomas Jefferson University School of Medicine **E**- University of Virginia (BS, MBA) **F-** owns 32,897—$8 million—shares of Prudential; Prudential compensation $320,000 (2016), Parks and Hotel compensation $2.4 million (2016), Hotel and Pack shares $8.4 million (2016)

Linda B. Bammann, US **CB-** Director: JPMorgan Chase & Co., Manulife Finance (Delaware) lp **PE-** Bank One, UBS Warburg, The Manufacturers Life Insurance Company **PC-** The Federal Home Loan Mortgage Corporation, Risk Management Association **E-** Stanford University (BS), University of Michigan (MA) **F-** JPMorgan compensation $350,000 (2016), JPMorgan shares 81,000 shares—$3.1 million (2016)

Oliver Bäte, Germany **CB-** CEO: Allianz SE **PE-** Westdeutsche Landesbank, McKinsey & Company, German Air Force, Professor: University of Cologne **PC-** Chairman: European Insurance CFO Forum, World Economic Forum **E-** University of Cologne, New York University (MBA) **F-** Allianz compensation $4.6 million (2016)

James A. Bell, US **CB-** Director: JPMorgan Chase & Co., Apple **PE-** Rockwell International, Dow Chemical, The Boeing Company **PC-** World Business Chicago, Chicago Economic Club, Trustee: Center for Strategic and International Studies **E-** California State University at Los Angeles **F-** JPMorgan compensation $354,375 (2016), Apple compensation $465,551 (2016), JPMorgan shares 25,032—$2.46 million (2016); Black Engineer of the Year "Pioneer Award" winner (2012)

Susan S. Bies, US **CB-** First Horizon, Director: Bank of America Merrill Lynch, VP: Zurich Financial Services AG **PE-** Professor of Economics: Rhodes College, Professor of Economics: Wayne State University **PC**- Securities and Exchange Commission, Board of Governors of the Federal Reserve System, Financial Accounting Standards Board, Financial Executives Institute, End Users of Derivatives Association, American Bankers Association, Bank Administration Institute, American Economic Association, Institute of Management Accountants, International Women's Forum, American Economic Association **E**- Buffalo State College, Northwestern University (PhD) **F**- Bank of America shares 152,056—$4.06 million (2016), Bank of America compensation $438,076 (2016), Zurich Financial compensation $410,000 (2016)

Lloyd C. Blankfein, US **CB**- Chairman and CEO: The Goldman Sachs Group **PE**- J. Aron & Co., Proskauer Rose llp **PC**- FICC, The Partnership for New York City, Governing Board of the Indian School of Business, Dean's Advisory Board and Dean's Council of Harvard University, World Economic Forum, Council on Foreign Relations, Catalyst **E**- Harvard (BA, JD) **F**- net worth $1.1 billion; Goldman Sachs compensation $20.2 million (2016), Goldman Sachs shares 2.66 million—$610.1 million (2016)

Iris Bohnet, Switzerland **CB**- Credit Suisse Group **PE**- Professor of Public Policy and Dean: Harvard Kennedy School, Research Fellow: University of California at Berkeley **PC**- World Economic Forum, Advisory Board of the Vienna University of Economics and Business Administration **E**- University of Zurich (PhD in Economics) **F**- Credit Suisse compensation $2.8 million (2016), Credit Suisse shares 38,809—$619,003 (2016)

Jack O. Bovender Jr., US **CB**- EP Health llc, HCA Realty, Montgomery Regional Hospital, Brookwood Medical Center of Gulfport, VH Holdings and Women's and Children's Hospital, Director: Bank of America Merrill Lynch **PE**- CEO: HCA Realty, Tennessee Valley Ventures lp **PC**- Business Council of the Committee for the Preservation of Capitalism, American Hospital Association, Trustee: Duke University **E**- Duke University (BA, MA) **F**- Bank of America compensation $450,000 (2016), Bank of America shares 87,588—$2.34 million (2016); received HCA stock worth $10 million in 1992

Crandall C. Bowles, US **CB**- Director: JPMorgan Chase & Co., Springs Global, Sara Lee Corporation **PE**- Wachovia Corporation **PC**- World Economic Forum International Business Council, The Business Council of the Council on Foreign Relations, Global Research Institute of UNC—Chapel Hill, The Committee of 200, Economic Club of New York, The University of North Carolina Press, Trustee: Brookings Institution **E**- Wellesley College, Columbia University (MBA); married to Erskine B. Bowles **F**- net worth $30–60 million; JPMorgan compensation $254,991 (2016), JPMorgan shares 86,631—$8.5 million (2016)

Erskine B. Bowles, US **CB**- BDT Capital Partners, Facebook, Norfolk Southern Corp., Erskine Bowles & Co., Intelisys Electronic Commerce, Lead Director: Morgan Stanley **PE**- Belk, Cousins Properties, General Motors, Krispy Kreme Doughnuts, Wachovia, McLeodUSA, Merck & Co., Community Health Systems, First Union Corp., Carousel Capital, President Emeritus: University of North Carolina system **PC**- United States Small Business Administration, National Commission on Fiscal

Responsibility & Reform, World Economic Forum, Deputy Special Envoy: United Nation, Chief of Staff: US Office of The President (under Bill Clinton) **E**- University of North Carolina at Chapel Hill (BS), Columbia University (MBA); married to Crandall C. Bowles **F**- estimated net worth $30–60 million (*New York Times*, 1999); JPMorgan compensation $369,375 (2016), Morgan Stanley compensation $383,333 (2016); owns Morgan Stanley stock worth $7.72 million

Frank P. Bramble Sr., US **CB**- Director: Bank of America Merrill Lynch, Lecturer: Towson University **PE**- Maryland National Bank, MBNA Corp. MNC Financial, Allfirst Financial, Allied Irish Banks plc, Constellation Energy Group, Wilmington Trust Retirement and Institutional Services Company, CEO: Allfirst Bank **E**- Towson University **F**- Bank of America shares 313,193—$8.37 million (2016), Bank of America compensation $300,000 (2016)

Tim Breedon, UK **CB**- Director: Barclays Bank plc, Index Funds Fidelity Investment (private), Apax Global Alpha Ltd. (private) **PE**- Legal & General Group plc, Standard Charter Bank, Mithras Investment Trust plc **PC**- Ministry of Justice, Association of British Insurers (ABI) [the UK government's non-bank lending taskforce], Investment Management Association, The Takeover Panel (UK), Financial Reporting Council **E**- Oxford University, London Business School (MS in Business) **F**- earned $2.5 million in 2012 on leaving L&G; Barclays compensation $288,200 (2016), Barclays shares 27,755—$269,501 (2016)

Marc Robert Bryant, US **CB**- Strategic Advisers, Deutsche Asset Management (private), Senior VP: FMR llc **PE**- GE Investment Management, Alliance Bernstein lp, ProFund Advisors llc **PC**-

World Economic Forum **E-** Colgate University (BA), Emory University School of Law (JD) **F-** FMR compensation N/A (private company)

Thomas Buberl, Germany **CB-** CEO: AXA Equitable Holdings **PE-** Zurich Financial Services AG, Winterthur Group, DBV Deutsche Beamtenversicherung AG **PC-** Forum of Young Global Leaders, World Economic Forum **E-** WHU Koblenz (MA in Economics), Lancaster University (MBA), University of St. Gallen (PhD in Economics) **F-** AXA annual compensation $2 million (2017), AXA shares 1,757,212—$44.1 million (2016)

Mortimer (Tim) J. Buckley, US **CB-** CEO, Managing Director, and Chief Investment Officer: The Vanguard Group **PE-** various positions at Vanguard Group **PC-** The Children's Hospital of Philadelphia **E-** Harvard College (BA in Economics), Harvard Business School (MBA) **F-** CEO of Vanguard compensation N/A (private)—though prior CEO earned $10 million

Stephen B. Burke, US **CB-** Comcast Corporation, Berkshire Hathaway, Director: JPMorgan Chase & Co., CEO: NBC Universal **PE-** Walt Disney Company, President: ABC Broadcasting **E-** Colgate University, Harvard Business School (MBA) **F-** Berkshire compensation $35.5 million (2016), JPMorgan compensation $309,375 (2016), JPMorgan shares 97,944—$9.6 million (2016), CEO of NBC compensation $37.5 million (2016), Berkshire Hathaway compensation $2,700 (Berkshire Hathaway pays directors $900 per meeting plus expenses)

Kennett F. Burnes, US **CB-** Director: State Street **PE-** Watts Water Technologies, Choate Hall & Stewart, CEO: Cabot

Corporation **E**- Harvard University (BA, JD) **F**- State Street compensation $425,000 (2016), State Street share value $6.1 million (2016)

M. Michele Burns, US **CB**- Goldman Sachs Group, Anheuser-Busch InBev SA/NV, Circle Internet Financial, Etsy, Alexion Pharmaceuticals, Cisco Systems **PE**- Mercer, Tresoro Mining Corp., Marsh & McLennan Companies, Mirant Corporation, GenOn Energy, Delta Air Lines, Arthur Andersen llp, Worldspan lp, Ivan Allen Company, Wal-Mart Stores **PC**- World Economic Forum, Elton John AIDS Foundation **E**- University of Georgia (BA in Business, MA in Accounting), Babson College (MBA) **F**- Marsh & McLennan earnings $204,906 (2016), Goldman Sachs compensation $600,000 (2016), Goldman Sachs shares 15,784—$3.7 million (2016), Cisco compensation $359,999 (2016), Anheuser-Busch compensation $204,906 (2016), Etsy compensation $201,906 (2016), Etsy shares 157,600—$2.5 million (2016), Alexion compensation $348,674 (2016), Alexion shares 9,646—$1.07 million (2016)

Mathis Cabiallavetta, Switzerland **CB**- Union Bank of Switzerland, Philip Morris International, General Atlantic Partners, Altria Group, Director: BlackRock **PE**- Marsh & McLennan Companies, Swiss Re Ltd. **PC**- Federal Reserve Bank of New York, UBS, Swiss American Chamber of Commerce, British-American Business Council **E**- University of Montreal, Queen's University at Kingston (MA in Economics) **F**- $600,000 compensation from BlackRock and Philip Morris; Marsh & McLennan Co. stock worth $18 million, BlackRock shares 5,092—$2.41 million (2016), Philip Morris shares 35,297—$3.65 million (2016)

Gilbert F. Casellas, US **CB-** Prudential Financial, Casellas & Associates, Diversity Advisory Board of Toyota Motor Corporation, Coca-Cola's Diversity Task Force, Joint Diversity Advisory Council of Comcast Corporation, Advisory Board at Catalyst **PE-** Swarthmore Group, McConnell Valdes llp, Q-linx, OMNITRU **PC-** General Counsel of the US Air Force, US Census Monitoring Board, US EEOC, Council on Foreign Relations, Congressional Hispanic Caucus Institute, Johnnetta B. Cole Global Diversity and Inclusion Institute, Hispanic Federation, Military Leadership Diversity Commission **E-** Yale University (BA), University of Pennsylvania (JD) **F-** Prudential compensation $323,750, Prudential shares 30,244—$33.4 million (2016)

Virginie Cayatte, France **CB-** Amundi Asset Management SA, SoLocal Group SA **PE-** various positions: AXA (for fifteen years total) **PC-** financial market regulation and economic forecasts: French Treasury (from 2002 to 2006) **E-** École Polytechnique (Economics), École Nationale Supérieure des Mines de Paris **F-** Amundi compensation $3,510 2016; left SoLocal by "mutual consent" in 2017

Noriko H. Chen, US **CB-** Capital Group Companies **PE-** Worldsec International Ltd., various positions: Capital Group **PC-** Board of Trustees for Williams College, World Economic Forum **E-** Williams College (BA in Economics), Keio University's Japanese Language Program **F-** compensation N/A (private company); owns a home in Northern California valued at $5.6 million as of 2015

Sir Ian Cheshire, UK **CB-** Menhaden Capital plc, Debenhams plc, Proland Corps llc, Medicinema Enterprises Ltd., Chairman

Designate: Barclays Bank UK plc **PE-** Kingfisher plc, British Retail Consortium, Sears plc, Boston Consulting Group, Guinness, Bradford & Bingley plc **PC-** United Kingdom Department for Work and Pensions, Prince of Wales Corporate Leaders Group on Climate Change, Business Disability Forum President's Group, Ecosystem Markets Task Force, World Economic Forum **E-** University of Cambridge (Economics and Law) **F-** netted $6.6 million from Kingfisher in 2015, Debenhams plc compensation $166,939 (2016); newly elected to Barclays's board in 2017

Jean-Pierre Clamadieu, France **CB-** various positions at Rhodia, Solvay SA, Chairman: Cytec Industries, CEO: Eco Services Operations Corp., Director: AXA **PE-** Ministry of Industry, Ministry of Labour **PC-** World Business Council for Sustainable Development, European Chemical Industry Council, World Economic Forum **E-** Group des École des Mines (Engineering degree) **F-** AXA stock $230,000, Rhodia compensation $2.3 million, AXA compensation $119,340 (2016), AXA shares 9000—$264,724 (2016)

Kevin G. Clifford, US **CB-** Capital Research and Management Company, Director: Capital Guardian Trust Company, CEO: American Funds Distributors **PC-** Board of Regents of Loyola High School in Los Angeles, Forum for Investor Advice, Financial Planning Association, Trustee: Wabash College **E-** Wabash College (BA in Political Science) **F-** compensation N/A (private company); owns a home in the LA area worth $2.2 million as of 2016

Todd A. Combs, US **CB-** Precision Castparts Corp., Berkshire Hathaway, Charter Brokerage llc, Duracell, Director:

JPMorgan Chase & Co. **PE**- Castle Point Capital Management llc, JPMorgan Chase Bank USA, Progressive Insurance Corp., Copper Arch Capital **PC**- Florida Office of Financial Regulation **E**- Florida State University, Columbia Business School **F**- Berkshire Hathaway $27 million+ 2013 bonus, with $1 million salary, JPMorgan compensation $25,500 (2016)

Linda Z. Cook, US **CB**- Bank of New York Mellon, Harbour Energy, Cargill, Chrysaor Holdings Ltd., EIG Global Energy Partners **PE**- Royal Dutch Shell, Boeing, KBR, Marathon Oil **PC**- National Petroleum Council, University of Kansas Endowment Association **E**- University of Kansas (BS in Petroleum Engineering) **F**- $7.5 million severance pay from Shell in 2010 with a $13.4 million pension transfer, Boeing annual compensation $250,000 (2008–2012), Bank of NY Mellon compensation $260,000+ (2017)

James S. Crown, US **CB**- JPMorgan Chase Bank, Henry Crown and Company, General Dynamics Corporation, Sara Lee Corporation, Bank One Corp., First Chicago NBD Corp. **PE**- Salomon Brothers, Capital Markets Service Group, Hillshire Brands Company **PC**- World Business Chicago, PEC Israel Economic Corp., Trustee: The Aspen Institute and University of Chicago **E**- Hampshire College, Stanford University Law School (JD) **F**- heir to $4 billion+ Crown Family fortune; JPMorgan compensation $355,000 (2016)

Pamela Daley, US **CB**- BG Group Ltd., Patheon NV, Secure-Works Corp., Director: BlackRock **PE**- Morgan, Lewis & Bockius, General Electric Co. **PC**- World Wildlife Fund **E**- Princeton University (BA in Literature), University of Pennsylvania Law School (JD) **F**- GE annual compensation $522,000 until 2014, BlackRock compensation $281,000 (2016), Black-Rock shares 1,607—$761,718 (2016)

Laurence Danon Arnaud, France **CB**- Amundi SA, Plastic Omnium SA, Tf1 Group SA, Groupe Bruxelles Lambert SA, Gecina SA, Soc Télévision Française 1 SA, Banque Privée Edmond de Rothschild, BPCE SA **PE**- Diageo plc, Plastic Omnium SA, Lafuma SA, Experian plc, Printemps, Rhodia SA **PC**- École des Mines de Nantes, Medef, French Ministry for the Economy and Finance **E**- École Normale Supérieure Paris (Organic Chemistry & Physics) **F**- net worth $12 million

Alistair Darling, UK **CB**- Morgan Stanley **PE**- Member of the House of Commons, Member of the House of Lords, Chancellor of the Exchequer at Her Majesty's Treasury, Secretary of State for the Department of Trade and Industry, Secretary of State for the Department of Work and Pensions, Secretary of State for Social Security, Secretary of State for Transport, Secretary of State for Scotland **PC**- World Economic Forum, Standard Life Foundation, Royal Institute of International Affairs, Chairman of the Better Together campaign in the Scottish referendum **E**- University of Aberdeen (LLB) **F**- Morgan Stanley compensation $415,000+, Morgan Stanley stock $631,000 (2016)

Ramon de Oliveira, France **CB**- Investment Audit Practice, JACCAR Holdings, Taittinger-Kobrand USA, MONY Life Insurance Co. of America (private), Director: AXA **PE**- JPMorgan Chase, AllianceBernstein Holding lp (AXA), Logan Pass Partners llc, Quilvest SA, The Hartford Insurance Company, American Century Company, Sungard Data Systems, FIS

Data Systems, Graduate School of Business at Columbia University, Stern School of Business at New York University, Fonds de Dotation du Musée du Louvre **PC-** Friends of Education, The Ewing Marion Kauffman Foundation **E-** Instituts D'Études Politiques, Université de Paris **F-** AXA compensation $210,268 (2016), AXA shares 11,300—$335,416 (2016), AllianceBernstein shares 7,059—$177,130 (2016)

Patrick de Saint-Aignan, US & France **CB-** European Kyoto Fund, Allied World Assurance Company Holdings AG, Director: State Street Corporation **PE-** Morgan Stanley, Bank of China Ltd., Natixis Corporate & Investment Bank **E-** École des Hautes Études Commerciales de Paris, Harvard University (MBA) **F-** State Street compensation $364,283, State Street shares worth $2.1 million

Phil de Toledo, US **CB-** President: The Capital Group Companies **PE-** Deloitte Haskins & Sells **PC-** Los Angeles Valley Executive Committee of the American Israel Public Affairs Committee **E-** UCLA (BA in Economics) **F-** owns two homes in LA worth collectively $2.8 million; Capital compensation N/A (private company)

Pierre J.P. de Weck, Switzerland **CB-** Piton Capital llp, General Atlantic llc, Director: Bank of America Merrill Lynch **PE-** Deutsche Bank, Citicorp, UBS, DWS Investments, Rhodia SA, Sal. Oppenheim Jr. & Cie. SCA **PC-** Parasol Unit Foundation for Contemporary Art **E-** Swiss Federal Institute of Technology (MS in Nuclear and Mechanical Engineering), MIT (MS in Management) **F-** Bank of America shares 39,770—$1.06 million (2016), Bank of America compensation $305,000 (2016)

Michel Demaré, Belgium & Switzerland **CB-** Syngenta AG, Global Markets, Director: UBS Group AG, CFO: ABB Group **PE-** Baxter International, Dow Chemical Company, Continental Illinois National Bank and Trust **PC-** World Economic Forum, IMD Foundation **E-** Université Catholique de Louvain, Katholieke Universiteit Leuven, Belgium (MBA) **F-** UBS compensation $975,000

William S. Demchak, US **CB-** Hilliard Lyons Research Advisors, The RBB Fund, Senbanc Fund, Director: BlackRock, CEO: PNC Financial Services Group **PE-** JPMorgan Chase & Co. **PC-** World Affairs Council of Pittsburgh, World Economic Forum, The Financial Services Roundtable **E-** Allegheny College, University of Michigan (MBA) **F-** PNC compensation $13.1 million (2016), PNC shares $63.3 million (2016), BlackRock shares 1,200—$568,800 (2016) [PNC holds 23 percent interest in BlackRock]

James (Jamie) Dimon, US **CB-** CEO: JPMorgan Chase **PE-** Citigroup, Travelers Group, Commercial Credit Company, American Express Company **PC-** The Federal Reserve Bank of New York, World Economic Forum, Council on Foreign Relations, Trustee: New York University Medical Center **E-** Tufts University, Harvard Business School (MBA) **F-** net worth $1.3+ billion; JPMorgan Chase compensation $27.5 million (2016), JPMorgan shares 12,790,959—$1.3 billion (2016); donated $50,000+ to the Council on Foreign Relations in 2016

Arnold W. Donald, US **CB-** Atlas Holdings llc, Wind Point Partners, Russell Brands llc, Crown Holdings, Bridgewell Resources llc, BJC Health System, BMO Financial Corp., Director: Bank of

America Merrill Lynch, CEO: Carnival plc **PE**- Bank of Montreal, VP: Monsanto Company and TransCanada Corp., CEO: Merisant Company **PC**- Boards of Carleton College and Washington University, Grocery Manufacturers of America, United States Russia Business Council, Eurasia Foundation, President's Export Council, Dean's Council of the Kennedy School of Government **E**- Washington University in St. Louis, Carleton College, University of Chicago (MBA) **F**- Carnival plc compensation $9.8 million, Bank of America compensation $300,000 (2016), Bank of America shares 58,342—$1.56 million (2016); sold Carnival shares worth $6.1 million in 2017

Nicholas M. Donofrio, US **CB**- Bank of New York Mellon, Sproxil, Wigix, Delphi Automotive, TopCoder, Advanced Micro Devices, Liberty Mutual Group **PE**- IBM, New York Hall of Science **PC**- National Association of Corporate Directors, The Council for the United States and Italy, Commission on the Future of Higher Education at the US Department of Education, National Action Council for Minorities in Engineering **E**- Rensselaer Polytechnic Institute (BS), Syracuse University (MS in Electrical Engineering) **F**- Bank of NY Mellon compensation $280,000 (2016), NY Mellon shares 64,842—$3.38 million (2016), AMD compensation $338,197 (2016), AMD shares 294,860—$4.38 million (2016)

Irene Dorner, UK **CB**- Rolls Royce, Control Risks Group Holding Ltd., Clearing House, Outleadership, HSBC, Director: AXA Group **PE**- Samuel Montagu and Co. Ltd. **PC**- Financial Services Roundtable, Committee Encouraging Corporate Philanthropy, South East Asia Rainforest Research Partnership, Partnership for New York City, Honorary Fellow: St. Anne's

College—Oxford, UK, University of Nottingham for Asia—UK
E- St. Anne's College (MA in Jurisprudence) F- AXA compen-
sation $97,127 (2016), AXA shares 2000—$58,820 (2016), Rolls
Royce compensation $82,300 (2016), HSBC compensation
$86,747 (2016)

Lynn A. Dugle, US **CB**- Engility Holdings, Texans Credit
Union, Raytheon Company, Director: State Street Corporation
PE- ADC Telecommunications, Texas Instruments **PC**- Intelligence and National Security Alliance, Defense Science Board,
CyberPatriot, Southern Methodist University Graduate Program **E**- Purdue University (BA in Technical Management and
Spanish), University of Texas at Dallas (MBA) **F**- State Street
compensation $290,250 (2016), State Street shares $488,051
(2017), Engility shares $624,252 (2017)

Denis Duverne, France **CB**- AllianceBernstein Holding llp,
Chair: Board of Directors of AXA **PE**- various positions at
AXA, Compagnie Financière IBI, French Consulate General in
New York **PC**- French Ministry of Finance **E**- Instituts D'Études
and Politiques École Nationale D'Administration **F**- AXA compensation $2.8 million (2016), AXA shares 1,348,524—$39.6
million (2016)

Joseph J. Echevarria, US **CB**- Bank of New York Mellon, Xerox,
Unum Group, Pfizer **PE**- Deloitte Touche Tohmatsu llp **PC**-
Association of Latino Professionals in Finance and Accounting,
Presidential Commission on Election Administration, Pres-
ident's Export Council, My Brother's Keeper Alliance, World
Economic Forum, Trustee: University of Miami **E**- University of
Miami (BA in Business) **F**- NY Mellon compensation $326,497

(2016), NY Mellon shares 15,372—$802,879 (2016), Xerox shares 12,803—$361,812 (2016)

Jessica P. Einhorn, US **CB**- Time Warner, Director: BlackRock, Dean: Paul H. Nitze School of Advanced International Studies at Johns Hopkins University **PE**- Clark & Weinstock, International Monetary Fund, World Bank, United States Treasury, International Development Cooperation Agency of the United States, Pitney Bowes **PC**- Trilateral Commission, Council on Foreign Relations, Peterson Institute for International Economics, Center for Global Development, National Bureau of Economic Research, Trustee: Rockefeller Brothers Fund **E**- Barnard College at Columbia University, SAIS (John Hopkins) (MA), Princeton University (PhD in Political Science) **F**- BlackRock compensation $246,000 (2016), BlackRock shares 1,452—$688,248 (2016), John Hopkins salary $300,000+ (2017), Time Warner shares worth $2 million as of 2016

Dame Amelia C. Fawcett, US & UK **CB**- Kinnevik AB, Director: State Street Corporation **PE**- Morgan Stanley, Guardian Media Group plc, Sullivan & Cromwell, Pensions First Group llp **PC**- Hedge Fund Standards Board, Prince of Wales's Charitable Foundation, London Business School, World Economic Forum, Commissioner: US–UK Fulbright Commission **E**- Wellesley College, University of Virginia (JD) **F**- State Street compensation $302,000 (2016), State Street shares $2.8 million (2017), Kinnevik AB compensation $83,000 (2016); awarded the title of Dame, Commander of the Order of the British Empire, in 2010

Laurence (Larry) D. Fink, US **CB**- PNC Financial Services Group, Innovir Laboratories (private), CEO: BlackRock **PE**- The

First Boston Corporation, VIMRx Pharmaceuticals **PC**- Financial Services Roundtable, Museum of Modern Art, World Economic Forum International Business Council, Director: Council on Foreign Relations, Trustee: New York University **E**- UCLA (BA, MBA) **F**- BlackRock compensation $25.4 million (2017), Black-Rock shares 1,041,711—$493.7 million (2016); awarded the title of CEO of the Decade by Financial News (2011); donated $50,000+ to the Council on Foreign Relations (2016)

Mark A. Flaherty, US **CB**- Goldman Sachs Group **PE**-Wellington Management Group, Standish Mellon Asset Management Company, Aetna **PC**- Trustee: Providence College and The Newman School **E**- Providence College **F**- Goldman Sachs compensation $575,000 (2016), Goldman Sachs shares 6,714—$1.6 million (2016)

Timothy P. Flynn, US **CB**- Walmart, Director: JPMorgan Chase & Co. **PE**- KPMG llp **PC**- World Economic Forum's International Business Counsel, Business Roundtable, Financial Accounting Standards Board, The Prince of Wales' International Integrated Reporting Committee **E**- University of St. Thomas (St. Paul, Minnesota) **F**- JPMorgan compensation $349,375 (2016), JPMorgan shares 38,817—$3.8 million (2016), Wal-Mart compensation $384,364 (2016), Wal-Mart shares 33,184—$3.23 million (2016)

Jean-Martin Folz, France **CB**- Jeumont-Schneider, Senior Independent Director: AXA SA **PE**- Groupe PSA, Eutelsat Communications SA, Carrefour SA, Banque PSA Finance, Alstom AG, Solvay SA, Compagnie de Saint-Gobain SA, Société Générale Group, Faurecia SA, Chair/CEO: Automobile Peugeot SA **E**-

École Polytechnique (Graduate), École Nationale Supérieure des Mines de Paris (degree in Engineering) **F**- AXA compensation $199,628 (2016), AXA shares 11,084—$325,980 (2016)

Reto Francioni, Switzerland **CB**- Swiss International Air Lines AG, Coca-Cola HBC AG, MedTech Innovation Partners AG, Consors, Director: UBS Group AG **PE**- Credit Suisse, SWX Europe Holdings Ltd., Consors Capital Bank AG, Hofmann-La Roche AG, Clearstream International SA, CEO: Deutsche Böerse Systems AG **PC**- Moscow International Financial Center, World Economic Forum **E**- University of Zurich (LLB, PhD) **F**- UBS compensation $580,000 (2016), Coca-Cola HBS compensation $94,770 (2016)

Mary Francis, UK **CB**- Fund Distribution Ltd., Ensco plc, Swiss Re AG, Director: Barclays plc **PE**- Aviva plc, Centrica plc, Cable & Wireless Communications Ltd. **PC**- UK Civil Service, Bank of England, Chatham House, Pensions Policy Institute, National Consumer Council, Press Complaints Commission, International Financial Services **E**- University of Cambridge (MA in History) **F**- Swiss RE compensation $64,000 (2016), Barclays compensation $37,990 (2016), Barclays shares 7,600—$73,796 (2016), Ensco plc compensation $302,252 (2016), Ensco shares worth $65,395 as of 2016

André François-Poncet, France **CB**- CIAM, Director: AXA SA **PE**- Morgan Stanley Dean Witter, Médica France SA, BC Partners **PC**- Club des Trente **E**- École des Hautes Études Commerciales de Montréal (MA in Business Administration), Harvard Business School (MBA) **F**- AXA estimated compensation $118,000 (2017)

Fabrizio Freda, Italy **CB**- Director: BlackRock, CEO: The Estée Lauder Companies **PE**- Procter & Gamble, Coca-Cola **E**- University of Naples **F**- BlackRock compensation $245,000 (2016), BlackRock shares 2,442—$1.15 million (2016), Estée Lauder compensation $15 million (2017); sold 300,000 shares of Estée Lauder for $31.7 million in 2017

William C. Freda, US **CB**- The Guardian Life Insurance Company of America (private), Hamilton Insurance Group Ltd. (private), Director: State Street Corporation **PE**- Deloitte llp **PC**- Committee on Capital Markets Regulation, American Institute of Certified Public Accountants' Insurance Companies Committee, International Accounting Standards Committee's Insurance Steering Committee, Economic Club of New York, National Italian American Foundation **E**- Bentley University (BS) **F**- State Street compensation $356,000 (2016)

Emerson U. Fullwood, US **CB**- Director: Vanguard Group, Professor: Rochester Institute of Technology, Director: North Carolina A&T University's College of Engineering Industry Advisory Group **PE**- Xerox Corporation, Amerigroup Corp., General Signal Corporation, SPX Corp. **PC**- United Way of Rochester, University of Rochester Medical Center, Monroe Community College Foundation, Rochester Urban League, Colgate Rochester Crozer Divinity School **E**- North Carolina State University, Columbia University (MBA) **F**- Vanguard compensation $237,000 (2016), Rochester compensation $160,000+ (2017)

Edward P. Garden, US **CB**- Bank of New York Mellon, Pentair, Trian Fund Management, General Electric (as of October

2017) **PE**- The Wendy's Company, Family Dollar Stores, Credit Suisse First Boston, Chemtura Corporation, BT Alex Brown **E**- Harvard (BA) **F**- NY Mellon compensation $268,746 (2016), Wendy's shares $3.6 million 2016; controls voting rights on 32.3 million shares of NY Mellon through Train Entities (2016); is also a Founding Partner of Train Fund Management, a private hedge fund with $12.4 billion under management as of 2016; purchased 421,800 shares in NY Mellon for $18.3 million in 2015

Rémi Garuz, France **CB**- Amundi SA, Caisse Régionale de Crédit Agricole Mutuel d'Aquitaine **PE**- Producta, CAMCA, Regional Bank of Gironde **PC**- Regional Economic, Social and Environmental Council **E**- awarded BEPC (Junior High School Certificate) and an Agricultural Technician Certificate **F**- compensation N/A

William W. George, US **CB**- Goldman Sachs Group, Novartis Consumer Health **PE**- Medtronic, Honeywell, ExxonMobil, Target Corp., Visiting Professor of Management: École Polytechnic Fédérale de Lausanne **PC**- US Department of Defense, The Carnegie Endowment for International Peace, The Global Center for Leadership and Business Ethics, World Economic Forum USA, Harvard Business School, American Red Cross, National Association of Corporate Directors, World Economic Forum, Trustee: Mayo Clinic **E**- Georgia Institute of Technology (BS in Industrial Engineering), Harvard University (MBA) **F**- Goldman Sachs compensation $600,000 (2016), Goldman Sachs shares 73,613—$17.6 million (2016)

Murry S. Gerber, US **CB**- Halliburton, United States Steel Corp., Director: BlackRock **PE**- Shell, CEO: EQT Corporation

PC- Pennsylvania Business Council, Trustee: Augustana College
E- Augustana College, University of Illinois (MA in Geology)
F- BlackRock compensation $301,000 (2016), BlackRock shares
38,686—$18.3 million (2016), US Steel compensation $200,000
(2016), US Steel shares 164,345—$4.4 million (2016), Halliburton
compensation $412,657 (2016), Halliburton shares 51,451—$2.3
million (2016)

Crawford Gillies, UK **CB**- Control Risks Groups Holdings Ltd.,
SSE plc, Director: Barclays plc, Chairman: The Edrington Group
Ltd. **PE**- Standard Life plc, Bain & Company, Mitie Group plc,
Reed International plc, Scottish Development International
Ltd. **PC**- UK Department of Trade and Industry's Manage-
ment Board and Strategy Board **E**- The University of Edinburgh
(LLB), Harvard Business School (MBA) **F**- Barclays compen-
sation $327,500 (2016), Barclays shares 70,208—$681,719 (2016),
SSE compensation $99,560 (2016), SSE shares 5,000—$9.2 mil-
lion (2016), Mitie compensation $100,000 (2016)

Mike C. Gitlin, US **CB**- Capital Group Companies Management Committee **PE**- Citigroup Global Markets, T. Rowe Price
Group **PC**- N/A **E**- Colgate University (BA) **F**- compensation
N/A (private company); owns a home in the LA area worth $6.9
million as of 2017

Thomas H. Glocer, US **CB**- Morgan Stanley, K2 Intelligence,
Publicis Groupe, Merck & Co. **PE**- Instinet Group, New York
City Investment Fund Manager, CEO: Thomson Reuters **PC**-
European Business Leaders Council, Partnership for New York
City, Madison Council of the Library of Congress, Advisory
Board of British-American Business Council, International

Business Council of World Economic Forum, Director: Council on Foreign Relations **E**- Columbia University (BA in Political Science), Yale Law School (JD) **F**- Morgan Stanley stock worth $2.1 million (2016), Morgan Stanley compensation $325,000 (2016), Merck compensation $305,000 (2016), Merck shares 49,291—$2.7 million (2016)

Ann F. Godbehere, UK & Canada **CB**- British American Tobacco plc, All Source Global Management AGM llc, Prudential plc, Rio Tinto Group, Atrium Underwriters Ltd., Arden Holdings Ltd., Director: UBS Group AG **PE**- Sun Life Financial (Canada), CFO: Northern Rock, CFO: Swiss Re Group **E**- Certified General Accountants Association of Canada **F**- UBS compensation $825,000 (2016), British American Tobacco compensation $146,720, British American Tobacco shares $200,252, Prudential shares $391,383, Rio Tinto shares $146,079 (2016)

Jeffrey A. Goldstein, US **CB**- Bank of New York Mellon, Hellman & Friedman llc, Edelman Financial Services, Westfield Corp. Ltd. **PE**- LPL Financial Holdings, BT Wolfensohn, Arch Capital Group, AlixPartners llc **PC**- Council on Foreign Relations, Foreign Policy Assn., Financial Stability Oversight Council, German Marshall Fund of the US, International Center for Research on Women, US Department of the Treasury **E**- Vassar College (BA in Economics), Yale University (MA, PhD in Economics) **F**- NY Mellon compensation $269,996 (2016), NY Mellon shares 20,332—$1.06 million (2016)

James P. Gorman, Australia & US **CB**- Chairman/CEO: Morgan Stanley **PE**- Merrill Lynch, Mckinsey & Co., Phillips Fox & Masel, MSCI, Visa USA **PC**- Federal Reserve Bank of New

York, Institute of International Finance, The Partnership for New York City, Metropolitan Museum of Art, Business Council, Council on Foreign Relations, World Economic Forum, Business Roundtable **E-** University of Melbourne (BA, LLB), Columbia University (MBA) **F-** Morgan Stanley compensation $9.6 million (2016); owns 183,687 Morgan Stanley shares worth $8.4 million, with options on 424,731 (2016)

Andreas Gottschling, Germany **CB-** Credit Suisse Group AG, Menkul Degerler A.S., Banca Comercială Română SA **PE-** Erste Group Bank AG, Erste&Steiermärkische Bank D.D, Oesterreichische Kontrollbank AG **PC-** N/A **E-** University of Freiburg, Germany (BA), Harvard University (postgraduate studies), UC San Diego (PhD in Economics) **F-** Credit Suisse compensation $2.8 million (2016)

Laurent Goutard, France **CB-** Amundi SA, Société Générale SA, Komerční Banka AS, Franfinance SA, Compagnie Générale d'Affacturage AS **PE-** Genefim SA, Sophia Bail SA, SG Financial Services Holding SA, Sogessur SA, Geneval SA **PC-** N/A **E-** Université Paris Dauphine (Economics), Institut d'Études Politiques de Paris (Economics) **F-** compensation N/A

Mark B. Grier, US **CB-** Vice Chairman: Prudential Financial **PE-** Chase Manhattan Corporation, Global Impact Investing Network, Achieve, Wachovia Securities Financial Holdings llc, RGS Energy Group, Annuity and Life Re (Holdings) Ltd. **E-** Eastern Illinois University (BA, MA), University of Rochester (MBA) **F-** Prudential compensation $14.2 million (2015); owns 920,869 shares of Prudential valued at $36.4 million

Sir Gerry Grimstone, UK **CB-** Tote Direct, Standard Life Investments Ltd., TheCityUK, Deloitte llp, Wilmington Capital Ltd., Abu Dhabi Commercial Bank P.J.S.C., Deputy Chairman: Barclays plc **PE-** Candover Investments plc, Schroders plc, F&C Global Smaller Companies plc, Aggregate Industries Ltd., Dairy Crest Group plc **PC-** Ministry of Defence, Horserace Totalisator Board, HM Treasury, UK Department of Health and Social Security, Financial Services Trade and Investment Board, Shareholder Executive, RAF Strike Command Board **E-** University of Oxford (MA, MS) **F-** Barclays compensation $327,500 (2016), Barclays shares 103,288—$2 million (2016), Standard Life compensation $497,800 (2016); owns 206,626 shares of Standard Life valued at $103 million

James Grosfeld, US **CB-** Copart, Interstate Bakeries Corporation, Addington Resources, Director: BlackRock **PE-** PulteGroup, Championship Liquidating Trust **PC-** Federal National Mortgage Association **E-** Amherst College, Columbia Law School (LLB) **F-** BlackRock compensation $264,000 (2016), BlackRock shares 513,780—$243.5 million (2016)

Rajiv L. Gupta, India & US **CB-** New Mountain Capital (private $6 billion investment firm), Delphi Automotive plc, Tyco International plc, Hewlett-Packard Company, Director: Vanguard Group **PE-** Scott Paper Company, Ducolite International, President: Rohm and Haas Co. **PC-** World Economic Forum, American Chemistry Council, Society of Chemical Industry, Trustee: The Conference Board and Drexel University **E-** Indian Institute of Technology, Cornell University, Drexel University (MBA) **F-** Vanguard compensation $250,333 (2016), Tyco International compensation $282,500 (2016), HP compensation

$360,354 (2017), HP shares 267,896—$5.8 million (2016), Tyco compensation 282,500 (2016), Tyco shares 30,803—$2.9 million, Delphi (chairman) compensation $525,072, Delphi shares 23,554—$2.3 million (2016)

Alexander Gut, UK & Switzerland **CB-** Credit Suisse Group AG, Holcim (Deutschland) AG, Adecco Group AG, Gut Corporate Finance AG **PE-** KPMG, Ernst & Young **E-** University of Zurich (MBA, PhD in Business Administration) **F-** Credit Suisse compensation $2.8 million (2016), Credit Suisse shares 7,866—$125,698 (2016)

Amy Gutmann, US **CB-** Director: Vanguard Group, President: University of Pennsylvania **PC-** Carnegie Corporation of New York, National Commission on the Humanities and Social Sciences, Presidential Commission for the Study of Bioethical Issues, Global Colloquium of the University Presidents, World Economic Forum, Trustee: National Constitution Center, Advisor: Secretary General of the UN **E-** Radcliffe Institute for Advanced Study, London School of Economics, Harvard University (PhD in Political Science) **F-** University of Pennsylvania salary $3.5 million (2017), Vanguard compensation $236,000 (2016)

Gerald L. Hassell, US **CB-** Comcast, Institute of International Finance, Chairman and CEO: Bank of New York Mellon **PE-** Private Export Funding Corporation **PC-** Financial Services Roundtable, Economic Club of New York, Financial Services Forum, Visitors of Duke University Fuqua School of Business, Big Brothers/Big Sisters of New York City, The Partnership for New York City, The Philharmonic-Symphony Society of New York, September 11 Memorial & Museum **E-** Duke University

(BA), New York University (MBA in Finance) **F-** NY Mellon compensation $19.1 million (2016), NY Mellon shares 2.52 million—$131.8 million (2016)

JoAnn Heffernan Heisen, US **CB-** Skytop Lodge Corporation, Director: Vanguard Group **PE-** Johnson & Johnson, Primerica Corporation, Kenmill Textile Corporation, Chase Manhattan Bank **PC-** Robert Wood Johnson Foundation, University Medical Center of Princeton at Plainsboro, Maxwell School of Citizenship and Public Affairs at Syracuse University, Center for Talent Innovation **E-** Syracuse University **F-** Vanguard compensation $248,833 (2016); also President of JoAnn Heffernan Heisen Family Foundation, which has $600,000 in assets as of 2015

Robert H. Herz, UK & US **CB-** Morgan Stanley, Workiva, itBit Trust Company (Bitcoin), Fannie Mae, Federal National Mortgage Association **PE-** Webfilings, Coopers & Lybrand llp, PricewaterhouseCoopers llp **PC-** Kessler Foundation, Financial Accounting Standards Board, International Accounting Standards Board, Public Company Accounting Oversight Board, Accounting Standards Oversight Council of Canada, Sasb Foundation **E-** University of Manchester (BA in Economics), Chartered Public Accountant **F-** Morgan Stanley stock worth $1.9 million (2016), Morgan Stanley compensation $325,000 (2016), Fannie Mae compensation $182,079 (2016)

Linda A. Hill, US **CB-** Director: State Street Corporation, Professor of Business Administration: Harvard University **PE-** Cooper Industries, Harvard Business Publishing **PC-** World Economic Forum, The Bridgespan Group, Nelson Mandela

Children's Fund USA, Trustee: Bryn Mawr College E- Bryn Mawr College, University of Chicago (PhD) F- State Street compensation $264,000 (2016), Harvard salary $198,000+ (2017), State Street shares 14,145—$4.4 million (2017)

John M. Hinshaw, US **CB**- Bank of New York Mellon, Docu-Sign, Clique Intelligence **PE**- Hewlett-Packard Company, Boeing, Cellco Partnership, Bell Atlantic **PC**- US Department of Commerce **E**- James Madison University (BA in Business) **F**- NY Mellon compensation $263,996 (2016), NY Mellon shares 14,145—$738,793 (2016)

Nobuyuki Hirano, Japan **CB**- Morgan Stanley, Mitsubishi UFJ Financial Group **PE**- The Bank of Tokyo-Mitsubishi UFJ Ltd. **PC**- Institute of International Finance, World Economic Forum, Japanese Bankers Association **E**- Kyoto University (Law degree) **F**- Bank of Tokyo-Mitsubishi compensation $1.3 million (2016); represents Mitsubishi's 23.5 percent ownership in Morgan Stanley

Joseph (Jay) L. Hooley, US **CB**- Boston Financial Data Services, National Financial Data Services, President: State Street Corp. **PC**- Boston College Center for Asset Management, Corporate Advisory Board Member: The Boston Club **E**- Boston College **F**- State Street compensation $13.5 million (2016), State Street shares $71.2 million (2016)

Linda Parker Hudson, US **CB**- Director: Bank of America Merrill Lynch, CEO: BAE Systems **PE**- General Dynamics Corp., Martin Marietta, Ford Aerospace, Harris Corporation **PC**- Aerospace Industries Association, International Women's

Forum, C200 **E-** University of Florida (Engineering) **F-** Bank of America compensation $280,000 (2015), Bank of America shares 56,365—$1.5 million (2016), BAE compensation $300,000 (2016), BAE CEO salary $2.9 million (2013), BAE shares 3,309—$1.77 million (2016)

Martina Hund-Mejean, Germany **CB-** Prudential Financial, Covidien International Finance SA, Topaz International Group SA, CFO: MasterCard Worldwide **PE-** Tyco International plc, General Motors Corporation, Dow Chemical **PC-** Trustee: University of Virginia **E-** University of Freiburg (MA in Economics), University of Virginia (MBA) **F-** MasterCard compensation $5.8 million (2016), Prudential compensation $305,000 (2016), Prudential shares 15,633—$1.6 million (2016)

Jacqueline Hunt, South Africa **CB-** Allianz SE **PE-** Prudential plc, Standard Life & Accident Insurance Co., Norwich Union Insurance, Aviva Group Ireland plc, Royal & SunAlliance Insurance plc, PricewaterhouseCoopers, National Express Group plc **PC-** World Economic Forum, Dormant Assets Commission, FXA Practitioner Panel, TheCityUK, ABI Board **E-** University of the Witwatersrand (BA), South African Institute of Chartered Accounts (Chartered Accountant) **F-** Allianz compensation $2,385,639 (2016)

Laban P. Jackson Jr., US **CB-** Clear Creek Properties, Gulf Stream Home, Garden Inc., TBN Holdings, Director: JPMorgan Chase & Co. **PE-** Home Depot, SIRVA, IPIX Corporation, Bank One **PC-** Federal Reserve Bank of Cleveland **E-** United States Military Academy **F-** JPMorgan compensation $532,500 (2016), JPMorgan shares 175,204—$17.2 million (2016)

Reuben Jeffery III, US **CB**- Director: Barclays plc, CEO: Rockefeller & Co. ($43 billion in asset management as of 2016) **PE**- Goldman Sachs & Co., Davis Polk & Wardwell llp, Morgan Guaranty Trust Company of New York, US Under Secretary of State for Economic Energy and Agriculture **PC**- National Security Council, The Ditchley Foundation, Council on Foreign Relations, World Economic Forum, Center for Strategic & International Studies, US Commodity Futures Trading Commission, International Advisory Council of the China Securities Regulatory Commission (CSRC), Atlantic Council, Trilateral Commission **E**- Yale University (BA in Political Science), Stanford University (MBA, JD) **F**- owns a $9 million Park Avenue apartment as of 2013; Goldman Sachs stock worth approximately $80 million; Barclays compensation $157,200 (2016), Barclays shares 200,196—$1.9 million (2016), Rockefeller compensation N/A (private firm); donated $25,000–50,000 to Council on Foreign Relations (2016)

Abigail Pierrepont Johnson, US **CB**- President: Fidelity Financial Services llc **PE**- Booz Allen & Hamilton **PC**- Trustee: Massachusetts Institute of Technology, Trustee: Fidelity Foundation **E**- Hobart and William Smith Colleges, Harvard Business (MBA) **F**- net worth $13.1 billion

Edward Johnson III, US **CB**- Crocker Realty Investors, CEO: FMR (retired), CEO: Regal Communications, Chair: Fidelity Investments **PC**- Beth Israel Hospital, American Academy of Arts and Science, Boston Museum of Fine Arts, Trustee: Fidelity Foundation **E**- Harvard (BA) **F**- net worth $8.4 billion (2016)

James A. Johnson, US **CB**- Goldman Sachs Group, Johnson Capital Partners, KB HOME/Shaw Louisiana llc **PE**- Fannie

Mae, Lehman Brothers, Dayton Hudson Corporation, Relypsa, Perseus llc, Gannett Co., Unitedhealth Group, Forestar Group, Temple-Inland, Cummins, TEGNA, AmpliPhi Biosciences Corporation, Executive Assistant to VP Walter F. Mondale **PC-** Council on Foreign Relations, American Institute of Certified Public Accountants Administrations, Trustee: The Brookings Institution **E-** University of Minnesota (BA), Princeton University (MPA) **F-** Goldman Sachs compensation $600,000 (2016), Goldman Sachs shares 42,312—$10.2 million (2016)

C. Bruce Johnstone, US **CB-** AP Capital Partners llc, Chairman and Trustee: Fidelity International **PC-** Needham Education Foundation, Harvard Business School Fund, Alexis de Tocqueville Society of the United Way, Inner City Schools Scholarship Fund **E-** Harvard University (BA, MBA) **F-** compensation N/A (private firms)

Helga Jung, Germany **CB-** Allianz SE, Deutsche Telekom AG **PE-** UniCredit SpA, Professor: University of Augsburg **PC-** World Economic Forum **E-** University of Augsburg (MBA, PhD in Business Administration) **F-** Allianz compensation $2.4 million (2016)

Robert S. Kapito, US **CB-** icruise.com, President: BlackRock **PE-** Bain & Co. **PC-** International Monetary Conference, The Financial Services Roundtable, Trustee: University of Pennsylvania **E-** Wharton School of the University of Pennsylvania (BA), Harvard Business School (MBA) **F-** BlackRock compensation $19.3 million (2017), BlackRock shares 411,144—$194.8 million (2016)

Edmund F. "Ted" Kelly, US & Ireland **CB**- Bank of New York Mellon, Liberty Mutual Group **PE**- Mellon Financial Corp., Aetna, EMC Corporation, Segue Software, Professor: University of New Brunswick, Professor: University of Missouri at St. Louis **PC**- Financial Services Roundtable, World Economic Forum, Alliance of American Insurers, United Way of Massachusetts Bay, American Red Cross of Massachusetts Bay, Boston Private Industry Council, American Ireland Fund, Bretton Woods Committee, Trustee: Boston College **E**- Queen's University of Belfast (BA), MIT (PhD) **F**- NY Mellon compensation $285,396 (2016), NY Mellon shares 45,807—$2.39 million (2016), Liberty shares 45,807—$824,526 (2016); retired as CEO of Liberty Mutual in 2013 with $50 million his final year

Angelien Kemna, Netherlands **CB**- Yellow&Blue Investment Management BV, Director: AXA, CEO: APG Asset Management NV **PE**- ING Investment Management BV, Robeco Group NV, Railpen Investments, Maastricht University, Erasmus University in Rotterdam, University of Leiden, Netherlands Authority for the Financial Markets **PC**- Child and Youth Finance International **E**- Erasmus University Rotterdam (MA in Econometrics, PhD in Finance) **F**- AXA compensation $91,494 (2016)

Isabelle Kocher, France **CB**- International Power plc, Electrabel SA, ENGIE SA, Lyonnaise Des Eaux France SA, Director: AXA SA, CEO: SUEZ SA **PE**- Compagnie Financière Edmond de Rothschild, Société Européenne de Propulsion, Arkema SA, French Ministry for the Economy and Finance, Industrial Affairs Adviser to the Prime Minister of France **PC**- World Economic Forum **E**- École Normale Supérieure (graduate degree), Corps des Mines (postgraduate degree in Physics) **F**- AXA compensation $78,000 (2016), AXA shares 5,960—$175,283 (2016), ENGIE compensation $1.13 million (2016)

Andreas N. Koopmann, Switzerland **CB**- Credit Suisse Group AG, Georg Fischer AG, Nestlé SA, CSD Holding AG **PE**- Bobst Group SA, Bruno Piatti AG, Motor Columbus AG **E**- Swiss Federal Institute of Technology (MA in Mechanical Engineering), International Institute for Management Development (MBA) **F**- Credit Suisse compensation $2.8 million (2016), Credit Suisse shares 81,746—$1.3 million (2016), Nestlé compensation $750,052 (2016), Nestlé shares 92,536—$6.6 million (2016)

Darcy Kopcho, US **CB**- Capital Group Companies Management Committee **PE**- Baker International, various positions at Capital Group Companies **PC**- Defenders of Wildlife **E**- University of California, Santa Barbara (BA in Religious Studies), University of California, Irvine (MBA) **F**- compensation N/A (private firm); owns a 7,340 sq. ft. house valued at $4.5 million in the LA area as of 2009

Karl J. Krapek, US **CB**- Prudential Financial, Northrop Grumman **PE**- Carrier Corp., United Technologies Corp., Otis Elevator Company, Pratt and Whitney Aircraft Engine Company, General Motors, The Connecticut Bank and Trust Company, Alcatel-Lucent USA, Delta Airlines **PC**- Visteon Corporation, Chairman and Trustee: Connecticut State University System **E**- Kettering University (BA), Purdue University (MS in Industrial Engineering) **F**- Prudential compensation $420,000 (2016), Prudential shares 45,606—$5.03 million (2016), Northrop Grumman compensation $354,011 (2016), Northrop shares 27,879—$8.27 million (2016)

Ellen J. Kullman, US CB- Goldman Sachs Group, Dell Technologies, Amgen, United Technologies, Temasek Holdings (Private) Ltd. **PE**- General Motors, General Electric, CEO: DuPont do Brasil SA **PC**- Council on Foreign Relations, Tufts University Board of Trustees, US–India CEO Forum, Business Council, National Academy of Engineering, World Economic Forum **E**- Tufts University (BS in Mechanical Engineering), Northwestern University (MBA) **F**- Goldman Sachs compensation $575,000 (2016), Goldman Sachs shares $50,028 (2016), Dell compensation $1.26 million (2016), United Technologies compensation $300,947 (2016), United Tech shares 14,798—$1.7 million (2016), Amgen compensation $79,790 (2017) (new appointment Oct. 2016), DuPont salary while CEO $9.7 million (2012)

Robert LeBlanc, France **CB**- Amundi SA, RL Conseil, SACI, Andersen Consulting, Chairman and CEO: Aon France **PE**- Société des Bourses Françaises, Meeschaert Rousselle, Uni Europe Assurance, APAX France, International Space Brokers France **PC**- Movement of Christian Entrepreneurs and Managers, MEDEF **E**- École Polytechnique (graduate degree), Université of Paris-Dauphine (PhD in Strategy of Organizations) **F**- Amundi compensation $3,510 (2016), Aon compensation $3.8 million (2016)

Suet Fern Lee, Singapore **CB**- Sanofi, Rickmers Trust Management Pte. Ltd., Director: AXA SA **PE**- Morgan Lewis & Bockius llp (Donald Trump's international law firm since 2005), Macquarie International Infrastructure Fund Ltd., Horsburgh Maritime Investments, SembCorp Industries Ltd., Transcu Group Ltd., Orangestar Investment Holdings Private

Ltd., Richina Pacific Ltd., Eng Wah Organization Ltd. **PC-** The World Justice Project, National Heritage Board, International Bar Association, Accounting Advisory Board, National University of Singapore Business School, Advisory Board: Singapore Management University School of Law, Executive Committee: Singapore Academy of Law **E-** University of Cambridge (First Master of Arts (Law)), Gray's Inn, London (Barrister-at-Law) **F-** Sanofi SA compensation $110,000 (2016), AXA compensation $118,000 (2016), AXA shares 8,000—$235,280 (2016)

Peter R. Lighte, US **CB-** Prudential Financial, JPMorgan Chase Bank (China) **PE-** Manufacturers Hanover Ltd. **PC-** Council on International Educational Exchange, Half The Sky Foundation **E-** George Washington University (BA), Princeton University (PhD in East Asian Studies) **F-** Prudential compensation $430,000 (2016), Prudential shares 4,260—$3.7 million

Stefan Lippe, Switzerland & Germany **CB-** Commerzbank AG, Yes Europe AG, CelsiusPro AG, Acqupart Holding AG, Acqufin AG, Director: AXA SA **PE-** Swiss Re AG, Bavarian Re **PC-** World Economic Forum, German Insurance Association for Vocational Training **E-** Universität Mannheim (BA in Mathematics, PhD in Economics) **F-** AXA compensation $214,181 (2016), AXA shares 1,200—$35,292 (2016), Commerzbank compensation $140,985 (2016)

F. Joseph Loughrey, US **CB-** Hillenbrand, SKF AB, Director: Vanguard Group **PE-** Cummins **PC-** National Association of Manufacturers, Kellogg Institute for International Studies at the University of Notre Dame, Chicago Council on Global Affairs, Lumina Foundation for Education, Oxfam America **E-** University of Notre Dame **F**- Hillenbrand compensation $246,852 (2016), Hillenbrand stock 43,786—$1.9 million (2016)

Mark Loughridge, US **CB**- Dow Chemical Company, Director: Vanguard Group **PE**- CFO: IBM (retired 2013) **E**- Stanford University (BE in Mechanical Engineering), University of Chicago (MBA), École Nationale Supérieure de Mécanique, France **F**- Vanguard compensation $281,333 (2016), Dow compensation $262,474 (2016), Dow shares 7,574—$534,724 (2016), IBM compensation $775,000 (2013), IBM shares 88,317—$13.2 million (2013)

Rob W. Lovelace, US **CB**- Capital Group Companies Management Committee **PE**- various positions at Capital Group Companies **PC**- Reef New World Fund, California Community Foundation, Pacific Council on International Policy, Council on Foreign Relations **E**- Princeton University (Mineral Economics (Geology)), Chartered Financial Analyst **F**- Capital compensation N/A (private firm); owns a home in the LA area valued at $4.8 million

Monica C. Lozano, US **CB**- The Walt Disney Co., Target Corporation, Sun America Asset Management Corp. (private), Director: Bank of America Merrill Lynch **PE**- Lozano Communications, ImpreMedia llc, Tenet Healthcare Corp., Union Bank Switzerland, CEO and Publisher: La Opinión lp **PC**- Council on Foreign Relations, California HealthCare Foundation, The Rockefeller Foundation, National Council of La Raza, President's Council on Jobs and Competitiveness, Trustee: University of Southern California, Regent: University of California **E**- University of Oregon **F**- Bank of America compensation $320,000

(2016), Bank of America shares 130,091—$3.48 million (2016), Disney compensation $124,964 (2016), Disney shares 23,019— $2.3 million (2016), Target compensation $196,630 (2016), Target shares 592—$33,080 (2016)

John A. Luke Jr., US **CB-** Bank of New York Mellon, Blue Heron Capital, The WestRock Company, The Timkin Company, Dominion Midstream Partners, Virginia Commonwealth University Health System, Factory Mutual Insurance Company **PE-** Rigesa **PC-** Council on Foreign Relations, The American Enterprise Institute for Public Policy Research, US Air Force, National Association of Manufacturers, American Forest & Paper Association, Virginia Museum of Fine Arts, Virginia Commonwealth University Health System, President's Export Council **E-** St. Lawrence University (BA), University of Pennsylvania (MBA) **F-** NY Mellon compensation $249,996 (2016), WestRock compensation $341,444 (2016), WestRock shares 2,935,272—$172 million (2016)

Seraina (Maag) Macia, Australia & Switzerland **CB-** Credit Suisse AG, Hamilton Insurance Group, BanQu **PE-** XL Insurance North America, Zurich Financial Services, Neue Zürcher Bank, Universal Underwriters Insurance Company **PC-** World Economic Forum Young Global Leaders, CFA Institute, Association of Professional Insurance Women **E-** Deakin University, Monash University (MBA), CFA Institute (Chartered Financial Analyst) **F-** Credit Suisse compensation $2.8 million (2016), Credit Suisse shares 19,799—$316,388 (2016)

Scott C. Malpass, US **CB-** Director: Vanguard Group, Manager: University of Notre Dame's $3.5 billion endowment **PE-** St.

Joseph Capital Corp., Bank of New York Mellon, Irving Trust Company **PC**- Round Table Healthcare Management llc, The Investment Fund for Foundations **E**- University of Notre Dame (BA, MBA) **F**- Vanguard compensation $230,300 (2016), Notre Dame University compensation $2.05 million (2016)

François Martineau, France **CB**- Conservateur Finance SA, Bred Banque Populaire, Director: AXA, Attorney: Lussan et Associés **PE**- École Nationale de la Magistrature **PC**- Council of Europe, Associations Mutuelles Le Conservateur **E**- Institut d'Études Politiques, Université Paris-Sorbonne, Paris IV (Philosophy degree), Université Paris I Panthéon-Sorbonne (MA in Law) **F**- AXA compensation $112,056 (2016), AXA shares 6,732—$197,988 (2016)

Christof Mascher, Austria **CB**- Allianz SE, CEO: ACORD Corporation **PE**- Volkswagen Autoversicherung AG, Wiener Allianz **E**- University of Vienna (MA), University of Innsbruck (PhD in Law) **F**- Allianz compensation $3.7 million (2016), ACORD compensation $2.3 million (2016)

Michel Mathieu, France **CB**- Amundi SA, Crédit Lyonnais SA, Cassa di Risparmio di Parma e Piacenza SpA, Crédit Agricole SA, Predica, SILCA **PE**- Banca Popolare FriulAdria SpA, Banco Espírito Santo SA **PC**- Commission de Politique Financière & Bancaire, Assn. Des Presidents, Commission Mixte Internationale, Cotec, Club IBM, Bureau Fédéral de la Fédération Nationale du Crédit Agricole **E**- Télécom ParisTech (PhD in Corporate and Business Law) **F**- Amundi compensation $923,161 (2015), Credit Agricole compensation $1.08 million

Sir Deryck Charles Maughan, UK **CB-** Nikko Securities Co., GlaxoSmithKline plc, Director: BlackRock **PE-** Salomon Brothers, Kohlberg Kravis Roberts & Co., Thomson Reuters Corporation, The Goldman Sachs Group, Citicorp. **PC-** Trilateral Commission, British-American Business Council, New York Stock Exchange, World Economic Forum, Advisory Councils at Harvard and Stanford, NYU Medical Center, Trustee: Lincoln Center **E-** King's College, University of London, Graduate School of Business, Stanford University (MS) **F-** BlackRock compensation $294,250 (2016), BlackRock shares 9,921—$4.7 million (2016)

Thomas J. May, US **CB-** NSTAR Communications, BEC Funding II llc, Connecticut Light and Power Company, Public Service Company of New Hampshire, Liberty Mutual Holding Company, Liberty Financial Companies, New England Business Service, DELUXEPINPOINT, Director: Bank of America Merrill Lynch **PE-** BankBoston Corp., RCN Corporation, CEO and President: Eversource Energy, CEO: Cambridge Electric Light Company and Boston Edison Company **PC-** Financial Executives International **E-** Stonehill College, Bentley College (MS in Finance), Harvard Business School's Advanced Management Program **F-** Bank of America compensation $300,000 (2015), Bank of America shares 254,224—$6.8 million (2016), Eversource compensation $19 million (2014), Eversource shares 1,297,588—$80.7 million (2016)

John McFarlane, UK **CB-** Barclays plc **PE-** Aviva plc, Australia and New Zealand Banking Group Ltd., Standard Chartered plc, The Royal Bank of Scotland Group plc, Citicorp, Capital Radio plc, First Group plc, Westfield Holdings Ltd., Carindale Property Trust, London Stock Exchange plc, National Westminster Bank plc **PC**- World Economic Forum, TheCityUK, Australian Bankers Association, The Securities Association, Economic Research Institute for Asean & East Asia, Financial Reporting Council, International Monetary Conference **E**- The University of Edinburgh (MA), Cranfield University (MBA) **F**- Barclays compensation $1.04 million (2016), Barclays shares 46,852— $454,932 (2016)

F. William McNabb III, US **CB**- CEO: Vanguard Group **PC**- Investment Company Institute's Board of Governors, Zoological Society of Philadelphia, United Way of Greater Philadelphia **E**- Dartmouth College (MBA), Wharton School of the University of Pennsylvania **F**- compensation N/A (private company)—though the prior Vanguard CEO's compensation was $10 million

Cheryl Mills, US **CB**- Director: BlackRock, CEO: BlackIvy Group **PE**- Cendant Corporation, Orion Power, Oxygen Media, Hogan & Hartson, VP: New York University, Chief of Staff to Secretary of State Hillary Clinton, Deputy Counsel to President Clinton **PC**- Clinton Foundation **E**- University of Virginia (BA), Stanford Law School (JD) **F**- BlackRock compensation $253,000 (2016), BlackRock shares 1,124—$532,776 (2016)

Judith A. (Jami) Miscik, US **CB**- Morgan Stanley, in-Q-Tel (CIA technology management foundation), EMC Corp. **PE**- Lehman Brothers Holdings, Barclays Bank plc, CEO: Kissinger Assoc., Deputy Director of Intelligence: CIA **PC**- National Security Council, American Ditchley Foundation, United Nations Assn., Director: Council on Foreign Relations **E**- Pepperdine University (BA), University of Denver (MA in International Studies) F- owns $807,953 in Morgan Stanley stock; Morgan Stanley compensation $345,000 (2016)

Lakshmi N. Mittal, India **CB**- Goldman Sachs Group, ISG, Incoal Company, CEO: APEram, ArcelorMittal (world's biggest steel maker) **PE**- Airbus Group SE **PC**- Indian Prime Minister's Global Advisory Council, Foreign Investment Council in Kazakhstan, International Investment Council in South Africa, the Investors' Council to the Cabinet of Ministers of Ukraine, World Economic Forum's International Business Council, World Steel Association's Executive Committee, Presidential International Advisory Board of Mozambique **E**- St. Xavier's College (BA) **F**- Goldman Sachs compensation $575,000 (2016), Goldman Sachs shares 40,079—$9.6 million (2016), APErm compensation $1.55 million (2016); net worth $16.4 billion (*Forbes*, 2017)

Hélène Molinari, France **CB**- Amundi SA, AHM Conseil, Lagardère SCA, BE-Bound **PE**- Cap Gemini, AXA, BE-Bound **PC**- MEDEF, Nos quartiers ont des talents, Centre d'Études Littéraires et Scientifiques Appliquées, Entreprendre pour Apprendre, Boyden Foundation **E**- graduate degree in Engineering **F**- Amundi compensation $64,657 (2016)

Jennifer B. Morgan, US **CB**- Bank of New York Mellon, SAP SE **PE**- Siebel Systems, Accenture **PC**- World Economic Forum, National Academy Foundation, GENYOUTH **E**- James Madison University (BA in Business) **F**- NY Mellon compensation $10,321 (2016), NY Mellon shares 416—$21,727 (2016), SAP compensation $185,000+ (2017)

Charles Sumner Morrison, US **CB**- Pyramis Global Advisors, President of Asset Management: FMR Co. ($2.1 trillion) **PE**- Fidelity Management & Research Company, Fidelity Investments **PC**- Forum Club SW Florida **E**- N/A **F**- compensation N/A (private firm)

Tushar Morzaria, UK **CB**- Director: Barclays plc **PE**- JPMorgan Chase, SG Warburg, Coopers & Lybrand Deloitte **PC**- World Economic Forum **E**- University of Manchester (BS in Computer Science and Accounting) **F**- Barclays compensation $4.8 million (2016), Barclays shares 5,518,841—$56.4 million (2016)

Brian T. Moynihan, US **CB**- CEO and President: Bank of America **PE**- Bank of America Merrill Lynch Preferred Capital Trust IV, BlackRock, Chairman: Merrill Lynch & Co. **PC**- World Economic Forum, Trustee: Brown University **E**- Brown University, University of Notre Dame Law School (JD), Miami University (MA) **F**- Bank of America compensation $15.4 million (2016), Bank of America shares 3,244,190—$86.7 million (2016)

Dambisa Moyo, Zambia **CB**- Barrick Gold Corporation, Chevron Corporation, Mildstorm Group, Director: Barclays plc **PE**- World Bank, Goldman Sachs, Lundin Petroleum AB, SABMiller plc, Seagate Technology plc **PC**- Berggruen Institute, World Economic Forum, Bilderberg Group **E**- American University (MBA), Kennedy School of Government, Harvard (MPA), St. Antony's College, Oxford (PhD) **F**- Chevron compensation $212,087 (2016), Chevron shares 1,391—$159,561 (2016), Barclays compensation $176,850 (2016), Barclays shares 51,192—$497,074 (2016), Barrick Gold compensation $200,000

(2016), Barrick shares 45,334—$724,437 (2016), Seagate shares 11,753—$461,892 (2016)

Xavier Musca, France **CB**- Pacifica SA, Capgemini SE, Crédit Agricole SA, Cassa di Risparmio di Parma e Piacenza SpA, Pacifica SA, CNP Assurances SA, Banco Espírito Santo, Chairman: Amundi SA **PE**- Gaz de France, PREDICA, Union de Banques Arabes et Françaises SA, Crédit Du Maroc, GDF Suez SA, BESPAR **PC**- Secretary General of the French Republic Presidency, French Ministry for the Economy and Finance, Club de Paris, Economic and Financial Committee of the European Union, African Development Bank **E**- Institut d'Études Politiques de Paris, Institut D'etudes Politiques, and École Nationale D'administration **F**- Amundi compensation $1.5 million (2016), Credit Agricole compensation $1.2 million (2016)

Dennis M. Nally, US **CB**- Morgan Stanley, Globality Inc. **PE**- PricewaterhouseCoopers **PC**- US Council for International Business, US Chamber of Commerce, The Business Roundtable, The Partnership for New York City, Advisory Board at Duke Kunshan University, World Economic Forum, Trustee: Carnegie Hall Corporation/The Carnegie Hall Society **E**- Western Michigan University, Columbia University, and Penn State University Executive Programs (CPA) **F**- Morgan Stanley compensation $165,416 (2016), Morgan Stanley shares 4,397—$215,848 (2016), PWC CEO compensation undisclosed, though the UK director of PWC made $4.8 million as of 2015

Kaikhushru (Kai) S. Nargolwala, Singapore **CB**- Credit Suisse Group, Singapore Telecommunications Ltd., Prudential plc, Clifford Capital Pte. Ltd., Duke-NUS Graduate Medical School

PE- Bank of America, Peat Marwick Mitchell & Co. PC- World Economic Forum E- University of Delhi (BA in Economics) F- Credit Suisse compensation $2.8 million (2016), Credit Suisse shares 226,362—$3.6 million (2016), Prudential compensation $159,820 (2016), Prudential shares 70,000—$3.5 million (2016)

Michael A. Neal, US **CB**- Director: JPMorgan Chase & Co. **PE**- GE Capital, Acasta Enterprises **PC**- US Advisory Board of the European Institute of Business Administration (INSEAD), World Economic Forum, Financial Services Forum, Georgia Tech Foundation **E**- Georgia Institute of Technology (BS) **F**- JPMorgan compensation $324,375 (2016), JPMorgan shares 29,100—$2.86 million (2017)

Gordon M. Nixon, Canada **CB**- BlackRock, Bell Canada, Acasta Enterprises **PE**- Royal Bank of Canada, Newmont Mining Corp. **PC**- Institute of International Finance, International Monetary Conference, Canadian Council of Chief Executives **E**- Queen's University (BA in Commerce) **F**- BlackRock compensation $262,500 (2016), BlackRock shares 252—$119,448 (2016), Bell Canada compensation $353,681 (2016), Bell Canada shares 20,000—$1.7 million

Mark A. Nordenberg, US **CB**- The Bank of New York Mellon, Pittsburgh Life Sciences Greenhouse, University of Pittsburgh Medical Center **PE**- Chancellor and Chief Executive Officer of the University of Pittsburgh **PC**- United States Supreme Court's Advisory Committee on Civil Rules, Pennsylvania Supreme Court's Civil Procedural Rules, Association of American Universities **E**- Thiel College (BA), University of Wisconsin Law School (JD) **F**- NY Mellon compensation $281,864 (2016), NY

Mellon shares 42,892—$2.23 million (2016), University of Pittsburgh salary $597,500 (2014)

Lionel L. Nowell III, US **CB**- American Electric Power Service Corporation, AEP Texas Central Company, VP and Director: Bank of America Merrill Lynch **PE**- RJR Nabisco, Pepsico, Reynolds American, Diageo plc, Pizza Hut, Church & Dwight Co., Bottling Group llc, CFO: Pillsbury North America **PC**- Executive Leadership Council, Financial Executive Institute, American Institute of Certified Public Accountants **E**- Ohio State University **F**- Bank of America compensation $3,000,000 (2016), Bank of America shares 66,375—$1.77 million (2016), Reynolds compensation $393,197 (2014), American Electric compensation $294,053 (2016), American Electric shares 34,015—$2.7 million (2016)

Adebayo O. Ogunlesi, Nigeria **CB**- Goldman Sachs Group, Kosmos Energy, Callaway Golf Company, SWAP Technologies and Telecomms (private), Global Infrastructure Partners (private), New York City Investment Fund Manager, Terminal Investment Ltd. SA (private), Harrisdirect (private) **PE**- Credit Suisse, Africa Finance Corporation, Global Energy Group, Freeport LNG Development **PC**- NAACP Legal Defense & Educational Fund, Prep for Prep, Americans for Oxford, Trustee: New York-Presbyterian Hospital **E**- Oxford University (BA), Harvard Law School (JD, MBA) **F**- Goldman Sachs compensation $600,000 (2016), Goldman Sachs shares 16,407—$3.9 million (2016), Kosmos Energy compensation $201,667 (2016), Kosmos shares $994 million (2016), Callaway compensation $127,700 (2016), Callaway shares 40,800—$587,928 (2016)

Hutham S. Olayan, Saudi Arabia & US **CB**- Morgan Stanley, IBM, Equity International, Olayan Group **PE**- Competrol Real Estate Ltd., Chase Manhattan Bank, Donaldson Lufkin & Jenrette, Saudi International Bank, The Blackstone Group lp, Trex Medical Corporation, Crescent Diversified Ltd., Thermo Fisher Scientific **PC**- The MasterCard Foundation, Arab Bankers Association of North America, Peter G. Peterson Institute for International Economics, Council on Foreign Relations, The Brookings Institution, World Economic Forum, Trustee: American University of Beirut **E**- American University of Beirut (BA), Indiana University (MBA) **F**- owns Morgan Stanley stock worth $6.7 million; Morgan Stanley compensation $345,000 (2016), IBM compensation $304,268 (2016), IBM shares 1,936—$300,087 (2016); donated $25,000–50,000 to the Council on Foreign Relations as of 2016; net worth $2.7 billion+

Deanna Oppenheimer, US & UK **CB**- Joshua Green Corporation (private), BoardReady (private), Vettd, Worldpay Group plc, Whitbread plc, Finsphere Corporation, Tesco plc, CEO: CameoWorks llc, Director: AXA **PE**- Anthemis Group SA, Barclays plc, Bain & Company, Washington Mutual, Catellus Development Corp., NCR Corporation, Tesco Personal Finance plc, Brooks Sports **PC**- Trustee: University of Puget Sound **E**- University of Puget Sound (BA in Political Science and Urban Affairs), Kellogg School of Management at Northwestern University Advanced Executive Program **F**- AXA compensation $142,975 (2016), AXA shares 9,800—$288,943 (2016), Tesco plc compensation $202,169, Tesco shares 57,350—$11.1 million (2016), Worldpay Group compensation $159,383 (2016), Whitbread co. compensation $100,870 (2016), Whitbread shares 1,600—$7.5 million

Peter Oppenheimer, US **CB**- Goldman Sachs Group **PE**- Apple, Automatic Data Processing, Coopers and Lybrand **PC**- Board of California Polytechnic State University Foundation **E**- California Polytechnic University (BA), University of Santa Clara (MBA) **F**- Goldman Sachs compensation $600,000 (2016), Goldman Sachs shares 11,354—$2.7 million (2016); retired as Apple's CFO in 2014 with $53 million in shares

Sean O'Sullivan, Canada & UK **CB**- Director: State Street Corporation **PE**- HSBC Holdings plc, HFC Bank Ltd. **PC**- Information Technology Advisory Committee at the University of British Columbia, York University Foundation **E**- The University of Western Ontario (BA) **F**- State Street compensation $250,000+ (2017), 46,115 HSBC shares sold in 2014—$22.6 million

James W. Owens, US **CB**- Morgan Stanley, IBM, Alcoa, Aludium Transformacion de Productos Sociedad Limitada, FM Global Insurance Company **PE**- Caterpillar, Peoria, Factory Mutual Insurance Company, Allianz SE **PC**- Council on Foreign Relations (Director 2006–2014), The Business Roundtable, World Resource Institute **E**- North Carolina State University (PhD in Economics) **F**- Morgan Stanley compensation $355,000 (2016), Morgan Stanley shares 58,797—$2.86 million (2016), IBM compensation $386,831 (2016), IBM shares 16,811—$2.5 million (2016), Alcoa compensation $83,346 (2016), Alcoa shares $1.39 million (2016)

Doina Palici-Chehab, Germany & France **CB**- Director: AXA (representing the employee shareholders), AXA Insurance Pte. Ltd. (Singapore) **PE**- various positions at AXA companies internationally, AGF **PC-** Chambre de Commerce Française (Singapore), Singapore College of Insurance, Advisory Board of Singapore Management University Lee Kong Chian School of Business **E-** University of Bucharest, Deutsche Versicherungsakademie (degree in Insurance Management) **F-** AXA compensation $118,331 (2016), AXA shares 27,041—$803,117 (2016)

William G. Parrett, US **CB-** Eastman Kodak Company, Blackstone Group LP, Conduent, Thermo Fisher Scientific, Director: UBS AG **PE-** CEO: Deloitte Touche Tohmatsu **PC-** World Economic Forum, United States Council for International Business, United Way Worldwide **E-** St. Francis College, NY (CPA) **F-** UBS compensation $727,000 (2016), Eastman Kodak compensation $270,000 (2016), Eastman Kodak shares 16,600+—$58,900 (2016), Conduent compensation $125,000 (2016), Conduent shares 5,161—$79,501 (2016), Blackstone compensation $329,910 (2016), Blackstone shares 80,543—$2.5 million (2016), Thermo Fisher compensation $290,731 (2016), Thermo Fisher shares 11,636—$2.25 million (2016)

George Paz, US **CB-** Prudential Financial, Express Scripts Holding Company, Aristotle Holding, Chairman: Honeywell International **PE-** Life Partners Group, Partner: Coopers and Lybrand llp **PC-** Federal Reserve Bank, Trustee: Washing University, St. Louis **E-** University of Missouri-Columbia (BA in Business) **F-** Prudential compensation $430,000 (2016), Prudential shares 4,677—$5.16 million (2016), Honeywell compensation $330,078 (2016), Honeywell shares 40,205—$6.01 million (2016), Express Scripts Holding Company compensation $11.9 million (2016)

André F. Perold, US & South Africa **CB**- Director: Vanguard Group, Managing Partner: HighVista Strategies ($3.2 billion under management) **PE**- Rand Merchant Bank, Professor of Finance and Banking: Harvard University **E**- University of the Witwatersrand, Johannesburg, Stanford University (PhD) **F**- Vanguard compensation $237,000 (2016)

Yves Perrier, France **CB**- Crédit Agricole, Société Générale Gestion SA, Crédit Agricole Cheuvreux SA, CEO: Amundi SA **PE**- Crédit Lyonnais, Calyon Bank Czech Republic A.S., LCH. Clearnet Group Ltd., CACEIS SA **PC**- French Financial Management Association **E**- ESSEC International School of Business Europe (MBA) **F**- Amundi compensation $2.8 million (2016)

Sandra Pianalto, Italy & US **CB**- Prudential Financial, JM Smucker Co., Eaton Corp. plc **PE**- President: Federal Reserve Bank of Cleveland **PC**- Budget Committee of the US House of Representatives, Team Neo, United Way of Greater Cleveland, Greater Cleveland Partnership, Northeast Ohio Council on Higher Education, University Hospitals Health System **E**- University of Akron (BA), George Washington University (MA in Economics) **F**- Prudential compensation $307,500 (2016), Prudential shares 3,965—$4.37 million (2016), Smucker compensation $228,000 (2016), Smucker shares 3,093—$344,467 (2016), Eaton compensation $301,198 (2016), Eaton shares 500—$37,980

Christine A. Poon, US **CB**- Prudential Financial, Crane Group Co. (private), The Sherwin-Williams Company, Regeneron Pharmaceuticals, Royal Philips Electronics North America, Johnson & Johnson **PE**- Barclays plc, Koninklijke Philips NV,

Kate Spade & Company, Liz Claiborne, Bristol-Myers Squibb Company, Dean: The Max M. Fisher College of Business at The Ohio State University **PC-** World Economic Forum, Fox Chase Cancer Center, US–China Business Council, Healthcare Businesswomen's Association **E-** Northwestern University (BA), St. Louis University (MS in Biology and Biochemistry), Boston University (MBA) **F-** Prudential shares 22,599—$2.5 million (2016), Prudential compensation $323,750 (2016), Johnson & Johnson compensation $189,295 (2016), Sherman Williams compensation $245,004 (2016), Sherman Williams shares 1,383—$544,943 (2016), Regeneron Pharmaceuticals compensation $2.06 million (2016), Regeneron Pharmaceuticals shares 82,433—$31.7 million (2016), Royal Philips Electronics compensation $169,065 (2016)

Lee R. Raymond, US **CB-** Decision Sciences Corporation, Director: JPMorgan Chase & Co. **PE-** Kohlberg Kravis Roberts & Co., CEO: ExxonMobil **PC-** Business Council for International Understanding, National Petroleum Council, American Enterprise Institute, The Business Council, The Business Roundtable, Council on Foreign Relations. President's Export Council, National Petroleum Council **E-** University of Wisconsin, University of Minnesota (PhD in Chemical Engineering) **F-** JPMorgan compensation $391,875 (2016), JPMorgan shares 225,711—$22.2 million (2016), ExxonMobil compensation $26.8 million (2005), ExxonMobil shares 3.2 million—$199 million (2005)

Joaquin J. Ribeiro, US **CB-** Credit Suisse Group **PE-** Deloitte llp **PC-** Institute of International Finance and Securities Industry, Financial Markets Association, World Economic Forum **E-**

Pace University (BA), New York University (MBA), Columbia Business School (Executive Business Certificate, CPA) **F-** Credit Suisse compensation $2.8 million (2016), Credit Suisse shares 7,865—$125,682 (2016)

Julie G. Richardson, US **CB-** Arconic, VEREIT, Yext, The Hartford Financial Services Group, Kroll Risk & Compliance Solutions (private), US Investigations Services llc, Director: UBS AG **PE-** Providence Equity Partners llc, JPMorgan Chase & Co., Merrill Lynch & Co., Open Solutions llc, SunGard, Stream Global Services **PC-** Make-A-Wish Foundation New York **E-** University of Wisconsin-Madison (BBA), Stanford Graduate School of Business **F-** UBS compensation $295,630 (2016), Arconic compensation $81,833 (2016), Arconic shares 3,112—$74,680 (2016), VEREIT compensation $235,087 (2016), VEREIT shares 49,979—$402,830 (2016), Hartford Financial compensation $191,505 (2016), Hartford Financial shares 26,517—$1.47 million (2016), Yext compensation $295,630, Yext shares 4,119—$191,505 (2016), Cisco shares 359,011—$11 million (2016)

Charles H. Robbins, US **CB-** BlackRock, CEO: Cisco Systems **PE-** Bay Networks, Ascend Communications **PC-** Atlanta Chapter of Business Executives for National Security, MS Society of Northern California, World Economic Forum **E-** University of North Carolina at Charlotte (BA) **F-** BlackRock compensation $250,000 (2017), Cisco compensation $16.7 million (2017), Cisco shares worth $37.9 million as of 2016

Elizabeth B. Robinson, US **CB-** The Bank of New York Mellon Corporation, Russell Reynolds Associates (private) **PE-** Goldman Sachs Group **PC-** Trustee: Williams College and

Massachusetts Museum of Contemporary Art E- Williams College (BA), Columbia University (MBA) F- NY Mellon compensation $250,000+ (2017)

Urs Rohner, Switzerland CB- Credit Suisse Group AG PE- ProSiebenSat.1 Media AG, Lenz & Staehelin, Sullivan & Cromwell llp PC- World Economic Forum, Institute of International Finance, Institut International d'Etudes Bancaires E- University of Zurich F- Credit Suisse compensation $2.8 million (2016), Credit Suisse shares 197,861—$3.16 million (2016)

Martin A. Romo, US CB- Capital Group Companies Management Committee, Fundamental Investors (private) PE- various positions at Capital Group Companies PC- Advisory Council for Stanford University - Stanford Graduate School of Business E- UC Berkeley (BA in Architecture), Stanford Graduate School of Business (MBA) F- compensation N/A (private firm)

Isabelle Romy, Switzerland CB- Federal Institute of Technology in Lausanne (EPFL), SIX Swiss Exchange, Director: UBS Group AG, Law Professor: University of Fribourg PE- Swiss Federal Supreme Court, Boalt Hall School of Law, University of California E- University of Fribourg (PhD), University of Lausanne (Law JD) F- UBS compensation $625,000 (2016), University of Fribourg compensation approx. $200,000 (2016)

Christian Rouchon, France CB- Amundi SA, Bforbank SA, Crédit Agricole Home Loan SFH SA, Capida SAS, Crédit Agricole Sud Rhône Alpes, InnovaFonds SAS PE- Crédit Agricole Loire Haute-Loire E- French Certified Public Accountant F- Amundi compensation $463,363 (2016)

Andrée Samat, France **CB-** Amundi SA, Crédit Agricole Group, Sofipaca SA, Crédit Foncier de Monaco, Carispezia, HECA, CFM Indosuez Wealth **PC-** Municipal Councilor and Deputy Mayor: Saint Cyr sur Mer **E-** undergraduate university degree **F-** Amundi compensation $3,000 (2016); other positions and shares N/A (private firms)

Charles W. Scharf, US **CB-** Microsoft Corporation, Visa International Service Association, CEO: The Bank of New York Mellon Corporation (effective Jan. 2018) **PE-** One Equity Partners llc, JPMorgan Chase & Co., Banc One Corporation, Citigroup, Smith Barney, Primerica, Commercial Credit Corporation, The Travelers Companies, SMARTRAC N.V, The St. Paul Companies **PC-** World Economic Forum, Board of Trustees for Johns Hopkins University, Financial Services Roundtable, Economic Club of Chicago **E-** Johns Hopkins University (BA), New York University (MBA) **F-** Microsoft compensation $325,000 (2016), Microsoft shares 36,162—$3 million (2016), Visa shares 88,316—$5.5 million (2015); NY Mellon compensation $7.6 million (CEO signing award) in 2017 and $16.5 million (in salary and incentives) in 2018

Diane Schueneman, US **CB-** The Capital Markets Company (private), N.V-Capco Consulting, Director: Barclays plc **PE-** Bank of America Merrill Lynch, McKinsey & Company, Penson Worldwide, Omgeo llc, ICAP plc, The Depository Trust & Clearing Corporation, United Bank of Africa **PC-** Year Up, National Cooperative Cancer Network Foundation **E-** UC San Diego (BA) **F-** Barclays compensation $303,920 (2016), Barclays shares 16,004—$161,320 (2016), Capco compensation approx. $75,980 (2017)

Severin Schwan, Austria & Germany **CB**- Credit Suisse AG, Genentech, CEO: Roche Holdings AG **PE**- Chugai Pharmaceutical Co. Ltd. **PC**- World Economic Forum, International Federation of Pharmaceutical Manufacturers, International Business Leaders Advisory Council for the Mayor of Shanghai **E**- University of Innsbruck (Economics, JD) **F**- Credit Suisse compensation $2.8 million (2016), Credit Suisse shares 82,803— $1.32 million (2016), Roche compensation $14.3 million (2016)

Douglas A. Scovanner, US **CB**- Prudential Financial, Hudson's Bay Company (private), Goldner Hawn Johnson & Morrison (private) **PE**- Target, Fleming Companies, Coca-Cola, TCF Financial Corp. **PC**- Greater Minneapolis Metropolitan Housing Corp. **E**- Washington and Lee University (BA), Colgate W. Darden Graduate School (MBA) **F**- owns 21,242—$2.4 million—shares of Prudential; Prudential compensation $335,000 (2016), Target compensation $3 million (2012)

Robert W. Scully, US **CB**- Zoetis, KKR & Co. lp, Ally Credit Canada Ltd., Chubb Corp., Director: UBS AG **PE**- Lehman Brothers, Salomon Brothers, Morgan Stanley, Chase Manhattan Bank **PC**- Global Fund for Children, Teach for America, Blyth Eastman Dillon & Co., Bank of America, General Motors Acceptance Corporation of Canada **E**- Princeton University, Harvard Business School (MBA) **F**- UBS compensation $295,000 (2016), KKR compensation $265,000, Zoetis compensation $295,000 (2016), Zoetis shares 9,436—$672,692 (2016), Chubb compensation $280,000 (2016), Chubb shares 23,922—$3.5 million (2016)

Ivan Seidenberg, US **CB**- Perella Weinberg Partners LP (private), Director: BlackRock **PE**- Cellco Partnership, American

Home Products Corporation, Wyeth llc, Honeywell Technology Solutions, Viacom, CEO: Verizon Communications **PC**- New York Academy of Sciences, US President's Export Council, Chairman: Business Roundtable **E**- City University of New York, Pace University (MBA) **F**- BlackRock compensation $282,500 (2016), BlackRock shares 11,330—$5.3 million (2016), Verizon compensation $26.4 million (2011)

Richard P. Sergel, US **CB**- Emera Inc., Director: State Street Corporation **PE**- New England Electric System (National Grid USA), CEO: North American Electric Reliability Corporation **PC**- Consortium for Energy Efficiency, Director: The Greater Boston Chamber of Commerce **E**- Florida State University, North Carolina State University, University of Miami (MBA) **F**- State Street compensation $318,000 (2016), State Street shares $4.4 million (2017), Emera compensation $210,311 (2016), Emera shares 10,235—$646,127 (2016)

David Sidwell, US & UK **CB**- Apollo Global Management-AGM llc, MSCI, PricewaterhouseCoopers, Director: UBS AG **PC**- National Council on Aging, Federal National Mortgage Association, International Accounting Standards Committee Foundation, Director: Fannie Mae **E**- Cambridge University, Institute of Chartered Accountants in England and Wales **F**- UBS compensation $1.07 million (2016), MSCI compensation $144,986 (2016), MSCI shares 704,118—$90.7 million, Pricewaterhouse (Chubbs) compensation $280,000 (2016), Pricewaterhouse shares 6,104—$581,894 (2016)

Marco Antonio Slim Domit, Mexico **CB**- Director: Black-Rock, CEO: Grupo Financiero Inbursa SAB de CV, Impulsora del Desarrollo y el Empleo en América Latina SAB de CV, Afore Inbursa SA de CV, Arrendadora Financiera Inbursa SA de CV, Operadora Inbursa de Sociedades de Inversión SA de CV, Seguros Inbursa SA, Sears Roebuck, America Telecom, América Móvil SA de CV, Carso Global Telecom SA de CV, US Commercial Corp. SA de CV, CompUSA, Grupo Carso SA de CV **PE**- Director: Teléfonos de México SAB de CV **PC**- World Economic Forum **E**- Universidad Anáhuac **F**- BlackRock compensation $264,000 (2016), BlackRock shares 2,538—$1.2 million (2016); personal net worth $4.1 billion+; son of Carlos Slim Helú, whose estimated net worth is $65 billion

James (Jes) Staley, US **CB**- BlueMountain Capital Management llc (private), CEO: Barclays plc **PE**- JPMorgan Chase, UBS AG **PC**- World Economic Forum, New York Federal Reserve Investor Advisory Committee, Institute of International Finance, Council on Foreign Relations, Robin Hood Foundation **E**- Bowdoin College (BA in Economics) **F**- Barclays compensation $5.5 million (2016), Barclays shares 4,242,848—$41.2 million (2016)

John R. Strangfeld, US **CB**- Chairman and CEO: Prudential Financial **PE**- N/A **PC**- New Jersey Performing Arts Center, Geneva Assoc., Director: American Council of Life Insurers **E**- Susquehanna University (BS), University of Virginia (MBA) **F**- Prudential compensation $17.3 million (2015), Prudential shares 1,893,286—$20.9 million (2016)

Gregory L. Summe, US **CB**- Global Buyout-Carlyle Group, Automatic Data Processing, Director: State Street Corporation **PE**- Goldman Sachs Capital Partners, Perkin Elmer, General Aviation Avionics, AlliedSignal (Honeywell International),

General Electric, McKinsey & Co. **PC-** Conference Board **E-** University of Kentucky, University of Cincinnati, Wharton School of the University of Pennsylvania (MBA) **F-** State Street compensation $308,360 (2016), State Street shares $6.7 million (2017); Automated Data compensation approx. $310,000 (2017)

Renée Talamona, France **CB-** Amundi SA, Crédit Agricole SA, LCL SA **PE-** CALF, BFT IM, GIE COOPERNIC **PC-** Syndicat National des Cadres Dirigeants **E-** degree in Economics **F-** compensation N/A (private firm)

Ryosuke Tamakoshi, Japan **CB-** Morgan Stanley, Persol Holdings, Temp Holdings Co., Chairman: Mitsubishi UFJ Financial Group (MUFG) **PE-** The Sanwa Bank, United California Bank, Bank of Tokyo, The Kansai Electric Power Company, Dah Sing Financial Holdings **F-** serves on Morgan Stanley without compensation, holding 23 percent voting share from MUFG, with annual profits of $1.1 billion as of 2017; MUFG compensation approx. $5 million (2016)

Eric Tazé-Bernard, France **CB-** Employee Representative Director: Amundi SA **PE-** Crédit Agricole, Invesco, SEDES, BNP, Banque Indosuez **E-** École Nationale de la Statistique et de L'administration Économique (degree in Statistics and Economics), Université Paris I Panthéon-Sorbonne (postgraduate diploma in Economics), Université Paris IV René Descartes (degree in Law), University of California in Berkeley (MA in Economics) **F-** compensation N/A (private firm)

Günther Thallinger, Austria **CB-** Allianz SE-PIMCO **PE-** Technical University of Vienna, McKinsey & Company **PC-** World

Economic Forum (European Business Council), Federal Finance Ministry, Principles for Responsible Investment Association, German Equity Institute **E-** Technical University of Graz and Technical University of Vienna (Mathematics), Technical University of Vienna (PhD, dissertation in Applied Mathematics) **F-** Allianz compensation $750,000+ stocks (2017)

Jassim Bin Hamad J.J. Al Thani, Qatar **CB-** Credit Suisse Group AG, Qatar Islamic Bank, Al Mirqab Capital, Damaan Islamic Insurance Co. (BEEMA), Qatar Navigation, Chair: QInvest, Chair: Qatar Insurance Company **PC-** Qatar National Cancer Society, World Economic Forum **E-** Royal Military Academy in Sandhurst, England **F-** Credit Suisse compensation $250,000, Credit Suisse shares 35,809—$572,227 (2016); net worth $1.3 billion (*Forbes*, 2016); member of the Royal Family of Qatar

Axel Theis, Germany **CB-** Allianz SE, Euler Hermes Group SA, ProCurand GmbH **PE-** Fireman's Fund Insurance Company, DEKRA eV, ThyssenKrupp Steel Europe AG **E-** Humboldt University Berlin, passed first and second state law exams; PhD in Law **F-** Allianz compensation $2.6 million (2016)

Richard E. Thornburgh, US **CB-** Corsair Capital ($220 billion), S&P Global (McGraw-Hill,) New Star Financial, CFO: Credit Suisse Group **PE-** First Boston Corporation, Reynolds American **E-** University of Cincinnati, Harvard (MBA in Finance) **F-** Credit Suisse compensation $10.4 million+ (2016), Credit Suisse shares 225,038—$35.9 million (2016), S&P compensation $234,639, S&P shares 7,989—$1.3 million (2017), New Star Financial shares 1.5 million—$17.7 million (2017)

John Tiner, UK **CB-** Credit Suisse Group, Lucida plc, Friends Life, Corsair Capital **PE-** FSA **PC-** Committee of European Insurance and Occupational Pensions Regulators, European Securities Regulators **E-** Kingston University, University of Innsbrook (MA in Economics, PhD in Law) **F-** Credit Suisse compensation $2.8 million+ (2017), Credit Suisse shares 140,910—$2.25 million (2016); awarded the title of Commander of the British Empire in 2008

Michael A. Todman, US **CB-** Prudential Financial, Brown-Forman Corporation, Newell Brands **PE-** Whirlpool, Wang Laboratories, Price Waterhouse and Co. **PC-** Loyola University Council of Regents **E-** Georgetown University (BS in Business) **F-** Brown-Forman compensation $236,856, Brown & Forman shares 10,489—$5.8 million (2016), Prudential compensation $430,000 (2016), Prudential shares 4,630—$5.1 million (2016), Newell compensation $262,488 (2016), Newell shares 51,954—$1.5 million (2016)

Perry M. Traquina, US **CB-** Morgan Stanley, eBay, Allstate **PE-** CEO: Wellington Management Group **PC-** World Economic Forum, Trustee: Brandeis University and Windsor School **E-** The London School of Economics (BA in Economics), Harvard Business School (MBA), Chartered Financial Analyst **F-** Morgan Stanley compensation $335,000 (2016), Morgan Stanley shares 20,307—$990,169 (2016), eBay compensation $328,000 (2016), eBay shares $969,000 (2016), Allstate shares 765—$75,796 (2016)

Ashok Vaswani, India **CB-** Brysam Global Partners, Chief Executive of Retail and Business Banking: Barclays Bank plc

PE- Citibank, Global Consumer Bank, US Cards Business **PC-** World Economic Forum, S.P. Jain Institute of Management **E-** Bombay University, Sydenham College of Commerce and Economics, Institute of Chartered Accountants of India **F-** owns 360,000 shares of Barclays stock worth $3.4 million

David A. Viniar, US **CB-** Goldman Sachs Group, Square Inc. **PC-** Goldman Sachs Foundation, Children's Aid & Family Services, Financial Accounting Foundation, Garden of Dreams Foundation **E-** Union College (BA), Harvard (MBA) **F-** Goldman Sachs compensation $575,000 (2016), Goldman Sachs shares 1.29 million—$308.7 million (2016), Square compensation $367,238 (2016), Square shares 335,700—$13.8 million (2016)

Brad Vogt, US **CB-** Capital Group Companies Management Committee **PE-** various positions at Capital Group Companies **PC-** Investment Company Institute **E-** Wesleyan University (BA in International Politics and Economics) **F-** Capital compensation N/A (private company)

Peter F. Volanakis, US **CB-** CCS Holding, Director: Vanguard Group **PE-** SPX Corporation, CEO: Corning Inc. **PC-** Overseer of Business Administration at Dartmouth College **E-** Dartmouth College (BA, MA) **F-** Vanguard compensation $250,000 (2016), Corning compensation $8.7 million (2010); sold 260,000 shares of Corning in 2010 for $4.68 million

Susan Lynne Wagner, US **CB-** RBB Fund, Bogle Small Cap Growth Fund, Founding Partner: BlackRock, Director: DSP BlackRock Investment India **PE-** Lehman Brothers **E-** Wellesley College, University of Chicago (MBA in Finance) **F-** BlackRock

compensation $244,000 (2016), BlackRock shares 494,629—
$243.4 million (2016)

Axel A. Weber, Germany **CB**- Director: UBS AG **PE**- President:
German Bundesbank, Professor of International Economics:
University of Cologne, Professor of Monetary Economics:
Goethe University **PC**- European Central Bank, Bank for International Settlements, International Monetary Fund, G7, G20,
World Economic Forum, European Systemic Risk Board, Financial Stability Board, German Council of Economic Experts,
Trilateral Commission, Group of Thirty, Berggruen Institute
E- University of Konstanz, University of Siegen (PhD) **F**- UBS
compensation $6.03 million (2016)

Beatrice Weder di Mauro, Switzerland & Italy **CB**- Director:
UBS AG, Professor of Economics: Johannes Gutenberg University of Mainz **PE**- International Monetary Fund (IMF),
National Bureau of Economic Research, Centre for Economic
Policy Research, World Bank, ThyssenKrupp AG, Roche
Holding AG, Economic Policy Adviser to the German Chancellor Angela Merkel **PC**- Federal Reserve Board of New
York, World Economic Forum, German Council of Economic
Experts **E**- University of Basel (PhD), visiting scholar: Harvard
University, National Bureau of Economic Research, United
Nations University (Tokyo), and INSEAD (Singapore) **F**- UBS
compensation $750,000 (2016), University of Mainz compensation approx. $200,000 (2017)

William C. Weldon, US **CB**- ExxonMobil, Director: JPMorgan
Chase & Co., Chairman: Johnson & Johnson **PE**- Korea McNeil
Ltd., Ortho-Cilag Pharmaceutical Ltd., Janssen Pharmaceu-

tica, Ethicon Endo-Surgery **PC-** US–China Business Council, The Business Council, Business Roundtable, Pharmaceutical Research and Manufacturers of America, World Economic Forum **E-** Quinnipiac University **F-** JPMorgan compensation $417,500 (2016), JPMorgan stock 89,379—$8.8 million (2016); ExxonMobil compensation $303,239 (2016); owns Johnson & Johnson stock worth $23 million+; retired as CEO of Johnson & Johnson with a $143 million retirement package

Dieter Wemmer, Switzerland & Germany **CB-** Allianz SpA, Director: UBS AG **PE-** Zurich Insurance Group AG **PC-** CFO Forum, European Central Bank, Systemic Risk Working Group Bank for International Settlements, Berlin Center of Corporate Governance, World Economic Forum, Chairman: Economic and Finance Committee of Insurance Europe **E-** University of Cologne (MA, PhD in Mathematics) **F-** Allianz compensation $3.3 million (2015), UBS compensation $2 million (2016)

Michael D. White, US **CB-** Kimberly-Clark Corporation, Whirlpool Corporation, Trian Fund Management lp, Director: Bank of America Corporation **PE-** Frito-Lay, Avon Products, Bain & Company, Arthur Andersen & Co. DIRECTV, CEO: PepsiCo **PC-** US–China Business Council, Partnership for Drug-Free Kids, World Economic Forum **E-** Boston College (BA), John Hopkins University (MA in International Relations) **F-** Bank of America compensation $252,330 (2016), Bank of America shares 97,730—$2.6 million (2016), Whirlpool shares 14,103—$2.3 million (2016), Whirlpool compensation $298,000 (2016), Kimberly-Clark compensation $265,000 (2016); sold Pepsi shares worth $6.18 million as of 2009

Rayford Wilkins Jr., US **CB**- Morgan Stanley, Valero Energy Corporation **PE**- H&R Block, AT&T, SBC, Southwestern Bell Telephone, Caterpillar **PC**- Tiger Woods Foundation, Advisor: McCombs School of Business at the University of Texas at Austin **E**- The University of Texas, Austin (BA in Business Administration) **F**- Morgan Stanley shares 21,041—$1.02 million (2016), Morgan Stanley compensation $345,000 (2016), Caterpillar stock worth $129,000 as of 2016, Valero Energy compensation $310,000 (2016); listed in *Fortune* as one of the "Nation's 50 Most Powerful Black Executives"

Mark O. Winkelman, Netherlands **CB**- Goldman Sachs Group **PE**- World Bank, J.C. Flowers & Co., Anheuser-Busch InBev SA/NV **PC**- World Economic Forum, Chairman of the Board: University of Pennsylvania Health System **E**- Erasmus University Rotterdam (BA in Economics), University of Pennsylvania (MBA) **F**- Goldman Sachs compensation $575,000 (2016), Goldman Sachs shares 96,517—$23.1 million (2016)

Thomas D. Woods, Canada **CB**- TMX Group, DBRS, Alberta Investment Management Corporation, St. Joseph's Health Centre, Canadian Imperial Bank of Commerce, Director: Bank of America **PE**- CIBC Wood Gundy Securities, Financial Corp., First Caribbean International Bank Ltd., Metrowerks Corporation **PC**- Covenant House, Invest in Kids Foundation, Hummingbird Centre for the Performing Arts **E**- University of Toronto (BA), Harvard Business School (MBA) **F**- Bank of America compensation $300,000 (2016), Bank of America shares 32,459—$862,760 (2016), Canadian Imperial Bank of Commerce compensation $300,000 (2016)

Robert David Yost, US **CB-** Marsh & McLennan Companies, Tyco International Ltd., Director: Bank of America Merrill Lynch **PE-** Exelis, HP Enterprise Services llc, Aetna, CEO: AmerisourceBergen Corp. **PC-** International Federation of Pharmaceutical Wholesalers, Trustee: University of Pennsylvania **E-** United States Air Force Academy, University of California at Los Angeles (MBA) **F-** Bank of America shares 138,568—$3.56 million (2016), Bank of America compensation $305,000 (2016), Marsh & McLennan compensation $270,000 (2016), Tyco International compensation $257,500 (2016)

Werner Zedelius, Germany **CB-** Allianz SE, FC Bayern München AG, Rosno **PE-** Cornhill Insurance plc, World Economic Forum **E-** Bankkaufmann (general qualification in Banking), University of Freiburg (PhD in Law), passed first and second state law examinations **F-** Allianz compensation $4.05 million (2016)

Alexandre Zeller, Switzerland **CB-** Credit Suisse Group AG, Kudelski SA, Maus Frères SA **PE-** Banque Cantonale Vaudoise SA, Nestlé, SIX Group AG **PC-** Vaud Canton Chamber of Commerce and Industry, Swiss Bankers Association, World Economic Forum **E-** University of Lausanne (BA in Economics), Harvard Business School Advanced Management Program **F-** Credit Suisse compensation $2.8 million (2016)

EVIDENCE OF TCC MANAGEMENT
GROUP SOLIDARITY

The 199 global Giants' directors are a very select set of people. They all know each other personally or know of each other. At least 69 have attended the annual World Economic Forum, where they often serve on panels or give public presentations. They mostly attended the same elite universities, and interact in upper-class social setting in the major cities of the world. They all are wealthy and have significant stock holdings in one or more of the financial Giants. They are all deeply invested in the importance of maintaining capital growth in the world. Some are sensitive to environmental and social justice issues, but they seem to be unable to link these issues to global capital concentration.

The power elite directors of these seventeen most central-ized/largest assets management firms represent the central core of international capital. These are the power elite managers for 2017. Individuals can retire or pass away, and other similar people will move into their place, making the overall structure a self-perpetuating network of global capital control. As such, these 199 people share a common goal of maximum return on investments for themselves and their clients, and they may seek to achieve returns by any means necessary—legal or not.

Again, we do not claim that any single person identified in this study, as one of the 199 Global Power Elite individuals at the financial core of the TCC, has necessarily done anything illegal. We only point out that the institutional and structural arrangements within the money management systems of global capital relentlessly seek ways to achieve maximum return on investment, and that the conditions for manipulations—legal or not—are always present. Adding in the fact that 199 individuals have easy access to each other makes for possibilities of cooper-ative activities even easier.

Developing this list of 199 directors of the largest money management firms in the world is an important step toward understanding how capitalism works globally today. These directors are responsible for making decisions regarding the investment of trillions of dollars. Given the fact that they could all fit into a medium-size university lecture hall, the concentration of power and control is absolutely amazing. They are supposedly in competition, but due to the concentrated wealth they share they are essentially required by the system to cooperate with each other for their greater good. This includes finding and supporting commonalities of investment opportunities and shared risk agreements, and working collectively for political arrangements that create advantages for their system as a whole.

This small group of 199 people are the central power elite core of global financial capitalism. They set the priorities for monetary investments in businesses, industry, and governments. Their number-one priority is to bring in average returns on investment of 3 percent to 10 percent or more. Where the investments occur is less important than that they yield continuous returns that supports growth in the overall market. Capital that supports tobacco products, war weapons, toxic chemicals, pollution, and other socially destructive goods and services and their byproducts are seen as investments that offer a return without a conscious concern for the social consequences of the investment.

Knowing Each Other

One of John McFarlane's duties is attending the International Monetary Conference's annual meetings. The International Monetary Conference is a private yearly meeting of the top few hundred bankers in the world. The American Bankers Association (ABA) serves as the secretariat for the conference. A rare press release for the 2015 Toronto conference read as follows:

The International Monetary Conference, for which ABA serves as secretariat, convenes today in Toronto, where the heads of financial institutions from 29 countries will hear from Federal Reserve Vice Chairman Stanley Fischer, Canadian Finance Minister Joe Oliver and other top banking and corporate leaders.

Attendees will discuss several critical global banking issues, including international competition, payments technology, financial conduct regulation and cybersecurity. ABA representatives at the conference include president and CEO Frank Keating and chairman John Ikard, president and CEO of FirstBank Holding Company, Lakewood, Colo.

Secretary of the Treasury Timothy Geithner spoke to the conference in 2011. His talk was released by the Department of the Treasury.[127]

...So let me describe why we are in a much stronger position today, and where we still have a lot of work to do.... The weakest parts of the US financial system—the firms that took the most risk—no longer exist or have been significantly restructured. That list includes Lehman Brothers, Bear Stearns, Merrill Lynch, Washington Mutual, Wachovia, GMAC, Countrywide, and AIG. Of the 15 largest financial institutions in the United States before the crisis, only nine remain as independent entities.

Those that survived did so because they were able to raise capital from private investors, significantly diluting existing shareholders. We used stress tests to give the private market the ability—through unprecedented disclosure requirements and clear targets for how much capital these institutions needed—to distinguish between those institutions that needed to strengthen their capital base and those that did not. The 19 firms that we put through that process have together increased common equity by more than $300 billion since 2008. . . .

The International Monetary Conference has been going on since 1956. The conference doesn't even have a website, using a password-protected site for members only.[128] Nothing on the agenda seems to address the socioeconomic consequences of investments to determine the impacts on people and the environment.

According to Andrew Gavin Marshall, the 2013 International Monetary Conference was held in Shanghai. Marshall lists the following bankers among the 200 attendees: Baudouin Prot (Chairman of BNP Paribas), Douglas Flint (Chairman of HSBC), Axel A. Weber (Chairman of UBS), Jacob A. Frenkel (Chairman of JPMorgan Chase International), Jamie Dimon (Chairman and CEO of JPMorgan Chase), Jürgen Fitschen (Co-CEO of Deutsche Bank), John G. Stumpf (Chairman and CEO of Wells Fargo), Francisco González (Chairman and CEO of BBVA), Peter Sands (CEO of Standard Chartered), Han Zheng (Member of the Political Bureau of the Communist Party of China (CPC)'s Central Committee and Secretary of the CPC Shanghai Municipal Committee), Jiang Jianqing (Chairman of the Industrial and Commercial Bank of China), Shang Fulin (Chairman of the China

Securities Regulatory Commission), Tian Guoli (Chairman of the Bank of China), Zhou Xiaochuan (Governor of the People's Bank of China, China's central bank), Mario Draghi (President of the European Central Bank), Jaime Caruana (General Manager of the Bank for International Settlements), and Janet Yellen, who was then the Vice Chair of the Federal Reserve Board, and became the Chair of the Federal Reserve System until 2018, when she was replaced by Jerome Powell.[129]

Donald Trump's Strategic and Policy Forum

CNBC reported on December 2, 2016 that President-elect Trump planned to meet regularly with key US business leaders and Wall Street executives shortly after the inauguration. Larry Fink and Jamie Dimon were included on the list shared by the Trump administration of the members of Trump's proposed business council:[130]

- Stephen A. Schwarzman (Forum Chairman), Chairman, CEO, and Co-Founder of Blackstone

- Paul Atkins, CEO, Patomak Global Partners llc, Former Commissioner of the Securities and Exchange Commission

- Mary Barra, Chairman and CEO, General Motors

- Toby Cosgrove, CEO, Cleveland Clinic

- Jamie Dimon, Chairman and CEO, JPMorgan Chase & Co

- Larry Fink, Chairman and CEO, BlackRock

- Bob Iger, Chairman and CEO, The Walt Disney Company*

- Rich Lesser, President and CEO, Boston Consulting Group

- Doug McMillon, President and CEO, Wal-Mart Stores

- Jim McNerney, Former Chairman, President, and CEO, Boeing

- Elon Musk, Chairman and CEO, SpaceX and Tesla*

- Indra Nooyi, Chairman and CEO of PepsiCo

- Adebayo (Bayo) O. Ogunlesi, Chairman and Managing Partner, Global Infrastructure Partners

- Ginni Rometty, Chairman, President, and CEO, IBM

- Kevin Warsh, Shepard Family Distinguished Visiting Fellow in Economics at the Hoover Institute, Former Member of the Board of Governors of the Federal Reserve System

- Mark Weinberger, Global Chairman and CEO, EY

- Jack Welch, Former Chairman and CEO, General Electric

- Daniel Yergin, Pulitzer Prize–winner, Vice Chairman of IHS Markit[131]

*By June 2017 both Bob Iger and Elon Musk had resigned because of Trump's Paris Agreement withdrawal decision.

When asked by Fox News if he would also resign from Trump's forum after being pressured by stockholders, Dimon simply said "no," according to a report from *Bloomberg News*. The leader of America's biggest bank by assets said that while he doesn't agree with all of the president's policies and ideas, he wants to help the leader of the free world be successful. "He's the pilot flying our airplane," Dimon reportedly said. "We're trying to help. I would try to help any president of the United States because I'm a patriot."

Before the 2016 election, thirteen corporate leaders jointly signed a policy letter on Commonsense Corporate Governance Principles. Jamie Dimon and Larry Fink were signers, along with Warren Buffett, CEO of Berkshire Hathaway, Mary Barra, CEO of General Motors, Jeff Immelt, CEO of GE, Mary Erdoes, CEO of JPMorgan Asset Management, Tim Armour, CEO of Capital Group, Mark Machin, CEO of CPP Investment Board, Lowell McAdam, CEO of Verizon, Bill McNabb, CEO of Vanguard, Ronald O'Hanley, CEO of State Street Global Advisors, Brian Rogers, chairman and CIO of T. Rowe Price, and Jeff Ubben, CEO of ValueAct Capital. Important sections of the letter to America are included below, giving us an insight into the ideological perspectives of the Global Power Elite.

The health of America's public corporations and financial markets—and public trust in both—is critical to economic growth and a better financial future for American workers, retirees and investors.

Millions of American families depend on these companies for work—our 5,000 public companies account for a third of the nation's private sector jobs. And these same families and millions more also rely on public companies to help improve their financial future—they are heavily invested in these companies through mutual funds, 401(k) and pension plans, college savings plans and other accounts to buy a home, send their children to college and save for retirement.

Our future depends on these companies being managed effectively for long-term prosperity, which is why the governance of American companies is so important to every American.... We represent some of America's largest corporations, as well as investment managers, that, as fiduciaries, represent millions of individual savers and pension beneficiaries. We include corporate CEOs, the head of the Canadian public pension fund and an activist investor, and the heads of a number of institutional investors who manage money on behalf of a broad range of Americans. Truly independent corporate boards are vital to effective governance, so no board should be beholden to the CEO or management. Every board should meet regularly without the CEO present, and every board should have active and direct engagement with executives below the CEO level. Diverse boards make better decisions, so every board should have members with complementary and diverse skills, backgrounds and experiences. It's also important to balance wisdom and judgment that accompany experience and tenure with the need for fresh thinking and perspectives of new board members. Every board needs a strong leader who is independent of management.... Our financial markets have become too obsessed with quarterly earnings forecasts.... A common accounting standard is critical for corporate transparency.... Effective governance requires constructive engagement between a company and its shareholders.... But we do hope our effort will be the beginning of a continuing dialogue that will benefit millions of Americans by promoting trust in our nation's public companies.[132]

Another example of TCC elite ideological unity is the response of the Strategic and Policy Forum's group to Trump's defense of white supremacists and neo-Nazis during the Charlottesville disturbances in mid-August 2017. A news account described Trump's position:

Trump responded to the events Saturday by immediately blaming the violence on "many sides." He later, on Monday, clarified his remarks, reading from a teleprompter: "Racism is evil and those who cause violence in its name are criminals and thugs, including KKK, neo-Nazis, white supremacists, and other hate groups repugnant to everything we hold dear as Americans."

But during a Tuesday press conference, Trump reverted back to giving cover to the white extremist movement. "Not all of those people were white supremacists," he said of individuals who rallied under white power organization and Nazi flags over the weekend.

"I do think there's blame on both sides," the President went on to say, equating antifa with rightwing extremists. "You look at both sides. I think there's blame on both sides and I have no doubt about it."[133]

In a conference call among the Strategic and Policy Forum's member's on August 16, 2017, the group collectively decided to disband the forum in protest of Trump's extreme racist statements. As the group was agreeing to disband, in a move to preempt the Forum, Trump tweeted, "Rather than putting pressure on the businesspeople of the Manufacturing Council & Strategy & Policy Forum, I am ending both. Thank you all!"[134]

Both Larry Fink and Jamie Dimon released letters to their employees regarding this political incident:

Message from Larry Fink

Dear colleagues,

Late last year, I joined President Trump's Strategic and Policy Forum because I believe we need to advance policies that can spur economic growth and improve life for all Americans. Engaging constructively with governments is central to advancing BlackRock's mission, and, in the United States, we desperately need to find common ground on which

Americans of different views and from different parties can come together to move the nation forward.

While I have disagreed with the President in certain instances this year, I continued to participate in the Forum because I believed it was important to have a voice at the table for investors, including our clients. Unfortunately, after the last few days, I concluded that I could no longer in good conscience participate in the Forum.

The events that occurred in Charlottesville, as I said on Monday, are nothing short of domestic terrorism. Such racism and bigotry must not just be condemned but must be condemned unequivocally. The diversity of America works because leaders from all walks of life have always been willing to step forward and reject intolerance without equivocation.

In the last 24 hours, I informed our clients on the Forum as well as the Forum's chairman of my decision to resign. I also made clear that while I won't be participating in the Forum, BlackRock will continue to engage on issues of public policy with governments at all levels and around the world. For the US economy, successfully enacting tax reform and rebuilding our infrastructure are of paramount importance.

BlackRock will continue to contribute to the debate on these and other important issues, but we will do so in ways that are consistent with our culture and values.

Sincerely,
Larry Fink[135]

Message from Jamie Dimon

I strongly disagree with President Trump's reaction to the events that took place in Charlottesville over the past several days. Racism, intolerance and violence are always wrong. The equal treatment of all people is one of our nation's bedrock principles. There is no room for equivocation here: the evil on display by these perpetrators of hate should be condemned and has no place in a country that draws strength from our diversity and humanity.[136]

Public statements of this sort are strong indications of a highly interconnected power elite at the financial core of the TCC. The effort to promote long-term benefits for all Americans with continuing market growth is a core ideological message of the TCC financial power elites. Extremist views and civil disruptions are not tolerated. Their efforts in this regard seem truthful and authentic, and based upon their perspective on the world.

It is not just these 199 power elites who support this system of capital investment and continuing growth. They are the central core of thousands of people from the Transnational Capitalist Class (TCC), collectively embedded in this system of mandatory growth. The interests of the Global Power Elite and the TCC are fully recognized by major institutions in society. Governments, intelligence services, policymakers, universities, police forces, military, and corporate media all work in support of their vital interests. Capitalism is an economic system that inevitably adjusts itself via contractions, recessions, and depressions. Yet we are entrapped in a web of enforced growth and profitmaking that has huge humanitarian consequences for billions of people. An honest, open look at real human options is vitally needed, and social movement activists seeking to end the crisis of humanity may find allies at the top willing to make radical readjustments needed to prevent wars, mass poverty, and environmental degradation.

CHAPTER 4

FACILITATORS
THE POWER ELITE POLICY PLANNING CENTER OF THE TRANSNATIONAL CAPITALIST CLASS

Both David Rothkopf and William I. Robinson discuss the importance of transnational institutions serving a unifying function for the TCC. Our research shows that the World Bank, International Monetary Fund, G20, G7, World Trade Organization (WTO), World Economic Forum, Trilateral Commission, Bilderberg Group, Bank for International Settlements, Group of 30 (G30), and International Monetary Conference serve as institutionalized mechanisms for TCC consensus building, and power elite policy formation and implementation. These international institutions serve the interests of the global financial Giants by supporting policies and regulations that seek to protect the free, unrestricted flow of capital and debt collection worldwide. The World Bank, IMF, G7, G20, WTO, Financial Stability Board, and Bank for International Settlements are institutions controlled by nation-state representatives and central bankers with proportional power/control exercised by dominant financial supporters, primarily the United States and European Union countries.

Our research focuses on transnational policy groups that are nongovernmental. These organizations help to unite TCC power elites as a class. The individuals involved in these organizations are the facilitators of international capitalism. They serve as policy elites who seek the continued growth of capital in the world.

The G30 and the Trilateral Commission are privately funded, staff-supported research organization/forums, whereby TCC power elites can speak openly on global capital and security issues, moving toward a consensus of understanding on needed policies and their implementations. These meetings offer TCC power elite individuals opportunities to personally interact with each other face-to-face in private, off-the-record settings that allow for personal intimacies, trust, and friendships to emerge. These interactions are the foundation of TCC class-consciousness and social awareness of common interests. The central activity of the TCC power elite is the management and protection of global capital. With this understanding, a wide variety of policy issues emerge for implementation by transnational entities, security institutions (military/police and intelligence agencies), and ideological organizations (media and public relations firms).

The Group of 30 (G30) and the Trilateral Commission, with a combined membership of 86 TCC power elites, are essentially the central core facilitators of the TCC power elite policy planning process. Both are nonprofit corporations, supported independently from government funding and regulations, that allow for open discussion of global capital and security needs by people with common class and financial interests. Twelve of the seventeen trillion-dollar Giants have one or more representatives on either or both the G30 or the Trilateral Commission

Executive Committee. Goldman Sachs Group has four directors on these core TCC policy-planning groups.

Certainly, other powerful nongovernmental organizations exist—such as the Friends of Europe/Security & Defense Agenda, a nonprofit policy group in support of the European Union—but like the United States's Council on Foreign Relations, the Friends of Europe primarily take policy positions in support of national agendas. One other organization that is a power elite core policymaking group, and which focuses on international security issues, is the Atlantic Council, which we will discuss in Chapter 5.

It is also important to note that US business leaders have long recognized the need for policies for growth. In 2005 the Business Roundtable in the United States joined with a transnational group of CEOs from the 500 largest corporations, in an organization known as the "World Business Leaders for Growth," to lobby the World Trade Organization for pro-growth policies. The group pushed sustained economic growth, and it was organized by CEOs from the US Business Roundtable, Business Council of Australia, Canadian Council of Chief Executives, Consejo Mexicano de Hombres de Negocios (Mexico), European Round Table of Industrialists, and Nippon Keidanren (Japan).[137]

Perhaps the most important TCC power elite private policy organization is the Group of Thirty (G30). The G30 describes itself as having "aims to deepen understanding of international economic and financial issues, and to explore the international repercussions of decisions taken in the public and private sectors."[138]

The G30 is a highly influential institution in the arena of global financial governance. The G30, founded in 1978, releases reports from study groups made up of top power elite bankers, financiers, policymakers, and academics. These reports are widely accepted and usually implemented across the globe.[139] The G30 is a nonprofit corporation originally funded by the Rockefeller Foundation. It now receives close to one million dollars per year in donated funds from various private sources.[140] According to Andrew Gavin Marshall,

> In 2012, the G30 published a report compiled by the Working Group on Long-term Finance, which was composed of nearly two-thirds of the membership of the G30. The report set out their concerns about "the efficient provision of a level of long-term finance sufficient to support expected sustainable economic growth in advanced and emerging economies." The report noted directly that it was not an "abstract exercise," but was "operational," complete with "practical recommendations for global and national actors and policy makers that would ... help create a system of long-term finance." In other words, for the Group of Thirty, they don't produce mere "recommendations," but rather "instructions," which they expect to be followed. It is of significance that many of those who produced the reports as members of the G30 conveniently hold other official positions so as to be able to dutifully implement those instructions.[141]

The most recent G30 reports from 2016 are as follows:

Shadow Banking and Capital Markets: Risks and Opportunities

Topics: Banking, Central Banks, Debt, Economic Policy, Emerging Markets, Financial Stability, Regulation, Risk

Thoughts on Monetary Policy: A European Perspective
Topics: Banking, Central Banks, Debt, Economic Policy, Economic Reform, the European Union, Financial Stability, Globalization, Monetary Policy

Oil and the Global Economy
Topics: Commodities, Economic Policy, Economic Reform, Emerging Markets, the European Union, Financial Stability, Globalization, Monetary Policy

The G30's October 2016 report on Oil and the Global Economy describes how US fracking technology has changed the industry, making the United States a global exporter of oil and resulting in lower prices and destabilization in the Middle East and North African (MENA) countries. The report calls on MENA countries to build more diversified/competitive economies. The report calls for "strong leadership," as "[t]he region needs bold and creative governments that show the way for the youth and new entrepreneurs, encourage private initiative without preserving vested interests, and change attitudes from idleness and dependency to diligence and self-reliance." In other words, if you are not a bold and creative government training your idle youth and complying with global capitalism's investment opportunities, you may just need to be replaced.[142]

The 32 G30 policy directors are deeply connected with TCC transnational institutions and central banks. Twelve are from the United States, with one US citizen having dual citizenship with Israel. Three members hold French citizenship, with one of those holding dual citizenship with the Ivory Coast. The two UK members both hold seats in the House of Lords. There are two directors each from Germany and Mexico, including the former president of Mexico. There is one director from each of the following countries: Poland, Canada, Spain, Argentina, Italy, Brazil, Switzerland, Japan, India, Singapore, and China. This is a highly educated group, with sixteen of the 32 holding PhD's from major universities. Nine hold degrees from Harvard, four from MIT, three from Yale, and two each from Chicago, Stanford, Princeton, and Oxford. The others attended elite universities in various part of the world. Twelve of the non-US/ UK members of the G30 attended university in the United States or the United Kingdom. The group has 31 men and one woman, Gail Kelly from the Australian Bankers' Association and the International Monetary Fund (IMF). The Group of 30 has directly linked membership at the IMF, Bank for International Settlements, World Bank, Basel Committee, Financial Stability Board, G7, G20, WTO, and the Federal Reserve. Additionally, 21 members of the G30 are current or former members of the Trilateral Commission. All 32 members of the G30 have been keynote speakers at the World Economic Forum in Davos. Six of the financial Giants have direct representation at the G30 through eight current members.

The G30 brings together 32 of the most powerful people in world. They are essentially the executive committee of the Global Power Elite for transnational capitalism. They formally develop policy recommendations outside of official government oversight. They organize behind-the-scenes study groups with other TCC elites to provide an international understanding of policies needed to protect global capitalism's need for continued growth and security.

Thirty-two key advisors are listed on the current G30 website for 2017. We have developed biographical briefs for each of the 32 members of the Group of 30. The leadership committee for the G30 is comprised of Paul Volcker, Jacob Frenkel, Jean-Claude Trichet, and Guillermo Ortiz Martínez.

G30 EXECUTIVE GROUP

CB- Corporate Boards/Current Corporate Employment
PE- Prior Corporate Employment/Boards
PC- Policy Councils, Philanthropic Organizations, Government
E- Education
F- Public Financials[143]

Note that in almost every case the financials cited constitute only a portion of total income and net worth. Some, especially those working with private investment groups, offer no information on compensation and shareholdings. Net worth information from various websites seems very much understated. Several times we found the value of stockholdings listed by corporate proxy reports far in excess of an individual's declared net worth.

Leszek Balcerowicz, Poland **CB**- President: Narodowy Bank Polski **PE**- Governor: European Bank for Reconstruction and Development, Deputy Prime Minister of Poland, Minister of Finance of Poland **PC**- Center for European Policy Analysis, Group of Thirty (G30), Trilateral Commission, World Economic Forum, Bilderberg Group, Director: Peterson Institute for International Economics, President: National Bank of Poland, Chairman: Bruegel, Trustee: Centrum für Europäische Politik **E**- St. John's University (MBA), Central School of Planning and Statistics (BA, PhD) **F**- winner of the Cato Institute 2014 $250,000 Milton Friedman prize

Ben S. Bernanke, US **CB**- Citadel ($27 billion hedge fund), Senior Advisor: PIMCO **PC**- Federal Open Market Committee, President's Council of Economic Advisers, Advisory Panel of the Federal Reserve Bank of New York, Bilderberg Group, Trilateral Commission, World Economic Forum, Group of Thirty (G30), Chairman: Federal Reserve System, Director: NBER Program in Monetary Economics, Editor: American Economic Review **E**- Harvard University (BA in Economics), Massachusetts Institute of Technology (PhD) **F**- net worth $3 million (celebritynetworth.com); Federal Reserve Salary $180,000

Mark J. Carney, Canada **CB**- Governor and Director: Bank of England, CEO: Canada Deposit Insurance Corporation, Director: Bank for International Settlements **PE**- Governor: Bank of Canada **PC**- Group of Thirty (G30), World Economic Forum, Bilderberg Group, Trilateral Commission, Chairman: Financial Stability Board **E**- Harvard University (BA), University of Oxford (MA, PhD) **F**- Bank of England compensation approx. $800,000+ (2016)

Jaime Caruana, Spain **PE**- Governing Council of the European Central Bank, General Manager: Bank for International Settlements, Director: International Monetary Fund, Governor: Bank of Spain (Spain's central bank) **PC**- Group of Thirty, Financial Stability Forum, International Organization of Securities Commissions (IOSCO), International Association of Insurance Supervisors (IAIS), Steering Committee Bilderberg Group, World Economic Forum, Chairman: Basel Committee on Banking Supervision, Chair: European Trilateral Commission **E**- Technical University of Madrid **F**- net worth $1.2 million (2017) (celebritynetworth.com); BIS annual salary $750,000 (ended 2017)

Domingo Cavallo, Argentina **CB-** Partner: Global Source Partners llc, Chairman and CEO: DFC Associates llc **PE-** Director: Bank of Cordoba, Executive Director: IERAL, President: Argentine Central Bank, Minister of Economy and Minister of Foreign Affairs of Argentina **PC-** The Group of Thirty (G30), World Economic Forum, Bilderberg Group, Trilateral Commission **E-** Universidad Nacional de Córdoba (UNC) (BA), Harvard University (PhD in Economics) **F-** N/A (private firms)

Mario Draghi, Italy **CB-** President: European Central Bank, Director: Bank for International Settlements, Chair: European Systemic Risk Board **PE-** Governor: Bank of Italy, Managing Director: Goldman Sachs International, Executive Director: World Bank **PC-** Group of Thirty (G30), World Economic Forum, Bilderberg Group, Trilateral Commission, Chairman: Financial Stability Board, Director General: Italian Treasury, Chairman: European Economic and Financial Committee, Chairman: OECD's Working Party No 3, Chairman: Italian Committee for Privatizations **E-** Sapienza University of Rome (BA), Massachusetts Institute of Technology (PhD in Economics) **F-** European Central Bank salary $400,000; net worth $4 million (getnetworth.com)

William C. Dudley, US **CB-** Director: Bank for International Settlements, President: Federal Reserve Bank of New York, Vice Chairman: Federal Open Market Committee (FOMC) **PE-** Goldman Sachs & Company, Executive VP: NY Fed, VP: Morgan Guaranty Trust Company **PC-** Council on Foreign Relations, World Economic Forum, Group of Thirty (G30), Partnership for New York City, Trilateral Commission, Director: Bank for International Settlements, Chair: Economic Club of New York,

Economist: Federal Reserve Board **E**- New College of Florida
(BA), University of California, Berkeley (PhD) **F**- net worth $8.5
million (*New York Times*); Federal Reserve salary $400,000+
(2016)

Roger W. Ferguson Jr., US **CB**- Brevan Howard Asset Management llp ($8.7 billion hedge fund as of 2017), General Mills,
Alphabet Inc., International Flavors & Fragrances, President
and CEO: TIAA (private) **PE**- Partner: McKinsey & Company,
Chair: Swiss Re America Holding Corporation **PC**- President's
Council on Jobs and Competitiveness, Group of Thirty (G30),
President's Economic Recovery Advisory Board, Economic
Club of New York, The Partnership for New York City, Regent
Smithsonian Institution, Council on Foreign Relations, Bilderberg Group, Trilateral Commission, World Economic Forum,
Vice Chair: Federal Reserve System, Chair: Conference Board
E- Harvard University (BA), Harvard Law School (JD) **F**- General Mills compensation $254,999 (2016), General Mills stock
9,000—$532,000 (2017), Alphabet Inc. stock award $1,004,789
(2017), International Flavors & Fragrances compensation
$237,790 (2016), International Flavors shares 9,860—$1.5 million (2016)

Arminio Fraga Neto, Brazil **CB**- Co-Founder: Gávea Investimentos Ltda. (now owned by JPMorgan Chase) ($7 billion
fund) **PE**- International Council JPMorgan Chase, Chairman of
the Board: BM&F Bovespa, President: Central Bank of Brazil,
Managing Director: Soros Fund Management **PC**- Group of
Thirty (G30), Advisory Board of the G7 group, Council on
Foreign Relations, Trilateral Commission, International Advisory Council of the China Investment Corp., World Economic

Forum **E-** Catholic University of Rio de Janeiro (BA, MA in Economics), Princeton University (PhD in Economics) **F-** N/A (private firms)

Jacob A. Frenkel, US & Israel **CB-** American International Group, Corsair Capital (private), Boston Properties (private), Loews Corp., Chair: JPMorgan Chase International **PE-** Professor of Economics: University of Chicago, Chair: Merrill Lynch International, Governor: Bank of Israel, Chair: Inter-American Development Bank, Vice Chair: European Bank for Reconstruction and Development, Governor: International Monetary Fund (IMF) **PC-** Economic Advisory Panel of the Federal Reserve Bank of NY, Japan Society, Peterson Institute for International Economics, Trilateral Commission, World Economic Forum, New York Economic Club, Aspen Institute Italia, The Council for the US and Italy, Temasek International Panel, Advisory Council of China Development Bank, Becker Friedman Institute, National Bureau of Economic Research, Chair: Group of Thirty (G30), Chairman of the Board: Council on Foreign Relations **E-** Hebrew University of Jerusalem (BA), University of Chicago (MA, PhD in Economics) **F-** Loews compensation $240,473 (2016), Loews shares $128,000 (2017)

Timothy F. Geithner, US **CB-** President: Warburg Pincus **PE-** Kissinger Associates, President and CEO: Federal Reserve Bank of NY **PC-** RAND Corporation, Group of Thirty (G30), World Economic Forum, Trilateral Commission, Bilderberg Group, International Rescue Committee, Wall Street Journal CEO Council, Undersecretary for International Affairs and Secretary of the Treasury of the United States, Director: International Monetary Fund, Vice-Chairman: Federal Open Market

Committee, Director: Council on Foreign Relations, Director: Center for Global Development E- Dartmouth College (BA), Johns Hopkins University (MA) F- net worth $6 million (celebritynetworth.com); Secretary of the Treasury salary $190,000 (2009–2013)

Gerd Häusler, Germany **CB**- Munich Re Group, RHJ International SA, Liquiditäts-Konsortialbank GmbH, Deutsche Kreditbank AG, MKB Bank Zrt. (private), Chair: Bayerische Landesbank, Director: BHF Kleinwort Benson Group (private) **PE**- Central Bank Council of Deutsche Bundesbank, International Advisory Committee of Federal Reserve Bank of New York, Chair and CEO: Bayerische Landesbank, Managing Director: Lazard Ltd., Executive Officer: International Monetary Fund (IMF), Senior Adviser: Deutsche Brse., Director: RHJ International SA **PC**- Group of Thirty (G30), World Economic Forum, Director: Institute of International Finance, European Chair: Trilateral Commission, Advisor: German Stock Exchange **E**- University of Frankfurt, University of Geneva (Law) **F**- Bayerische Landesbank compensation $112,000 (2017), Munich Reinsurance Group compensation $122,320 (2016)

Philipp Hildebrand, Switzerland **CB**- Vice Chairman: Black-Rock **PE**- Chair: Swiss National Bank (SNB) **PC**- Financial Stability Board (FSB), Strategic Committee of the French Debt Management Office, Group of Thirty (G30), World Economic Forum, Bilderberg Group, Director: Bank for International Settlements (BIS), Swiss Governor: International Monetary Fund (IMF) **E**- University of Toronto (BA), Graduate Institute of International Studies (MA), University of Oxford (PhD in International Relations) **F**- Swiss National Bank compensation

$900,000 (2012); recognized father of twins with Margarita Louis-Dreyfus; net worth $8 billion (2017)

Gail Kelly, Australia (born in South Africa) **CB**- Woolworths Holdings Ltd., St. George Bank Ltd., CEO: Westpac Group, Director: Australian Bankers' Association **PE**- Nedbank Group, Director: BHP Billiton, Vice President: International Monetary Conference, Director: Business Council of Australia **PC**- Wall Street Journal CEO Council, Group of Thirty (G30), McKinsey Advisory Council, US Council on Foreign Relations, World Economic Forum, Australian Prime Minister's Indigenous Advisory Council, Senior Global Advisor: UBS Group AG **E**- University of Cape Town (BA), University of Witwatersrand (MA), Charles Sturt University (PhD) **F**- net worth $35 million (celebritynetworth.com)

Mervyn A. King, UK **CB**- Professor of Economics and Law: New York University **PE**- Governor: Bank of England **PC**- Bank of International Settlements (BIS), Group of Thirty (G30), Baron King of Lothbury, House of Lords, World Economic Forum, Professor: London School of Economics **E**- King's College, Cambridge, St John's College, Cambridge, Harvard University (Law) **F**- Bank of England pension $306,000 (2017), NYU salary approx. $200,000+ (2017)

Paul Krugman, US **CB**- Professor of Economics: City University of NY, Columnist: *New York Times* **PE**- Professor: Princeton Woodrow Wilson School of Economics **PC**- President's Council of Economic Advisers, National Bureau of Economic Research, Group of Thirty (G30), World Economic Forum (rarely by his own admission), World Bank, International Monetary

Fund, United Nations, Council on Foreign Relations, Consultant: Federal Reserve Bank of New York, Fellow: Econometric Society **E-** Yale University (BA), Massachusetts Institute of Technology (MIT) (MA, PhD) **F-** City University of NY salary $250,000+ (2017); won the Nobel Memorial Prize in Economic Sciences in 2008, worth $1.2 million; net worth $2.5 million (2017) (celebritynetworth.com)

Haruhiko Kuroda, Japan **CB-** Governor: Bank of Japan, President: Asian Development Bank, Professor: Graduate School of Economics at Tokyo's Hitotsubashi University, Kuroda Partners LP ($180 billion hedge fund) **PE-** Governor and Chair: The Policy Board at Bank of Japan (ADB) **PC-** Bank of International Settlements, Group of Thirty (G30), World Economic Forum, Financial Stability Board, Trilateral Commission, Director: Bank for International Settlements (BIS), Advisor: International Monetary Fund **E-** University of Tokyo (BA), All Souls College University of Oxford (MA in Economics) **F-** Hitotsubashi University salary $150,000+, Bank of Japan compensation $294,000+ (2016); net worth $5 million (2016) (networthpost.com)

Christian Noyer, France **CB-** European Central Bank, Governor: Banque de France, Chairman: Bank of International Settlements **PE-** Power Corporation of Canada, Société Générale SA, Le Crédit Lyonnais SA, Le Groupe des Assurances Nationales, Dassault Aviation SA, Pechiney SA, Air France, Électricité de France SA **PC-** Monetary Policy Council, Group of Thirty (G30), World Economic Forum, Trilateral Commission, Bilderberg Group, Suez SA **E-** Institut d'Etudes Politiques de Paris **F-** Banque de France compensation private; net worth $15 million (networthpost.com)

Guillermo Ortiz Martínez, Mexico **CB**- BTG Pactual SA, Grupo Aeroportuario del Sureste (private), Senior Advisor: First Reserve Corporation (private), Director: Vitro SAB de CV, Independent Director: Weatherford International plc **PE**- World Bank, Inter-American Development Bank, Governor: Bank of Mexico, Chair: Grupo Financiero Banorte, Secretary of Finance and Public Credit of the Mexican Federal Government, Governor: International Monetary Fund **PC**- Group of Thirty (G30), World Economic Forum, Center for Financial Stability, SWIFT Institute, Institute of Globalization and Monetary Policy of the Federal Reserve Bank of Dallas, China International Finance Forum, GO & Asociados, Quality of Life Advisory Board of the Mexico City Government, Zurich Insurance Group Ltd., Council of Bombardier Inc., Chairman: Per Jacobsson Foundation **E**- National Autonomous University of Mexico (BA in Economics), Stanford University (MSc, PhD in Economics) **F**- Weatherford compensation $420,939 (2016), Weatherford shares 155,732—$544,390

Raghuram Rajan, India **CB**- 21st Century Council, Advisory Board of MCap Fund Advisors, Senior Advisor: Booz and Co. **PE**- Governor: Reserve Bank of India, Chief Economist: International Monetary Fund **PC**- Berggruen Institute, Group of Thirty (G30), World Economic Forum, FDIC Systemic Resolution Advisory Committee, President: American Finance Association, Director: Bank for International Settlements **E**- Information Technology and Technical Education Council (BA), Indian Institute of Management (MA), Massachusetts Institute of Technology (PhD) **F**- net worth $1 million+ (HighlightsIndia.com)

Kenneth Rogoff, US **CB-** Federal Reserve Bank NY **PE-** Professor: Harvard Economics **PC-** Group of Thirty (G30), Trilateral Commission, World Economic Forum, Council on Foreign Relations, Bilderberg Group, Chief Economist: International Monetary Fund **E-** Yale University (BA), MIT (PhD) **F-** net worth $18 million (networthpost.com); Rogoff writes on January 8, 2018, "But while politics is not, at least for now, impeding global growth nearly as much as one might have thought, the long-run costs of political upheaval could be far more serious. First, post-2008 political divisiveness creates massive long-term policy uncertainty, as countries oscillate between governments of the left and the right … Harder to assess, but potentially far more insidious, is the erosion of public trust in core institutions in the advanced economies. Although economists have endless debates about whether culture or institutions lie at the root of economic performance, there is every reason to be concerned that the recent wave of populism is a threat to both."[144]

Masaaki Shirakawa, Japan **CB-** Director: Mitsubishi Estate Co. Ltd. (private) **PE-** Governor: Bank of Japan **PC-** World Economic Forum, Trilateral Commission, Bilderberg Group, Group of Thirty (G30), Vice-Chairman: Bank of International Settlements **E-** University of Tokyo (BA), University of Chicago (MA in Economics) **F-** net worth $1 million (networthpost.com)

Lawrence Summers, US **CB-** Lending Club, Square, D. E. Shaw & Co. lp, Alliance Partners, Citigroup, The Santander Group, Xapo, Genie Oil and Gas, Advisor: Andreessen Horowitz, Professor and President (2001–2006; rehired 2017): Harvard University, Director: Revolution Money **PE-** US Secretary of Treasury for Clinton, Director of the National Economic

Council for Obama, President: Center of Global Development, Chief Economist: World Bank **PC-** Atlantic Council, Council on Foreign Relations, Center for American Progress, World Economic Forum, Group of Thirty (G30), Bilderberg Group, Trilateral Commission, Council on Competitiveness, Berggruen Institute **E-** MIT (BA), Harvard (PhD in Economics) **F-** net worth $40 million (celebritynetworth)

Tharman Shanmugaratnam, Singapore **CB-** Singapore's Deputy Prime Minister and Coordinating Minister for Economic and Social Policies, Director: GIC Private Ltd. **PE-** Minister for Education-SG **PC-** World Economic Forum, Group of Thirty (G30), Chair: Monetary Authority of Singapore (MAS), Chair: International Monetary and Financial Committee (IMFC), Deputy Chair: National Research Foundation (NRF) **E-** London School of Economics (LSE) (BA), University of Cambridge (MA in Economics), Harvard University (MA in Public Administration) **F-** net worth $67 million (2017) (toprichests.com)

Tidjane Thiam, Ivory Coast & France **CB-** 21st Century Fox, CEO: Credit Suisse Group **PE-** Chief Executive: Prudential plc, Managing Director: Aviva International **PC-** Group of Thirty (G30), World Economic Forum, Bilderberg Group, Chairman: Association of British Insurers, Côte d'Ivoire's Minister of Development and Planning, Global Advisory Board: Council on Foreign Relations, CEO: National Bureau for Technical Studies and Development **E-** École Polytechnique France (BA), INSEAD (MBA) **F-** Prudential compensation $15.4 million (2015), Credit Suisse compensation $12 million (2016)

Jean-Claude Trichet, France **CB**- Bank for International Settlements, Director: Airbus Group SE **PE**- President of Executive Board: European Central Bank, Secretary General: Interministerial Committee for Improving Industrial Structures (CIASI) **PC**- Honorary Chairman: Group of Thirty, Chair: Bruegel, Steering Committee: Bilderberg Group, European Chairman: Trilateral Commission, President: Societé de Gestion de Participations Aéronautiques, Governor: Banque de France, Adviser to the cabinet of the Minister of Economic Affairs, Deputy Director of Bilateral Affairs: Treasury Department, President: Group of Governors and Heads of Supervision (GHOS) in Basel, Paris Club, World Economic Forum, European Systemic Risk Board (ESRB) **E**- École Nationale Supérieure des Mines de Nancy (BA), University of Paris (MA) **F**- Airbus Se compensation $187,200 (2017); ranked fifteenth in *Forbes*'s list of most powerful people in 2010

Adair Turner, UK **CB**- House of Lords **PE**- Standard Chartered plc, Director General: CBI (Confederation of British Industry), Vice-Chairman: Merrill Lynch Europe, Director: Prudential plc **PC**- Institute for New Economic Thinking, UK Financial Services Authority, Group of Thirty (G30), World Economic Forum, Energy Transitions Commission, Pensions Commission, Low Pay Commission, Chairman: Financial Services Authority, Chairman: International Financial Stability Board, Chair: Climate Change Committee **E**- Gonville and Caius College (Cambridge University) (MA in Economics) **F**- N/A

Paul A. Volcker, US **CB**- Mevion Medical Systems (private), Director: Deutsche Bank Trust Corporation (private) **PE**- President: Federal Reserve Bank (FRB) of New York, Economist:

Chase Manhattan Bank, Chairman: Wolfensohn & Co., Senior Advisor: Shinsei Bank Ltd. **PC**- Group of 30 (G30), Bilderberg Group, World Economic Forum, Japan Society, the Institute of International Economics, American Assembly, and the American Council on Germany, Honorary Chairman: Trilateral Commission, Chair of Governors: Federal Reserve System, Director: Council on Foreign Relations (1988–1999), Trustee: International House NY, Trustee: International Accounting Standards Committee (IASC), Director: Treasury's Office of Financial Analysis, Senior Advisor: Pro Mujer **E**- Princeton University (BA), Harvard University Graduate School of Public Administration (MA), London School of Economics (MA) **F**- net worth $700,000 (2017) (networthpost.com)

Kevin M. Warsh, US **CB**- Hoover Institute, UPS **PE**- Morgan Stanley & Co. NY **PC**- Group of Thirty (G30), Board of Governors of the Federal Reserve System, Federal Open Market Committee (FOMC), White House National Economic Council, President Trump's Strategic and Policy Forum, World Economic Forum, Bilderberg Group **E**- Stanford University (AB), Harvard Law School (JD) **F**- UPS compensation $272,461 (2016), UPS shares 8,922—$1.05 million, Hoover compensation $70,000+ (2017); married to Jane Lauder, heir to the Estee Lauder company; net worth $2 billion (Forbes)

Axel A. Weber, Germany **CB**- Chairman: UBS **PE**- University of Chicago, Governing Council of the European Central Bank, President: Deutsche Bundesbank **PC**- Bank for International Settlements, Group of Thirty (G30), Council for the Future of Europe (CFE), International Monetary Fund, G7 and G20 Ministers and Governors, Financial Stability Board, Berggruen

Institute, World Economic Forum **E-** University of Constance (MA), University of Siegen (PhD in Economics) **F-** UBS compensation $6.03 million (2016)

Ernesto Zedillo, Mexico **CB-** Procter & Gamble, Citigroup, International Advisory Board of Rolls Royce, Professor of International Economics: Yale University, Director: Alcoa **PE-** President of Mexico, Credit Suisse, BP **PC-** Foundation Board of the World Economic Forum, Trilateral Commission, Group of Thirty (G30), Bilderberg Group, Global Advisory Board of Council on Foreign Relations, International Commission on Nuclear Non-proliferation and Disarmament, Director: Institute for International Economics, Director: Inter-American Dialogue, Chairman: Global Development Network, Chairman: Oversight Board of the Natural Resources Charter, Advisor: Bill and Melinda Gates Foundation **E-** National Polytechnic Institute in Mexico (BA), Yale University (PhD in Economics) **F-** Alcoa compensation $84,595, Alcoa shares 43,813—$1.8 million (2016), Procter & Gamble compensation $285,000 (2016), Procter & Gamble shares 38,191—$3.4 million (2016), Citigroup compensation $286,322 (2016), Citigroup shares 27,131—$2 million (2016), Yale salary $200,000+ (2017)

Zhou Xiaochuan, China **CB-** China Construction Bank, Governor: People's Bank of China, Central Committee of the Communist Party of China **PC-** National Committee of Economic Reform, Economic Policy Group of the State Council, Group of Thirty (G30), Bank for International Settlements (BIS), G20, World Economic Forum, Trilateral Commission **E-** Beijing Chemical Engineering Institute (BA), Tsinghua University (PhD) **F-** N/A; voted *Forbes*'s fifteenth most powerful person in 2011

Systemic Risk Council

A more recently formed global financial policy group, closely linked to the G30, is the Systemic Risk Council, which was formed in 2012 to protect against another economic crisis similar to the one in 2008. They received funding from the Pew Charitable Trusts and CFA Institute. The CFA Institute is the international organization of chartered financial analysts, with 142,000 members in 73 countries. The CFA Institute is a $280 million organization pledged to "lead the investment profession globally by promoting the highest standards of ethics, education, and professional excellence for the ultimate benefit of society."[145]

The Systemic Risk Council is chaired by Sir Paul Tucker, fellow at the Harvard Kennedy School and former deputy governor of the Bank of England. Chair Emeritus is Sheila Bair, president of Washington College and former chair of the FDIC. The G30 members on the Systemic Risk Council are Jean-Claude Trichet, Paul Volcker, and Adair Turner. The sixteen other Systemic Risk Council directors are current and former members of the US Senate, European Parliament, Securities and Exchange Commission, UK House of Commons, US Secretary of the Treasury, Federal Reserve Board, and Basel Committee on Banking Supervision, as well as elite university professors at MIT, Wharton School of the University of Pennsylvania, and Goethe University, and key investors at Citigroup and Bank of America.

In 2017 the Systemic Risk Council made a formal policy statement to the G20. The recommendations called for

> support for maintaining minimal international standards in global financial reform measures...

underlining the vital importance of five core pillars
of the global reform program: (1) mandating much
higher common tangible equity in banking groups
to reduce the probability of failure ... ; (2) requiring
banking-type intermediaries to reduce materially
their exposure to liquidity risk; (3) empowering regulators to adopt a system-wide view through which
they can ensure the resilience of all intermediaries
and market activities ... ; (4) simplifying the network
of exposures among intermediaries by mandating
that, wherever possible, derivatives transactions
be centrally cleared by central counterparties that
are required to be extraordinarily resilient; and (5)
establishing enhanced regimes for resolving financial intermediaries of any kind, size, or nationality so
that, even in the midst of a crisis, essential services
can be maintained to households and businesses
without taxpayer solvency support.[146]

The Systemic Risk Council is a demonstration of the continuing evolution of TCC power elite policymaking efforts.
Since the economic crisis of 2008, serious efforts to limit the
possibility of recurring crises are ongoing for TCC power elites.

World Economic Forum

As reported in Chapter 1, the World Economic Forum is not
a formal policymaking body. It serves an educational consensus-building function for thousands of TCC elites, with
exclusive discussions and open meetings. One thousand global
corporations with $5 billion in income or more pay some

$25,000 per person to attend. Three thousand people attended the 2017 World Economic Forum in Davos, Switzerland, in the January snows at 5,000 feet elevation. Eighty percent were men mostly from the leading corporations in the world, and several hundred more were from civil society, or were governmental ministers or heads of state. Companies are allowed to bring up to five people as long as one is a woman.[147] There were more than 200 sessions in 2017 on a range of topics held over a five-day period. (For a list of the current Governing Board of the World Economic Forum, see Appendix B.)

The mission statement of the World Economic Forum reads as follows:

> The World Economic Forum, committed to improving the state of the world, is the International Organization for Public–Private Cooperation. The Forum engages the foremost political, business and other leaders of society to shape global, regional and industry agendas.
>
> It was established in 1971 as a not-for-profit foundation and is headquartered in Geneva, Switzerland. It is independent, impartial and not tied to any special interests. The Forum strives in all its efforts to demonstrate entrepreneurship in the global public interest while upholding the highest standards of governance. Moral and intellectual integrity is at the heart of everything it does.
>
> Our activities are shaped by a unique institutional culture founded on the stakeholder theory, which asserts that an organization is accountable to all parts of society. The institution carefully blends and

balances the best of many kinds of organizations, from the public and private sectors, international organizations and academic institutions.

We believe that progress happens by bringing together people from all walks of life who have the drive and the influence to make positive change.[148]

As the World Economic Forum's 2015–2016 annual report noted,

In 2015-2016 the World Economic Forum published 37 reports, including its globally recognized indexing reports: The Global Competitiveness Report 2015–2016; The Global Gender Gap Report 2015; and Global Risks 2015. The Forum also unveiled two new reports: The Inclusive Growth and Development Report 2015, representing its first major publication focused on addressing global inequalities and strengthening economic growth; and The Future of Jobs, Employment, Skills and Workforce Strategy for the Fourth Industrial Revolution, which assesses the impact of disruptions on employment levels, skill sets and recruitment patterns in different industries and countries.[149]

The World Economic Forum is a TCC cultural experience facilitating socialization among thousands of wealthy and powerful people. The World Economic Forum serves as a network within networks. For example, the Wall Street Journal CEO Council holds its annual luncheon at Davos every year.

The cultural experience for new and returning attendees is undoubtedly very much a self-affirming experience. Sharing the

FACILITATORS **185**

same space with heads of state, CEOs of the largest firms in the world, and top academic scholars gives one the impression of being inside the uppermost power network in the world. This social consciousness carries over into daily life for the Davos crowd, giving them a continuing sense of importance and prestige. Shared connections obtained at Davos continue in the business world and the TCC networks, serving as a reinforcing mechanism of solidarity and perceived insightfulness.

Lewis Lapham described his visit to Davos in 1998 in his book, *The Agony of Mammon: The Imperial Global Economy Explains Itself to the Membership in Davos, Switzerland.*[150] Lapham describes the meetings as a quorum of investors, whose number-one topic is security for the markets.

Bilderberg Group

The smaller and older Bilderberg meetings take place annually in June at various exclusive resorts around the world. Bilderberg meetings are attended by about 150 invited TCC power elites. Founded in 1954, the annual meetings were designed to foster dialogue between Europe and North America after World War II. The Bilderberg website states, "Thanks to the private nature of the meeting, the participants are not bound by the conventions of their office or by pre-agreed positions. As such, they can take time to listen, reflect and gather insights. There is no detailed agenda, no resolutions are proposed, no votes are taken, and no policy statements are issued."

The 2016 Bilderberg meeting was held in Dresden, Germany. Topics on the agenda included China, Europe, migration, growth, reform, vision, unity, the Middle East, Russia, the US political landscape, debt, cyber security, the geo-politics of energy and commodity prices, the precariat and the middle class, and technological innovation.[151] Like the World Economic Forum, the Bilderberg meetings serve primarily as educational consensus-building sessions. Bilderberg Group meetings are of a smaller, more intimate/exclusive nature than those held in Davos. The topics reflect key sociopolitical issues in the world, but clearly are addressed from an elite TCC perspective. The discussion of the precariat and middle class as a top topic in Dresden implies concerns with voters in democracies that could be swayed by populist agendas, a development that may threaten capital priorities. The author of 2016's *The Precariat: The New Dangerous Class* is Professor Guy Standing at the University of London. He has been invited to attend several recent Bilderberg meetings. (See the list of current Bilderberg Group steering committee members in Appendix A.)

Council on Foreign Relations

The Council on Foreign Relations (CFR) was founded in 1921 and is the premier policy group for international affairs in the United States. It has an annual budget of $60 million, and assets of $490 million. It has more than 5,000 individual members and 170 corporate sponsors. CFR has a long history of promoting US expansionism, with the goal of solidifying the United States's global hegemonic power. Sometimes referred to as the advisory board to the US State Department, CFR has taken a leadership role for US policy and globalization for close to a century.[152] Corporate members paying $100,000 per year for membership include Bank of America Merrill Lynch, JPMorgan Chase, Goldman Sachs Group, Citigroup, NASDAQ OMX Group, Chevron, ExxonMobil, and PepsiCo.[153]

CFR has historically viewed international affairs from the perspective of US interests. The CFR continues very much in that vein today alongside an increasing involvement in transnational capital security, as US interests have penetrated worldwide. In 1995 CFR formed an international council of advisors that was revised in 2012 to a group of 23 TCC power elites referred to as the Global Board of Advisors.[154] Six of the financial Giants are members of CFR, and a dozen second-tier investment firms are members as well. Laurence H. Shoup writes, "One of the overall core functions of the CFR is a no-holds-barred ongoing effort to facilitate the expansion of opportunities for capital accumulation for the US capitalist class and its corporations."[155]

CFR is strongly neoliberal and free trade–oriented. As such, the Council pays close attention to international financial policies. The Council's global-dominance hegemonic agenda is supported by the US State Department and Pentagon involvements worldwide.

Trilateral Commission

The Trilateral Commission (TC) was formed in 1973 to bring together unofficially (that is, without official government oversight) the highest-level elites to address important international problems. In 1972 CFR leaders David Rockefeller and Zbigniew Brzezinski participated in the Bilderberg meetings. Seeking to bring something like the Bilderberg meetings to the United States, they had the Rockefeller Foundation fund the initial development of the Trilateral Commission.[156]

Original representatives were from the United States, Europe, and Japan only. However, recently representatives from around the globe have been included. Currently there are 375 members from 40 countries, with 87 members from the United States, 20 members from Germany, and 18 members each from France, Italy, and the United Kingdom. The Asia group has 100 members, with the remaining 124 members hailing from various countries throughout the world. Each country has a quota and can nominate people as openings become available. Members who take formal positions in their governments are asked to step down so others can join. The goal is to keep the Trilateral Commission a policy-influencing body free of direct government involvement.

Trilateralists hold an annual meeting that all members attend, in addition to at least three regional meetings. The three regional committees serve Europe, North America, and Asia. G30 member Jean-Claude Trichet is chair for the European group, and G30 member Paul Volcker is honorary chair for the North American group. Harvard professor and former assistant secretary of defense Joseph Nye Jr. is the chair of the North American group. Yasuchika Hasegawa, chairman of Takeda Pharmaceutical Co. and former chair of the Japan Association of Corporate Executives, is the Asia/Pacific chair for the Trilateral Commission. There are 55 people from 30 nations listed on the extended executive committee.[157] More than half of the extended executive committee are directly involved in international finance/investment and banking.

The Trilateral Commission has played a major role in development of the Transnational Capitalist Class. Direct foreign investment by Japan in the United States and by US investors in Japan was facilitated by various Trilateralist meetings. In 2004 Nobuyuki Idei from Sony and Yotaro Kobayashi, chair of the Trilateral Commission's Asian-Pacific group, attended a meeting of 450 foreign investors in cooperation with Bill

Clinton and George Shultz, former secretary of state, both of whom are longtime members of the TC. In 2008 Japan's direct foreign investment in the United States reached $226 billion, and its direct foreign investment in Europe reached $161 billion. Conversely, US direct investment in Japan in 2008 was $74 billion, and Europe's direct investment in Japan was $86 billion. Increasingly, US investors such as JPMorgan Chase, Goldman Sachs Group, and Morgan Stanley & Co. helped encourage a more transnational neoliberal perspective among traditional Japanese elites. The TC clearly encouraged the formation of a TCC power elite consciousness in the Asia-Pacific region.[158] As of 2017, 36 members of the Trilateral Commission hail from Japan.

Among the TC's seventeen Executive Committee members (though Rockefeller passed away in March 2017), ten have direct interests in international investment and finance and represent such TCC institutions as the Group of 30, World Economic Forum, World Bank, Bank for International Settlements, Atlantic Council, World Trade Organization, and a number of policy groups, such as the Council on Foreign Relations, Heritage Foundation, and Aspen Institute.

Barack Obama appointed eleven members of the Trilateral Commission to top-level and key positions in his administration within his first ten days in office. This represented a very narrow source of international leadership inside the Obama administration. Obama was groomed for the presidency by key members of the Trilateral Commission. Most notably, Zbigniew Brzezinski, co-founder of the Trilateral Commission with David Rockefeller in 1973, was Obama's principal foreign policy advisor.

Obama's Trilateral appointees included:

- Secretary of the Treasury Timothy Geithner

- Ambassador to the United Nations Susan Rice

- National Security Advisor Gen. James L. Jones

- Deputy National Security Advisor Thomas Donilon

- Chairman of the Economic Recovery Committee Paul Volcker

- Director of National Intelligence Admiral Dennis C. Blair

- Assistant Secretary of State for East Asian and Pacific Affairs Kurt M. Campbell

- Deputy Secretary of State James Steinberg

- State Department Special Envoy Richard Haass

- State Department Special Envoy Dennis Ross

- State Department Special Envoy Richard Holbrooke

The seventeen Executive Committee members of the Trilateral Commission are a highly educated group, with four holding PhDs and eight others with MA and MBA degrees. They attended the world's top-ranked universities, including Harvard (4), University of London (3), Yale (2), with one member each from Princeton, Chicago, Stanford, University of Paris, and Swarthmore. The Trilateral Commission issues regular in-depth task force reports. The most recent of these reports include "Nuclear Disarmament and Nonproliferation," "The Global Economic Crisis," "Engaging Iran and Building Peace in the Persian Gulf Region," and "Energy Security and Climate Change."

The annual meeting, held April 15–17 in 2016, was hosted in Rome and included presentations and discussion on the following topics:

- The Middle East in Turmoil: From an Arab Spring to a Deep Winter?

- Where Is Russia Heading? With Issue Brief Update of the 2014 Trilateral Report on Engaging

- The North Korean Nuclear and Missile Threats
  The United States Presidential Elections

A 2013–2014 Trilateral Commission Task Force Report was entitled "Engaging Russia: A Return to Containment?" The authors were Paula Dobriansky, former US under secretary of state, Andrzej Olechowski, professor at Vistula University, Warsaw, and former Polish minister of foreign affairs, Yukio Satoh, former Japanese ambassador to the UN, and Igor Yurgens, chairman of the Institute of Contemporary Development, Moscow. The report was prepared in 2013 in consultation at multiple meetings of the Trilateral Commission in Mexico City, Manila, Kraków, Washington, DC, and at Harvard University.

The report expressed alarm caused by the Russian "invasion" of the Crimea. President Putin was described as bringing about a ruthless break with the West, abandoning Mikhail Gorbachev's vision of Russia joining its "common European Home." The Trilateral Commission feels that Russia is not contributing to global stability, but rather aspires to superpower status. And US business leaders are concerned about the anemic growth and economic climate in Russia:

> In short, Russia always was and will remain different. Acceptance of that 'otherness' should be a premise for forming our views on Russia's future and our relations with her. . . . Even if Moscow seeks 'normalization' with the West, the nature of Putin's regime permits little more than a transactional US–Russia relationship on a narrow range of issues. Putin's departure from office however may produce a transformational moment that portends real systemic change in the Russian system. Russian politics will have to be invented almost from the ground-up, perhaps creating possibilities for a rapprochement.[159]

Concerns with Putin and the topic of his removal are clearly uppermost in the minds of Trilateralists. TCC power elite business leaders are salivating over the opportunities Russia's vast economic resources offer for capital investment. Clearly since 2014 an increasing anti-Putin message has been offered in the US corporate media.

The Trilateral Commission releases annual reports from their meetings to all their members, but the most recent meeting report on their website is from 2009. The 40th Plenary meeting of the Trilateral Commission was held in Tokyo on April 25–26, 2009. The report states: "They met (170 attending) amidst fears that the global financial crisis would be more intense than any economic downturn since the great depression.... [O]ne underlying theme of the meeting was that global governance is in a period of transition away from domination by the United States and Europe ... and [there is] a need for a joint response to the fiscal crisis."[160] It was at the TC Tokyo meeting in 2000 that discussions on the new role of NATO took place. The 2000 report stated that "NATO is not now an alliance against anything. It's an alliance on the basis of common interests and common values."[161]

The Trilateral Commission publishes their reports through the Brookings Institution Press. Recent titles shown on the Brookings website include

- Energy Security and Climate Change in the Trilateral Context (2016)

- Engaging Russia (2015)

- Irregular Migration, Trafficking, and Smuggling of Human Beings (2016)

- Challenges in the Process of China's Urbanization (2017)

The Trilateral Commission does maintain a listing of their members' key news reports and published policy papers. The TC is composed of Transnational Capitalist Class power elites and continually works to maintain the security of global capital investments and opportunities. Trilateral Commission policy papers are taken seriously by the institutional managers and politicians inside the G7, G20, WTO, World Bank, IMF, Financial Stability Board, Bank for International Settlements, NATO, US military, and various world governments. They lay the foundation for actionable steps in international governance, and they strongly influence future actions and decisions throughout the world.

The 55 members of the Trilateral Commission's extended executive committee are an important set of TCC power elites engaged in making global policy recommendations. They offer policy positions on global financial matters in a manner similar to the G30 group, and they also address such broader sociopolitical issues as climate change, refugees, urbanization, and concerns regarding Russia. Thirty-one countries have participants on the extended executive committee. Twenty-six (46 percent) hold current positions with global capital investment firms, and eleven are university professors, mostly in economics, at major institutions. Sixty-seven percent of the extended executive committee attended universities in the United States or United Kingdom. All of the Trilateral Commission extended executive committee members should be considered Global Power Elite members of the Transnational Capitalist Class. They share similar lifestyles and incomes, know each other, and have frequent opportunities to meet and interact. They have similar university education backgrounds, with strong interests in policymaking to protect and expand capital investment opportunities for themselves and their associates.

We have developed biographical briefs for each of the 55 members of the extended executive committee of the Trilateral

Commission. These individuals are among the central facilitators of the Global Power Elite. Again, we recommend that you read the biographies of these people to understand the broad, powerful reach of this TCC policy group. Watch for prime ministers, intelligence directors, National Security Council members, ambassadors, members of Parliament, media and PR executives, peers in the House of Lords, Defense Policy Board members, and recipients of the Légion d'honneur and the Woodrow Wilson Award.

TRILATERAL COMMISSION EXECUTIVE GROUP

CB- Corporate Boards/Current Corporate Employment
PE- Prior Corporate Employment/Boards
PC- Policy Councils, Philanthropic Organizations, Government
E- Education
F- Public Financials

Note that in almost every case the financials cited constitute only a portion of total income and net worth. Some, especially those working with private investment groups, offer no information on compensation and shareholdings. Net worth information from various websites seems very much understated. Several times we found the value of stockholdings listed by corporate proxy reports far in excess of an individual's declared net worth.

Esko Aho, Finland **CB**- Aalto University, VP: Nokia **PE**- Centre Party of Finland, Harvard University, Prime Minister of Finland **PC**- Trilateral Commission Executive Group, Finnish Arctic Society of Finland, Skolkovo Foundation, President: SITRA, Fellow: Iinstitute of Politics at Harvard University **E**- University of Helsinki (MA in Social Science) **F**- N/A

C. Fred Bergsten, US **PE**- Putnam Reinsurance Co., Transatlantic Holdings **PC**- Trilateral Commission Executive Group, Director and Founder: Peter G. Peterson Institute for International Economics, Under Secretary of the United States Department of the Treasury, Staff: National Security Council, Visiting Fellow: Council on Foreign Relations **E**- Central Methodist College (BA), The Fletcher School of Law (MA, PhD) **F**- N/A

Catherine Bertini, US **CB**- Tupperware Brands, Professor of Public Administration: Syracuse University **PE**- Executive Director: UN World Food Program, Assistant Secretary of Food and Consumer Services at the US Department of Agriculture **PC**- Trilateral Commission Executive Group, Board for International Food and Agricultural Development, USAID **E**- State University of New York at Albany (BA) **F**- Syracuse salary $200,000 (2016), Tupperware compensation $232,391 (2016), Tupperware shares 25,452—$1.6 million (2017)

Chen Naiqing, China **CB**- Vice President of the Chinese People's Institute of Foreign Affairs, Former Chinese Ambassador to Norway, Trilateral Commission Executive Group **E**- N/A **F**- N/A; married to Zhang Yesui, former Chinese Ambassador to the US

Richard Conroy, Ireland **CB**- Chairman and Founder: Karelian Diamond Resources plc (private), Chairman: Conroy Gold and Natural Resources plc (private) **PE**- Professor of Physiology: Royal College of Surgeons in Ireland, Chairman and CEO: Arcon International Resources plc, Senator in the Republic of Ireland Parliament **PC**- Trilateral Commission

Executive Group, Dublin County Council **E**- BlackRock College, Royal College Of Surgeons **F**- N/A

Alfonso Cortina, Spain **CB**- YPF Sociedad Anónima, TPG Growth, Banco Hispano Americano Group, Sociedad de Crédito Hipotecario SA **PE**- Inmobiliaria Colonial **PC**- European Advisory Council of Rothschild, European Round Table of Industrialists, Trilateral Commission Executive Group, Portland Valderrivas **E**- Higher Technical School of Industrial Engineers (ETSII) (Advanced Industrial Engineering degree), Madrid University (Economics/Business degree) **F**- net wealth $1.3 billion as of 2017 (*Forbes*)

Tarun Das, India **CB**- Trans Asia Hotel Ltd. (private), John Keells Hotels plc (private), International Advisory Board of Coca-Cola **PE**- Haldia Petrochemicals Ltd., New Delhi Television **PC**- Confederation of Indian Industry, Indo-US Strategic Dialogue, Trilateral Commission Executive Group, Give Foundation Ltd., President: Aspen Institute **E**- Calcutta University, Manchester University (Economics/Commerce degree), University of Warwick, UK (Honorary Doctorate) **F**- N/A

Roberto de Ocampo, Philippines **CB**- ARGOSY Fund (private), ABCapitalOnline.com (private), PSi Technologies (private), Universal LRT Corporation (BVI) Ltd. (private), Alaska Milk Corp. (private), PSi Technologies, House of Investments Inc., SPC Power Corporation, Robinsons Land Corporation, EEI Corporation, PHINMA Corporation, Director and Founding Partner: Centennial Group, Advisor: Planters Bank, CEO and Chair: Philippine Veterans Bank (private) **PE**- Secretary of Finance of the Republic of the Philippines, World Bank **PC**- Trilateral Commission Executive Committee, President: Asian Institute of Management **E**- De La Salle College and Ateneo de Manila University (BA), University of Michigan (MBA), The London School of Economics (Political Science degree) **F**- N/A

Kenneth M. Duberstein, US **CB**- Dell, Promontory Interfinancial Network, Duberstein Group (private), The Boeing Company **PE**- Fannie Mae, Conoco Phillips, White House Chief of Staff (under Ronald Reagan), US Department of Labor, US General Services Administration **PC**- National Endowment for Democracy, Trilateral Commission Executive Group, Brookings Institution, Council on Foreign Relations, American Council for Capital Formation **E**- Franklin & Marshall College (BA, Honorary Doctor of Laws degree), American University (MA) **F**- Boeing compensation $371,000 (2016), Boeing shares 54,966—$15.9 million (2016)

Antonio Garrigues Walker, Spain **CB**- GAWA Capital Partners SL (private) **PE**- Global Law Chair: University of Navarra **PC**- Garrigues Foundation, Foundation Council Spain–Japan, Foundation Council Spain–USA, Trilateral Commission Executive Group, Honorary Chairman: United Nations High Commissioner for Refugees **E**- Universidad Autónoma de Madrid (Law degree) **F**- N/A

David R. Gergen, US **CB**- Professor: John F. Kennedy School of Government at Harvard University **PE**- CNN **PC**- Council on Foreign Relations, The Aspen Institute, Adviser to the Nixon, Reagan & Clinton administrations, Trilateral Commission Executive Group, Bohemian Club **E**- Yale University (BA), Har-

vard Law School (JD) **F**- Harvard salary approx. $200,000+
(2017)

John J. Hamre, US **CB**- Center for Strategic and International
Studies, The MITRE Corporation (private), Science Appli-
cations International Corporation **PE**- Exelis, Leidos, ITT
Corporation, Xylem **PC**- Department of Defense, Trilateral
Commission Executive Committee, Council on Foreign Relations, Congressional Budget Office, Senate Armed Services
Committee, National Petroleum Council **E**- Augustana University (BA), Paul H. Nitze School of Advanced International
Studies at Johns Hopkins University (PhD) **F**- SAIC compensation $232,543 (2016), SAIC shares 26,537—$2.05 million (2016);
sold previous SAIC shares for $76,198 in 2015

Han Sung-Joo, Korea **CB**- Chairman: International Policy
Studies Institute of Korea (IPSIKOR) **PE**- President Emeritus:
Korea University, Ambassador of Korea to the United States
PC- United Nations, East Asia Vision Group, Trilateral Com-
mission Executive Committee **E**- Seoul National University, UC
Berkeley (PhD in Political Science) **F**- N/A

Jane Harman, US **CB**- President and CEO: Woodrow Wilson
International Center for Scholars **PE**- United States House of
Representatives, Lawyer: United States Department of Defense
PC- Trilateral Commission Executive Committee, Defense
Policy Board, Homeland Security Advisory Council, Council
on Foreign Relations, Aspen Institute, Trustee: USC **E**- Smith
College (BA), Harvard Law School (JD) **F**- net worth $244 mil-
lion as of 2017 (getnetworth.com)

Yasuchika Hasegawa, Japan **CB**- Asahi Glass Co., Ltd. (private), Chairman: Takeda Pharmaceutical Company Ltd. (private) **PE**- Tokyo Electric Power Company Holdings, Takeda Chemical Industries Ltd. **PC**- Keizai Doyukai (Japan Association of Chief Executives), Trilateral Commission Executive Committee, World Economic Forum **E**- Waseda University (BS) **F**- N/A

John R. Hewson, Australia **CB**- Gsa Ltd. (private), Churchill Resources NL (private), Energy Mad (private) **PE**- KidsXpress Ltd., Pulse Health Ltd., Biometric Ltd., Liberal Party of Australia, Australian Parliament, Macquarie Bank, Macquarie University Graduate School of Management **PC**- Trilateral Commission Executive Committee, Reserve Bank of Australia, Australian Department of the Treasury, Special Advisor to the Undersecretary of the United Nations **E**- University of Sydney (BA), University of Regina (MA), Johns Hopkins University (MA, PhD) **F**- N/A

Nigel Higgins, UK **CB**- Managing Partner and Co-Head: Rothschild Co. **PE**- Tetra Laval Group, Sadlers Wells, Rothschild Bank AG, Director: Rothschild North America, Co-Chief Executive Officer: Rothschild Group at Rothschild Europe B.V., Executive Director: N.M. Rothschild & Sons Ltd., Director: Rothschild Bank AG (35 years with Rothschild) **PC**- Trilateral Commission Executive Committee **E**- Oxford University (BA) **F**- net worth $1.07 billion (Company Check Ltd.)

Carla A. Hills, US **CB**- Chair: Hills & Company **PE**- JPMorgan Chase & Co., The TCW Group, Coca-Cola, Chevron, AIG, Time Warner, American International Group, Alcatel-Lucent USA, Chevron Corp., Assistant Attorney General: United States

Department of Justice, Secretary: US Department of Housing and Urban Development, Partner: Latham & Watkins llp, **PC**- Trilateral Commission Executive Committee, Inter-American Dialogue, Center for Strategic and International Studies, Urban Institute, Peterson Institute for International Economics, Americans for Generational Equity, Council of the Americas, US Trade Representative: Office of the United States Trade Representative, Trustee: Institute for International Economics and Center for Strategic and International Studies, Co-Chairman: Council on Foreign Relations, Chair: National Committee on United States-China Relations, Trustee: US–China Business Council **E**- Oxford University, Stanford University (BA), Yale (JD) **F**- Chevron shares 5,500—$275,000 (2004), Gilead shares 157,393—$5.9 million (2010), Gilead Science compensation $389,937 (2010), Alcatel-Lucent USA compensation $135,000 (2006), Alcatel-Lucent USA shares 179,133—$492,615 (2006); owned 96,500 shares—worth $2.4 million—of Time Warner as of 2006; donates $25,000 annually to the Council on Foreign Relations

Akinari Horii, Japan **CB**- Promontory Financial Group llc, (IBM), Tokio Marine Holdings (private) **PE**- The Canon Institute for Global Studies, Supervisory Committee of ABF Pan Asia Bond Index Fund, Director of International Department: Bank of Japan, Executive Director: Bank of Japan **PC**- BIS in Basel, Switzerland, The Canon Institute for Global Studies, Bank for International Settlements' Financial Stability Board, Trilateral Commission Executive Committee, Institute for International Policy Studies in Tokyo, Japan's Ministry of Finance, Chairman: Asian and Pacific Central Banks **E**- University of Tokyo (BA in Economics), Wharton School (MBA) **F**- N/A

Karen Elliott House, US **CB**- Dow Jones of CNBC Europe and CNBC Asia Pacific (a business-television partnership of Dow Jones and NBC Universal) **PE**- Vice President and Publisher: The Wall Street Journal (of Dow Jones & Company) **PC**- Trilateral Commission Executive Committee, WTA Tour, Asia Society, Director: Council on Foreign Relations, Chairman: The RAND Corporation, Trustee: Boston University **E**- University of Texas at Austin (BA in Journalism) **F**- net worth $6 million as of 2017 (networthpost.com); won the Pulitzer Prize for International Reporting

Mugur Isărescu, Romania **CB**- Governor: National Bank of Romania, Bucharest (15 years) **PE**- Prime Minister of Romania **PC**- Trilateral Commission Executive Committee **E**- Bucharest Academy of Economic Studies (International Trade degree) **F**- National Bank of Romania compensation $259,448 (2017)

Lord Kerr of Kinlochard, UK **CB**- Scottish American Investment Trust, House of Lords, Vice Chair: Scottish Power Ltd. **PE**- Scottish Power, Royal Dutch Shell, Rio Tinto, Treasury, British Diplomatic Service, Chancellor of the Exchequer, Ambassador: European Commission, Ambassador: United States, Secretary: Diplomatic Service, Secretary: Foreign and Commonwealth Office **PC**- Baron of Kinlochard, UK/Korea Forum for the Future, Centre for European Reform, Fulbright Commission, National Gallery, Rhodes Trust, Steering Committee of the Bilderberg Group, Trilateral Commission Executive Committee, Trustee: Carnegie Trust for the Universities of Scotland, President: St Andrew's Clinics for Children, Vice President: European Policy Centre, Chairman: Imperial College London **E**- Oxford (BA, Honorary Doctorate of Law) **F**-

Shell compensation $389,000 (2011), Rio Tinto compensation $231,000 (2014), Rio Tinto shares 15,000—$53.4 million (2014)

Jovan Kovačić, Serbia **CB**- East-West Bridge, CEO: GCA Global Communications Associates Ltd., Senior Partner: Kovačić & Spaić, Partner: Hill & Knowlton **PE**- Former International Reporter and War Correspondent: CNN, ABC, NPR, and BBC **PC**- Trilateral Commission Executive Committee, Serbian National Group of the Trilateral Commission, GCA and CEO: Global, Political Advisor: Strategic Partnerships Group, Consultant: Republika Srpska and President Milorad Dodik in Bosnia **E**- British, Serbian and American schools; American MA in Communications and Media Management **F**- net worth $11 million (networthpost.com)

Kurt Lauk, Germany **CB**- Magna International, Co-President and Founding Partner: Globe Capital Partners (private) **PE**- BCG Inc., Charles Bernd AG, I-D Media AG, TomTom Licensing, Gehring Maschinenbau, Fortemedia, Gehring GmbH & Co. KG and Charles Bernd SA, Solera Holdings, TowerBrook Capital Partners lp, CIBER Inc., Veritas Software Corporation, Corus Group Ltd., Innovation Group plc, Diligence London, Silver Lake, Senior Vice President: DaimlerChrysler AG, Senior Vice President: Audi AG, CEO: Zinser Textile Machinery **PC**- Franco-German Institute in Ludwigsburg, Trilateral Commission Executive Committee, Bilderberg Group, Trustee: International Institute for Strategic Studies in London **E**- Stanford University (MBA), University of Munich (MA in History and Theology), University of Tübingen, University of Kiel (PhD in International Relations) **F**- Magna compensation $238,000 (2016), Magna shares valued at $1.1 million as of 2016

Eli Leenaars, Netherlands **CB**- VP: UBS **PE**- ING Group, ING Poland, and ING Latin America **PC**- Trilateral Commission Executive Committee, ABN Amro Bank **E**- Catholic University of Nijmegen (Civil Law degree), Harvard Business School, European University Institute in Florence (LLM) **F**- N/A

Jean Lemierre, France **CB**- TEB Holding AS (Turkey), Chair: BNP Paribas SA, Director: TOTAL SA **PE**- President: The European Bank for Reconstruction and Development **PC**- International Advisory Council at China Investment Corporation, Trilateral Commission Executive Committee **E**- École Nationale d'Administration (graduate degree in Science) **F**- BNP Paribas compensation $1.17 million (2016)

Monique Leroux, Canada **CB**- President: International Cooperative Alliance **PE**- BCE Inc., S&P Global, President and CEO: Alimentation Couche-Tard **PC**- Conference Board of Canada, Global Agenda Council of the World Economic Forum, Trilateral Commission Executive Committee, HEC Montréal's Council of Governors, Investissement Québec, Quebéc Economic and Innovation Council, Order of Canada, L'Ordre national du Québec, Chevalier of the Légion d'honneur, Recipient of the Woodrow Wilson Award (United States), Chair: International Summit of Cooperatives, Chair of the Board of Governors: the Society for the Celebrations of Montreal's 375th Anniversary **E**- eight Canadian university honorary degrees **F**- S&P Global share value $85,000 (2017), S&P compensation approx. $100,000 (2017)

Thomas Leysen, Belgium **CB**- KBC Bank NV, KBC Insurance, Corelio NV, Corelio Media, Eurométaux, Rubenianum Fund,

Heritage Fund of the Fondation Roi Baudouin, Aurubis Belgium nv/sa, Toyota Motor Corporation in Japan, Norddeutsche Affinerie AG, Metzler Bank, UCB SA, Chairman: Federation of Belgian Enterprises, Chairman: Umicore SA **PE-** Umicore NV, Sydes NV, Atlas Copco, Aurubis AG, CEO: Transcor Group **PC-** Executive Committee of the Belgian Employers Federation (FEB/VBO), Trilateral Commission Executive Committee, European Round Table of Industrialists, European Friends of Versailles, Vice President: "Vrienden van het Rubenshuis," President: BJA **E-** University of Leuven, Belgium (Law degree and Masters of Law) **F-** Umicore & KBC compensation $585,000 (2016)

Bo Lidegaard, Denmark **CB-** Editor: Politiken **PC-** Climate Change Secretariat under the Danish Ministry of State, Trilateral Commission Executive Committee **E-** University of Copenhagen (PhD in History) **F-** net worth $1.7 million as of 2017 (celebritybio.org)

Franjo Luković, Croatia **CB-** UniCredit Bank, President: Management Board of Zagrebačka Banka **PE-** Coning in Varaždin, Deputy Chairman: Jugobanka in Zagreb **PC-** Trilateral Commission Executive Committee **E-** University of Zagreb (Economics degree) **F-** Zagrebacka Banka shares valued at $3.5 million as of 2016

Minoru (Ben) Makihara, Japan **CB-** International Advisory Council of Allianz SE **PE-** International Council of JPMorgan Chase & Co., Coca-Cola, Director: IBM, Senior Corporate Advisor: Mitsubishi Corporation, Advisor: Holdingham Group **PC-** Trilateral Commission Executive Committee, Shinsei

Bank **E**- Harvard University (BA, MPA), **F**- IBM compensation $627,701, IBM shares valued at approx. $1.03 million as of 2010; awarded an Honorary Knighthood of the Most Excellent Order of the British Empire 2013

Mario Monti, Italy **CB**- International Advisor: Goldman Sachs **PE**- Prime Minister of Italy, European Commission, President: Italian Council of Ministers, President: Bocconi University **PC**- American European Community Association, Council for the Future of Europe (CFE), Attali Commission on Economic Growth, Trilateral Commission Executive Committee, Patron: European Advisory (real estate), Director: Peterson Institute for International Economics, Creator: International Competition Network **E**- Bocconi University (BA), Yale (MA in Management) **F**- net worth $50 million (celebritynetworth.com)

Joseph S. Nye Jr., US **CB**- The Chertoff Group **PE**- Defense Policy Board, US Assistant Secretary of Defense, Professor: John F. Kennedy School of Government at Harvard University **PC**- Defense Policy Board, Belfer Center for Science and International Affairs, Trilateral Commission Executive Committee, Director: Council on Foreign Relations (2004–2013), Trustee: Wells College and the Center for Strategic and International Studies, Chairman: Trilateral North American Group **E**- Princeton University (BA), Exeter College (MA), Harvard University (PhD) **F**- net worth $1.5 million as of 2017 (networthpost.com)

Akio Okawara, Japan **CB**- President and CEO: Japan Center for International Exchange **PE**- Sumitomo Corporation Global Research, Mazda Motors America **PC**- Japan Conference on Cultural and Educational Interchange (CULCON), Trilateral

Commission Executive Committee E- Keio University (BA) F-N/A

Andrzej Marian Olechowski, Poland **CB**- Central Europe Trust, Chair: Bank Handlowy W Warszawie SA **PE**- Minister of Finance of Poland, Minister of Foreign Affairs of Poland, World Bank, ICENTIS Capital Sp., Layetana Developments Polska, Euronet Worldwide, Polski Koncern Naftowy Orlen SA, VCP Capital Partners, Governor: National Bank of Poland **PC**- Trilateral Commission Executive Committee **E**- Szkola Glówna Handlowa w Warszawie (PhD), Graduate Institute of International and Development Studies, Geneva **F**- N/A

Meghan L. O'Sullivan, US **CB**- Jeane Kirkpatrick Professor of the Practice of International Affairs: John F. Kennedy School of Government at Harvard University **PE**- National Intelligence Council, Intelligence Director and Senior Director for Strategic Planning: National Security Council **PC**- Trilateral Commission Executive Committee, Aspen Strategy Group, Council on Foreign Relations, Trustee: German Marshall Fund of the United States, Fellow: Brookings Institution **E**- Georgetown University (BA), Oxford University (MA, PhD) **F**- Harvard salary $300,000+ (2017)

Ursula Plassnik, Austria **CB**- Ambassador to Switzerland **PE**- Foreign Minister of Austria, Ambassador to France **PC**- European Council on Foreign Relations (ECFR), Foreign Policy and United Nations Association of Austria (UNA-AUSTRIA), Trilateral Commission Executive Committee **E**- University of Vienna (JD), College of Europe (Certificate of Advanced European Studies) **F**- N/A

Adam Simon Posen, US **CB**- Congressional Budget Office Panel of Economic Advisers, President: Peterson Institute for International Economics **PC**- Okun Memorial Fellow, Brookings Institution, Council on Foreign Relations, Trilateral Commission Executive Committee, World Economic Forum, Senior Fellow: Institute for International Economics **E**- Harvard University (BA, PhD) **F**- N/A

Luis Rubio, Mexico **CB**- President: The Consejo Mexicano de Asuntos Internacionales (COMEXI) **PE**- Planning Director: Citibank Mexico **PC**- Mexico Institute, Center of Research for Development (CIDAC), Trilateral Commission Executive Committee **E**- Brandeis University (MA, PhD) **F**- N/A

Jin (Roy) Ryu, Korea **CB**- PMX Industries, BIAC, Chair and CEO: Poongsan Corporation (metals and munitions) **PC**- The Federation of Korea Industries, International Wrought Copper Council (IWCC), Korea Defense Industry Association, Federation of Korean Industries, Korea International Trade Association, Vice Chairman: Korea–US Economic Council, Director: Trilateral Commission Executive Committee **E**- Seoul National University (BA) **F**- Poongsan shares valued at $123 million as of 2017

Ferdinando Salleo, Italy **CB**- VP: Banca Del Mezzogiorno-MedioCredito Centrale Spa (private) **PE**- Safei SA, Italy's Ambassador to the US (1995–2003) **PC**- Trilateral Commission Executive Committee **E**- University of Rome (JD) **F**- N/A

Carlo Secchi, Italy **CB**- Mediaset, Allianz RAS, A2A SpA (private), Rector and Professor of Economic Policy: University

Bocconi, Director: Pirelli SpA, Italcementi SpA **PE-** Parmalat, VP: CEMS, President: European Association of Development Research and Training Institutes (EADI), Professor of Economics: Universities of Milano, Sassari, and Trento **PC-** Foundation NovaResPublica, ISLA at University of Bocconi, University Association for European Studies (AUSE), Scientific Committee of the IReR, I-CSR (Italian Foundation for the Dissemination of Corporate Social Responsibility), Italian Senate, European Parliament in the IV Legislature, Vice-President: Economic, Monetary Affairs and Industrial Politics Commission, President: Italian Group of the Trilateral Commission **E-** Bocconi University (BA), Erasmus University (Graduate degree) **F-** Mediaset compensation $100,620 (2017), Italcementi compensation $46,800 (2016)

Kristin Skogen Lund, Norway **CB-** Umoe AS, Schibsted Group, Trivano-Ericsson **LM-B PE-** Unilever, Nordic Semiconductor ASA, Coca-Cola, Sweden, Aftonbladet AB, Head of Digital Services & Broadcast: Telenor ASA, Managing Director: Aftenposten AS, CEO: Aftenposten at Media Norge ASA, Executive Officer and CEO: Scanpix Scandinavia AB, Editor: Scandinavia Online AS (SOL), Director: Orkla ASA **PC-** Confederation of Norwegian Enterprise (NHO), Council of Stiftelsen Det Norske Veritas, Trilateral Commission Executive Committee, Bilderberg Group, VP: Confederation of Norwegian Business (NHO) **E-** University of Oregon (BA in Business), INSEAD (MBA) **F-** Trivana compensation $116,721 (2017); CNN described her as Norway's most powerful woman as of 2012

James B. Steinberg, US **CB-** Professor of International Affairs: Syracuse University **PE-** Brookings Institution, RAND Corporation, Center for a New American Security, National Security Advisor to Clinton, Deputy Secretary of the State Department, Staff: Senate Armed Services Committee, Dean: LBJ School of Public Affairs, University of Texas **PC**- Trilateral Commission Executive Committee, Atlantic Council, Council on Foreign Relations, Markle Task Force on National Security in the Information Age, America Abroad Media **E**- Harvard University (BA), Yale University (JD) **F**- Syracuse compensation $200,000+ (2017)

Shigemitsu Sugisaki, Japan **CB**- Goldman Sachs Japan Co. (private) **PE**- Ministry of Finance, Deputy Director General: International Finance Bureau, Commissioner: Tokyo Regional Taxation Bureau, Deputy Managing Director: International Monetary Fund (IMF) **PC**- Trilateral Commission Executive Committee **E**- University of Tokyo (BA), Columbia University (MA in International Affairs) **F**- N/A

György Surányi, Hungary **CB**- Chair: Banca Intesa Beograd, Professor: Central European University **PE**- Chairman of the Supervisory Board: Vub AS, CEO: CIB Bank, President: Hungarian National Bank, Regional Head: Intesa Sanpaolo Group **PC**- Trilateral Commission Executive Committee, World Economic Forum **E**- Corvinus University of Budapest (BA) **F**- Central European University compensation approx. $100,000

Peter Sutherland, Ireland **CB**- Chair: Goldman Sachs International **PE**- Eli Lilly & Co., BP Amoco plc, ABB Ltd., BP Solar International, BW Group Ltd., Chair: British Petroleum, Director: WTO, Chair: Allied Irish Bank, Chairman: BP plc **PC**- The Royal Irish Academy, Foundation Board of World

Economic Forum, Global Advisory Board of the Council on Foreign Relations, Council for the Future of Europe (CFE), Bilderberg Group, President: European Policy Centre Advisory Council, Chair: Court of Governors at The London School of Economics and Political Science, Chair: UN Special Representative for Migration and Development, Vice-Chair: European Round Table of Industrialists, Honorary Chairman: The Trilateral Council **E-** University College Dublin (BA) **F-** BP shares 30,079—$17 million (2006), BP compensation $585,000 (2006); net worth $45 million (1999)[162]

Tarisa Watanagase, Thailand **CB-** Independent Director: Siam Cement Public Company Ltd. **PE-** Governor: Bank of Thailand, Deputy Governor: Financial Institutions Stability at Bank of Thailand (BOT), Chair: Financial Institutions Policy, Chairman: Bank of Thailand, Director: US Securities and Exchange Commission **PC-** Trilateral Commission **E-** Keio University (BA, MA in Economics), PhD Washington University, St. Louis (PhD in Economics) **F-** Siam Cement compensation $100,000 (2015), Siam Cement 40,100 shares—$1.3 million (2015)

Jean-Claude Trichet, France CB- Bank for International Settlements, Director: Airbus Group SE **PE-** President: Executive Board at European Central Bank, Secretary General: Interministerial Committee for Improving Industrial Structures (CIASI) **PC-** World Economic Forum, Steering Committee of the Bilderberg Group, European Systemic Risk Board (ESRB), Paris Club, Honorary Chairman: Group of Thirty, Chairman: Board of Directors of Bruegel, European Chairman: Trilateral Commission, President: SOGEPA, Governor: Banque de France,

212 OF 384 Global Power Elite

Adviser to the Cabinet of the Minister of Economic Affairs, Deputy Director of Bilateral Affairs at the Treasury Department, President: Group of Governors and Heads of Supervision (GHOS) in Basel E- École nationale supérieure des Mines de Nancy (BA), University of Paris (MA) F- Airbus SE compensation $187,200 (2017)

Raivo Vare, Estonia **CB**- Sthenos Group, & OÜ RVVE Group (private), SmartCap Ltd. (private), CEO: Pakterminal Ltd. (private) **PE**- AS Eesti Raudtee, Director: Tallinna Pank Ltd. **PC**- President's Academic Advisory Board, Minister of State and Minister of Transport and Communication in Tallinn, Council Estonian Development, Trilateral Commission Executive Committee, Chairman: Council of the Parliament's Development Fund, Vice-Chair: Council Estonian Cooperation Assembly **E**- Estonian Business School (MBA), University of Tartu (Law degree) **F**- approx. $1 million+ (2017); "Raivo Vare, CEO at the oil transit company Pakterminal, one of the largest companies in Estonia, told the daily newspaper Postimees that he did not support revealing the salaries of private-sector employees. 'Estonian society is not yet ready for that,' he said. 'The gaps at different levels of life in Estonia are still huge, and news about high salaries would cause only anger.'"[163]

George Vassiliou, Cyprus **PE**- President of Cyprus, Member of Parliament and Leader of the United Democrats **PC**- European Council on Tolerance and Reconciliation, Trilateral Commission Executive Committee **E**- University Budapest, University of London (PhD) **F**- N/A

Paul A. Volcker, US **CB-** Mevion Medical Systems, Senior Advisor: Pro Mujer, Director: Deutsche Bank Trust Corporation **PE-** President: Federal Reserve Bank (FRB) of New York, Economist: Chase Manhattan Bank, Chairman: Wolfensohn & Co., Senior Advisor: Shinsei Bank Ltd. **PC-** Group of Thirty (G30), Bilderberg Group, World Economic Forum, Japan Society, the Institute of International Economics, American Assembly, American Council on Germany, Honorary Chairman: Trilateral Commission, Director: Council on Foreign Relations (1988–1999), Chairman of Governors: Federal Reserve System, Trustee: International House New York and International Accounting Standards Committee (IASC), Director: Treasury's Office of Financial Analysis **E-** Princeton University (BA), Harvard University Graduate School of Public Administration (MA), London School of Economics (MA) **F-** net worth $700,000+ as of 2017 (networthpost.com)[164]

Marko Voljč, Slovenia **CB-** Chief Officer of Corporate Change & Support: KBC Group, Brussels Chairman: Supervisory Board of DZI plc **PE-** Chief Executive Officer: Nova Ljubljanska Banka, CEO: Kereskedelmi és Hitelbank Zártköruen Muködo Részvénytársaság, CEO: Central & Eastern Europe and Russia Business Unit at KBC Group **PC-** National Bank of Slovenia, World Bank, Supervisory Board at CIBANK EAD, Trilateral Commission, Chairman: Supervisory Board at CIBANK EAD **E-** Univerzitet u Beogradu, University of Ljubljana **F-** N/A

Panagis Vourloumis, Greece **CB-** Senior Adviser: N.M. Rothschild **PE-** Head of the South-East Asia division of the International Finance Corporation (IFC), Chairman and Chief Executive Officer: Hellenic Telecommunications Organization (O.T.E.), Chairman and Chief Executive Officer: ALPHA Finance, ALPHA Mutual Funds, and ALPHA Bank Romania **PC**- Board of the Federation of Greek Industries, Trilateral Commission **E**- The London School of Economics and Political Science, Economic Development Institute **F**- Cosmote Mobile Telecommunications OTE 1 million shares valued at $28.9 million as of 2007

Jusuf Wanandi, Indonesia **CB**- Senior Fellow and Co-Founder: Centre for Strategic and International Studies, Jakarta, Vice Chairman: Board of Trustees of the CSIS Foundation **PE**- Governor: East West Centre in Hawaii **PC**- International Advisory Board at the Council on Foreign Relations, Trilateral Commission, Co-Chair: Indonesian National Committee of the Council for Security Cooperation in the Asia Pacific (CSCAP), Member of Board of Trustees and Senior Fellow: Centre for Strategic and International Studies in Jakarta **E**- University of Indonesia **F**-net worth $304 million (2017)[165]

The Global Power Elite facilitators listed in this chapter share interest in insuring that capital growth and open opportunities for investment worldwide continues as the driving force of capitalism. Global policymaking thereby develops an important transnational function. The power elite policy groups inside the Transnational Capitalist Class are made up of persons with shared educational experiences, similar lifestyles, and common ideologies. They are rapidly becoming an essential component of global capitalism.

Institutions within capitalist countries, such as government ministries, defense forces, intelligence agencies, judiciaries, universities, and representative bodies, recognize to varying degrees that the overriding demands of transnational capital reach beyond the boundaries of nation-states. The idea of legal boundaries of nation-states has long been held as sacrosanct in traditional liberal capitalist economies. However, globalization has placed a new set of demands on capitalism that requires transnational mechanisms to support continued capital growth worldwide, and that imperative increasingly falls beyond the boundaries of individual states.

The TCC viewed the financial crisis of 2008 as an acknowledgment that the global system of capital is under threat. We see the TCC's demands for global investment as allowing for the abandonment of nation-state rights altogether via occupations, wars, trade agreements, and enforced economic rules. Failed states, manufactured civil wars, regime changes, and direct invasions/occupations are manifestations of the new world order requirements for protecting transnational capital.

The Global Power Elites understand fully the need for transnational agreements and institutional mechanisms in support of capital expansion and growth. They have very rapidly built organizations to support the Transnational Capitalist Class and bring together capitalist power elites from every region in the world. Knowing exactly the core players in the new world order of things is an important part of understanding what needs to be done. Perhaps it is not too late for democracy movements to divert this onslaught of concentrated global wealth and power, but rapid adjustments must be implemented very soon if we hope to maintain our human rights and freedoms.

CHAPTER 4, APPENDIX A
Bilderberg Group Steering Committee

Source: Bilderberg Meetings, undated, http://www.bilderbergmeetings.org/
steering-committee.html.

CHAIRMAN
Henri de Castries (France)—Chairman and CEO: AXA Group

Paul M. Achleitner (Austria)—Chairman of the Supervisory
Board: Deutsche Bank AG
Marcus Agius (Great Britain)—Non-Executive Chairman: *PA
Consulting Group*
Roger C. Altman (US)—Executive Chairman: Evercore
Matti Apunen (Finland)—Director: Finnish Business and
Policy Forum EVA
José M. Durão Barroso (Portugal)—Former President of the
European Commission
Nicolas Baverez (France)—Partner: Gibson Dunn
Svein Richard Brandtzæg (Norway)—President and CEO:
Norsk Hydro ASA
Juan Luis Cebrián (Spain)—Executive Chairman: PRISA and
El País
John Elkann (Italy)—Chairman and CEO: EXOR, Chairman:
Fiat Chrysler Automobiles
Thomas Enders (German)—CEO: Airbus Group
Ulrik Federspiel (Denmark)—Group Executive and Chief:
International and Public Affairs
Lilli Gruber (Italy)—Editor-in-Chief and Anchor: *"Otto e
mezzo," La7 TV*
Victor Halberstadt (Netherlands)—Chairman: Bilderberg
Meetings, *Professor of Economics: Leiden University*

Kenneth M. Jacobs (US)—Chairman and CEO: Lazard
James A. Johnson (US)—Chairman: Johnson Capital Partners
Alex Karp (US)—CEO: Palantir Technologies
Klaus Kleinfeld (Germany)—Chairman and CEO: Alcoa
Ömer M. Koç (Turkey)—Chairman: *Koç Holding AS*
Marie-Josée Kravis (Canada)—President: American Friends of
    Bilderberg, Senior Fellow: Hudson Institute
André Kudelski (Switzerland)—Chairman and CEO: Kudelski
    Group
Thomas Leysen (Belgium)—Chairman: KBC Group
Craig J. Mundie (US)—Principal: Mundie & Associates
Michael O'Leary (Ireland)—CEO: Ryanair plc
Dimitri Papalexopoulos (Greece)—CEO: Titan Cement Co.
Heather M. Reisman (Canada)—Chair and CEO: *Indigo Books
    & Music*
John Sawers (Great Britain)—Chairman and Partner: *Macro
    Advisory Partners*
Eric E. Schmidt (US)—Executive Chairman: Alphabet Inc.
Rudolf Scholten (Austria)—CEO: *Oesterreichische
    Kontrollbank AG*
Peter A. Thiel (US)—President: Thiel Capital
Jacob Wallenberg (Sweden)—Chairman: Investor AB
Robert B. Zoellick (US)—Chairman of the Board of Interna-
    tional Advisors for the Goldman Sachs Group

CHAPTER 4 APPENDIX B
Members of the World Economic Forum
Board of Trustees
(as of 24 August 2017)

Klaus Schwab—Chairman of the Board of Trustees of the
World Economic Forum

Peter Brabeck-Letmathe—Vice-Chairman of the Board of
Trustees of the World Economic Forum

H.M. Queen Rania Al Abdullah of the Hashemite Kingdom of
Jordan

Mukesh Ambani—Chairman and Managing Director: Reliance
Industries, India

Marc R. Benioff—Chairman and Chief Executive Officer:
Salesforce, US

Mark Carney—Chairman: Financial Stability Board, Governor:
Bank of England

Orit Gadiesh—Chairman: Bain & Company, US

Al Gore—Vice-President of the United States (1993–2001),
Chairman and Co-Founder: Generation Investment Management llp, US

Herman Gref—Chairman of the Board and Chief Executive
Officer: Sberbank, Russia

Ángel Gurría—Secretary-General: Organisation for Economic
Co-operation and Development

André S. Hoffmann—Non-Executive Vice-Chairman: Roche
Holding Ltd., Switzerland

Jim Yong Kim—President: The World Bank, Washington, DC

Christine Lagarde—Managing Director: International Monetary Fund (IMF), Washington, DC

Yo-Yo Ma—Cellist, US

Peter Maurer—President: International Committee of the Red
Cross (ICRC), Geneva

Luis Alberto Moreno—President: Inter-American Development Bank, Washington, DC

Indra Nooyi—Chairman and Chief Executive Officer: PepsiCo,
US

L. Rafael Reif—President: Massachusetts Institute of Technology (MIT), US

Jim Hagemann Snabe—Chairman: A.P. Møller-Maersk, Denmark

Heizo Takenaka—Minister of State for Economic and Fiscal
Policy of Japan (2002–2006)

Ursula von der Leyen—Federal Minister of Defense of Germany

Min Zhu—President: National Institute of Financial Research,
People's Republic of China, Deputy Managing Director:
International Monetary Fund

CHAPTER 5

PROTECTORS
THE POWER ELITE AND THE US MILITARY NATO EMPIRE, INTELLIGENCE AGENCIES, AND PRIVATE MILITARY COMPANIES[166]

The power elite inside the Transnational Capitalist Class continually worry about the unruly exploited masses rising in rebellion. As a result of these class insecurities, the Global Power Elites work hard to protect their structure of concentrated wealth. The US military empire has long been the protector of global capitalism. The United States has more than 800 military bases in 70 countries and territories. The United Kingdom, France, and Russia have about 30 foreign bases.[167] US military forces are now deployed in 70 percent of the world's nations. US Special Operations Command (SOCOM) has troops in 147 countries, an increase of 80 percent since 2010. Most of the missions are training exercises, but direct action counterterrorism strikes occur regularly, including drone assassinations and kill/capture raids.[168]

US special forces are currently engaged in more than 100 missions in Africa. A recent journal article by senior SOCOM leaders discusses the ongoing critical stituation in Africa and predicts a generation of continuing conflict:

For the men and women of SOCAFRICA the African continent offers every possible physical, political, and psychological environment an operational command could possibly confront. This terrain creates opportunity for threat groups to conceal themselves in the population, move unhindered across borders and transit information and material throughout the SOCAFRICA area of operations. The definition for this type of environment has been termed "The Gray Zone." ... The Violent Extremist Organization (VEO) threat operates in a non-state, trans-regional and trans-national, decentralized, and dispersed operational construct, exploiting and exacerbating instability in Africa. The threat survives in ungoverned and under-governed safe-havens and sanctuaries created by ineffective governance resulting in a population that has lost hope.[169]

Remaining unexplained are the reasons why many African populations have lost hope, as well as the rationale for VEO groups to resist. What hope could possible exist for generations of families living on a few dollars a day with zero possiblity of bettering their situation? Of course some will accept the resisters to empire within their ranks and at times even come to their aid. The US military empire stands on hundreds of years of colonial exploitation and continues to support repressive, exploitative governments that cooperate with global capital's imperial agenda. Governments that accept external capital investment, whereby a small segment of a country's elite benefits, do so knowing that capital inevitably requires a return on investment that entails using up resources and people for economic gain. The whole system continues wealth concentration for elites and expanded wretched inequality for the masses. The daily violence in the Gray Zones is in fact manifested by empire, producing thousands of deaths from misery and poverty. Many VEO resisters—so-called "terrorists"—are in reality acting in a rational manner, using the only means available to challenge the empire of exploitative capital concentration.

We wish to declare here an abhorrence for all acts of terrorism and violence. We fully support the Universal Declaration of Human Rights (reproduced in Chapter 7). However, it remains clear to us that the structural terror of poverty and powerlessness is a contributing factor to VEO resistance movements. It is far too simple for justifiers of empire to claim that resisters are simply evil people who have no belief in the value of human life. After 9/11, George W. Bush declared, "We will rid the world of the evil-doers,"[170] and "They hate our freedoms— our freedom of religion, our freedom of speech, our freedom to vote and assemble and disagree with each other."[171] Both statements are simply a meaningless demonization of others as a political justification of permanent war. Presidents since Bush have done little better in justifying continuing war worldwide. Understanding permanent war as an economic relief valve for surplus capital is a vital part of comprehending capitalism in the world today. War provides investment opportunity for the Giants and TCC elites and a guaranteed return on capital. War also serves a repressive function of keeping the suffering masses of humanity afraid and compliant.

Protection of global capital is the prime reason that NATO countries now account for 85 percent of the world's defense spending, with the United States spending more on the military than the rest of the world combined.[172] Fears of inequality, rebellions, and other forms of unrest motivate NATO's gobal agenda in the war on terror.[173] The Chicago 2012 NATO Summit Declaration reads:

> As Alliance leaders, we are determined to ensure that NATO retains and develops the capabilities necessary to perform its essential core tasks— collective defence, crisis management and cooperative security—and thereby to play an essential role promoting security in the world. We must meet this responsibility while dealing with an acute financial crisis and responding to evolving geo-strategic challenges. NATO allows us to achieve greater security than any one Ally could attain acting alone.
>
> We confirm the continued importance of a strong transatlantic link and Alliance solidarity as well as the significance of sharing responsibilities, roles, and risks to meet the challenges North-American and European Allies face together.... [W]e have confidently set ourselves the goal of NATO Forces 2020: modern, tightly connected forces equipped, trained, exercised and commanded so that they can operate together and with partners in *any* [emphasis added] environment.[174]

NATO is quickly becoming a US military empire supplemental police force for the Global Power Elite and the Transnational Capitalist Class. As the TCC more fully emerged in the 1980s, coinciding with the USSR's collapse, NATO began broader operations. United Nations Security Council resolutions provided NATO with a mandate for operations in Afghanistan, outside of its traditional North Atlantic region, and a framework for the NATO training mission in Iraq.[175] NATO's military structure is divided between two strategic commands: Supreme Headquarters Allied Powers Europe, located near Mons, Belgium; and the Allied Command Transformation, located in Norfolk, Virginia. The Supreme Allied Commander Europe oversees all NATO military operations and is always a US general officer. The North Atlantic Council is NATO's main political body, made up of high-level delegates for each member state.[176] The power elite civilian-based Atlantic Council is the primary advisory planning nonprofit group that sets the parameters of US–NATO operational expectations and global security priorities.

Germany and other European powers have taken a strong interest in modernizing NATO's defense infrastructure. In a meeting of NATO defense ministers in Brussels in late June 2017, it was reported that member nations were meeting their agreement by spending 2 percent of their GDP on defense. The EU NATO budget is set at 38.5 billion euros ($45 billion) for 2018 and will go up to 42.4 billion euros by 2021 ($50 billion).[177] Additionally, in March 2017 EU defense ministers agreed to set up a joint command center for military planning and operations independent of NATO and the United States.[178]

NATO's first military venture took place in the Balkans, where it remains, and it then held direct operations in Afghanistan, Libya, and Iraq. NATO now conducts operations all around the world, including a Counter-Piracy Task Force in the Gulf of Aden and missions in Somalia, Sudan, Mali, Ethiopia, Nigeria, Kenya, Lithuania, Estonia, Latvia, Georgia, Hungary, Slovakia, Bulgaria, Poland, Turkey, Pakistan (disaster relief), and

Romania.[179] NATO also cooperates with its partner countries in Central Asia: Kazakhstan, Kyrgyzstan, Tajikistan, Turkmenistan, and Uzbekistan.[180] Russian leaders believe that NATO's expansion into former Soviet Union countries is a betrayal of agreements from 1990 by then–US Secretary of State James Baker, who promised no eastern expansion of NATO during the negotiations for reuniting Germany.[181]

While NATO's intrusions outside of Europe are justified as peacekeeping humaniarian missions, it has become clear that the Global Power Elite uses NATO and the US military empire for its worldwide security. This is part of an expanding strategy of US military domination around the world, whereby the US/NATO military empire, advised by the power elite's Atlantic Council, operates in service to the Transnational Corporate Class for the protection of international capital everywhere in the world.[182]

Sociologists William I. Robinson and Jerry Harris anticipated this situation in 2000, when they noted a "shift from the social welfare state to the social control (police) state, replete with the dramatic expansion of public and private security forces, the mass incarceration of the excluded populations (disproportionately minorities), new forms of social apartheid ... and anti-immigrant legislation."[183] Robinson and Harris's theory accurately predicted the agenda of today's Global Power Elite, such as:

- President Trump's continuation of the police state agendas of his executive predecessors, Barack Obama, George W. Bush, Bill Clinton, and George H.W. Bush;

- the long-range global dominance agenda of the Global Power Elite, which uses US/NATO military forces to discourage resisting states and maintain internal police repression, in service of the capitalist system's orderly maintenance;

- and the continued consolidation of capital around the world without interference from governments or egalitarian social movements.[184]

Furthermore, this agenda entails further pauperization of the botton half of the world's population and an unrelenting downward spiral of wages for 80 percent of the world.[185] The world is facing economic crisis, and the neoliberal solution is to spend less on human needs and more on security.[186] It is a world of financial institutions run amok, where the answer to economic collapse is to print more money through quantitative easing, flooding the population with trillions of new inflation-producing dollars. It is a world of permanent war, whereby spending for destruction requires further spending to rebuild, a cycle that profits the Giants and global networks of economic power. It is a world of drone killings, extrajudicial assassinations, death, and destruction, at home and abroad.

As Andrew Kolin notes in *State Power and Democracy*, "There is an Orwellian dimension to the [Bush, Obama, and now Trump] Administration's perspective. It chose to disregard the law, instead creating decrees to legitimate illegal actions, giving itself permission to act without any semblances of power sharing as required by the Constitution or international law."[187]

"The bottom line, the fundamental division of our society," Dennis Loo writes, "is between, on the one hand, those whose interests rest on the dominance and the drive for monopolizing the society and planet's resources and, on the other hand, those whose interests lie in the husbanding of thoses resources for the good of the whole rather than the part."[188]

The Occupy Movement used the 1 percent vs. 99 percent mantra as a master concept in its demonstrations, disruptions, and challenges to the practices of the Transnational Corporate Class. Occupy was exactly what the Global Power Elites fear the most—a global democratic movement that exposes the agenda of capitalism and the continuing theater of government elections, where the actors in each performance may change but the marquee remains the same.

The military empire dominated by the United States and the North Atlantic Treaty Organization (NATO) serves to protect power elite capital investments around the world. Wars, regime changes, and occupations performed by military and intelligence agencies remain in service to investors' access to natural resources, free flow of capital, debt collection, and speculative advantages in the world marketplace.

GIANTS AND THE GLOBAL POWER ELITE INVEST IN WAR

The following are the top three Weapons Producers in the world and the Giants that invested in them in 2017.

Lockheed Martin Corporation: State Street ($15.2 billion), Capital Group ($12.17 billion), Vanguard Group ($6.5 billion), BlackRock ($6.1 billion), Bank of America ($3.1 billion), UBS ($902 million), Bank of NY Mellon ($733 million), Fidelity Investments (FMR) ($721 million), Morgan Stanley & Co. ($703 million), Goldman Sachs Group ($474 million), Prudential Financial ($449 million), Credit Suisse ($149 million), Allianz SE (PIMCO) ($82 million), JPMorgan Chase ($55 million), Amundi/ Crédit Agricole ($54 million), Barclays plc ($50 million)

Northrop Grumman Corporation: State Street ($5.9 billion), Vanguard Group ($4 billion), BlackRock ($4 billion), Fidelity Investments (FMR) ($2.4 billion), Capital Group ($1.8 billion), JPMorgan Chase ($1.5 billion), Bank of America ($666 million), Goldman Sachs Group ($488 million), Bank of NY Mellon ($410 million), UBS ($248 million), Morgan Stanley & Co. ($211 million), Prudential Financial ($200 million), Allianz SE (PIMCO) ($176 million), Credit Suisse ($67 million), AXA Group ($55 million), Amundi/Crédit Agricole ($51 million), Barclays plc ($44 million)

Boeing Company: Capital Group ($12.8 billion), Vanguard Group ($11.9 billion), BlackRock ($10.3 billion), State Street ($8 billion), Fidelity Investments (FMR) ($1.9 billion), Bank of NY Mellon ($1.6 billion), Morgan Stanley & Co. ($1.5 billion), Goldman Sachs Group ($1.2 billion), Bank of America ($1.01 billion), UBS ($729 million), JPMorgan Chase ($711 million), Prudential Financial ($440 million), Allianz SE (PIMCO) ($337 million), Credit Suisse ($273 million), Barclays plc ($245 million), Amundi/Crédit Agricole ($195 million), AXA Group ($119 million)

INTELLIGENCE AGENCIES IN SERVICE TO THE VITAL INTERESTS OF THE GLOBAL POWER ELITE

Intelligence agencies operate in every country in the world. The CIA is active in every country as well. Many of these agencies work closely together to protect the freedom of global Giants to invest anywhere in the world without interference from governments and nationalist resistance movements. In particular, the CIA has close working relationships with intelligence agencies in Britain, Australia, Canada, Germany, Poland, France, Jordan, and Saudi Arabia.[189] These government agencies share common concerns for protecting the shared vital interests of economic growth.

Robert Blackwill, the Henry Kissinger senior fellow for the Council on Foreign Relations and national security advisor to George W. Bush, stated clearly in a January 25, 2017 article that defending vital US interests should be of primary concern to President Trump. In addition to protecting the United States from nuclear threats, Blackwill called for ensuring the "viability and stability of major global systems: trade, financial markets, supplies of energy, and climate." He wrote, "we must maintain a regional and global balance of power that promotes peace and stability through domestic American robustness, US international primacy, and strengthening and defending US alliance systems, including the alliance with Israel."[190]

The Heritage Foundation, in their Index of US Military Strength, describes US vital interests as

- Defense of the homeland;

- Successful conclusion of a major war having the

potential to destabilize a region of critical interest
to the United States; and

- Preservation of freedom of movement within
  the global commons: the sea, air, and outer space
  domains through which the world conducts business.[191]

Peter Dale Scott, in his book *The American Deep State*,
describes the importance of Wall Street in offering intelligence
agencies key personnel and policies. Certainly, Allen Dulles, a
Wall Street lawyer and CIA director, is a good example of this
close relationship between Wall Street and national intelligence.
Scott believes that the mushrooming of intelligence agencies
after 9/11 has also allowed for the emergence of "Deep State"
intelligence networks with independent capabilities, even while
still in support of Wall Street's agenda.[192]

Dana Priest and William Arkin in 2011 described the United
States as two governments, "one [that] the citizens are familiar
with which operates more or less in the open, and the other [a]
parallel top-secret government whose parts have mushroomed
in less than a decade into a gigantic, sprawling universe of its
own, visible to only a carefully vetted cadre—and in its entirety
visible only to God."[193]

Scott reports that global intelligence agencies work together
as Deep State networks. He cites how countries fighting com-
munism organized in the mid 1970s when the CIA was under
restrictions imposed by Congress and enforced by President
Carter. Intelligence representatives from France, Egypt, Saudi
Arabia, and Iran met in Kenya at the Safari Club with CIA oper-
atives, including former CIA Director George H.W. Bush, to

overcome constraints imposed by Washington. This led to the emergence of the Bank of Credit and Commerce International (BCCI) as the depository of money for off-the-books covert operations and the formation of what Scott calls a supranational Deep State.[194]

As the Global Power Elite increasingly concentrate wealth, the requirement from the overlords for security and protection will magnify. Responding to that call will be the intelligence agencies of the capital-vested nation-states cooperating with each other, and coordinating regime changes, wars, occupations, assassinations, and covert actions deemed necessary. The Atlantic Council reflects these concerns of the Global Power Elite and offers recommendations on the parameters of needed actions.

ATLANTIC COUNCIL

The Atlantic Council is a nonprofit organization established in 1961 as a voluntary alliance of countries in the North Atlantic Treaty Organization (NATO).[195] Its stated goal is to build policies and institutions that promote collective security and peace. With an annual budget of $20 million, and with 74 percent of those funds raised from member contributions and grants, the Atlantic Council produces numerous policy reports, books, and papers.[196] Global capital protection and US/NATO military/security issues are a high priority for the Atlantic Council.

The Atlantic Council lists 146 Global Power Elites from 28 countries on their board of directors. Among the listed directors are four former NATO commanders and thirteen representatives from several major defense contractors, including Boeing, Raytheon, Bechtel, Lockheed Martin, BAE Systems, SAIC,

Carlyle Group, and Booz Allen Hamilton. Eleven directors are current or former military generals and admirals. Forty-one directors are active in government or private security organizations such as the US National Security Council, as well as various public and private security policy groups focusing on cyber security. G4S, an international security company and the second largest private employer in the world, is represented on the Atlantic Council.

Major corporate donors to the Atlantic Council include Airbus, Chevron, Google, Lockheed Martin, Raytheon, Southern Company, Thomson Reuters, BP, ExxonMobil, General Electric, Northrop Grumman, Panasonic, SAIC, United Technologies, Barclays Capital, Coca-Cola, ConocoPhillips, Eni, FedEx, McAfee, Microsoft, Target, Boeing, Bloomberg, Caterpillar, Daimler, Gallup, HSBC, Dow Chemical, Comcast, Rolls-Royce, and Bank of Tokyo–Mitsubishi UFJ.[197] Included also on the Atlantic Council's donor list is the US Airforce, US Marines, US State Department, US Army, Clinton Foundation, United Arab Emirates, and Bahrain.

Global capital management and the protection of concentrated capital investment practices are a top priority for the Atlantic Council. We found 40 individuals on the board of governors who are connected with capital investment management. People serving on the boards of six of the financial Giants' corporations are directors of the Atlantic Council. Many other financial management/investment firms have members on the Atlantic Council as well.

Most major corporate media companies have representatives on the Atlantic Council, including Time Warner, CBS, NBC, and Reuters. Additionally, we found four representatives from the world's largest public relations firms on the Atlantic Council.

These links tie the corporate media, public relations industry, and propaganda firms directly to capital management and military/security policies.

We also found power elite representatives on the Atlantic Council from the World Economic Forum (6 members), Trilateral Commission (5 members), Aspen Institute (7 members), and one or two members each from the World Bank, IMF, Bilderberg Group, and Bohemian Club.

The Atlantic Council, in distinction to the World Economic Forum and Bilderberg Group, publishes regular weekly reports and policy recommendation updates as a key part of their activities. These reports are created without direct government involvement, and as such offer more of a TCC power elite interpretation on world affairs than government reports subject to congressional or democratic reviews.

The Atlantic Council provides Global Power Elites policy recommendations and offers government officials and intelligence agencies direction and guidance for implementation of security pacts and the protection of global capital. Some of the Atlantic Council's reports from the first few months of 2017 include "Strategy of 'Constrainment'" (on Russia), "European Economic Growth and Its Importance to American Prosperity," and "Evaluating Western Sanctions on Russia."

In 2016 the Atlantic Council issued a report entitled "The Future of the Army." The report sought to ensure that the US Army remains the "preeminent fighting force in the world for the remainder of this century."[198] Key policy recommendations for 2016–2020 include increasing Special Operations Forces, Security Assistance Brigades, and Homeland Defense. For 2020–2025 the report calls for more forces overseas, units trained in urban operations, overseas staging areas, and counter-drone systems. Out to 2040 and beyond the report suggests the need for independent, small, mobile fighting companies both within the military and through private sources. "The Future of the Army" also calls for training with virtual reality, with the use of battlefield robotics and artificial intelligence.

An Atlantic Council report from the Middle East Strategy Task Force chaired by Madeleine Albright and Stephen Hadley was released in November 2016. The report acknowledged a continuing global crisis emanating from the Middle East, with ongoing violence and terrorism, and it called for a new strategic approach emphasizing partnership with regional leaders who would take full responsibility for charting a new and positive vision for their societies.[199] The report stated that top-down security issues required "heavy lifting" by external forces should take a "whole region approach." The report claims that Daesh (ISIS) succeeds due to the humanitarian abuses of the Assad regime in Syria. Military action against the Assad regime will probably prove necessary. The report concluded that in Iraq continued military support of the Iraqi national army is necessary to defeat Daesh. In Libya, the United States must continue to take a leadership role in support of a government of national accord. In Yemen, a political solution must be sought, while maintaining counterterrorism efforts against al-Qaeda. The report called for a sustainable two-state solution for the Israel–Palestine conflict and continuing determent of Iran's influence in the region.

It is clear that the Atlantic Council is recommending a continuation of US–NATO policies in the Middle East while calling for regional dialogue and cooperation. Interestingly, the report calls for a new social contract in the region whereby governments will provide security in exchange for the right to rule.

A needed new social contract would be based on citizen–government relations that are inclusive, effective, and accountable, moving to the "big bang" regulatory reform that supports business entrepreneurs and spurs needed foreign investment.[200] It appears that US–NATO military policy, as recommended by the Atlantic Council, is in support of building compliant nation-states in the Middle East that offer safe investment opportunities for power elite TCC investment capital.

Again, we ask readers to peruse the full biographies of the Atlantic Council Executive Committee. Doing so allows for a qualitative understanding of the dimensions of power represented by these 35 people on the Executive Committee, united by similar backgrounds, capital interests, and political involvements. In particular, watch for a Commander of the British Empire, Under Secretaries of State (2), an Under Secretary of Commerce, an Under Secretary of the Treasury, ambassadors to the UN and other countries (3), membership in the Council on Foreign Relations (10), National Security Council (6), Project for the New American Century (2), Cato Institute, Aspen Institute (5), Trilateral Commission (2), NATO (2), World Economic Forum (6), military intelligence, major defense contractors (4), and former members of Congress.

ATLANTIC COUNCIL EXECUTIVE COMMITTEE (35 MEMBERS)[201]

CB- Corporate Boards/Current Corporate Employment
PE- Prior Corporate Employment/Boards
PC- Policy Councils, Philanthropic Organizations, Government
E- Education
F- Public Financials[202]

Note that in almost every case the financials cited constitute only a portion of income and net worth.

Robert J. Abernethy, US **CB-** President: American Standard Development Company and Self-Storage Management Company (private), Director: Metropolitan Investments (private) **PE-** Hughes Aircraft's Phoenix Missile Program, Director: Public Storage **PC-** US Department of State Advisory Committee on International Economic Policy, Council on Foreign Relations, Peabody Institute, California State Board of Education, Brookings Institution, Atlantic Council Executive Committee, William H. Parker Los Angeles Police Foundation, California Arts Council, Truman National Security Project, RAND Center for Global Risk and Security, Aspen Institute, Trustee Emeritus: John Hopkins University, Trustee: Loyola Marymount University **E-** Johns Hopkins University (BA in Math and Electrical Engineering), Harvard (MBA), UCLA (Construction Management/Real Estate degree) **F-** Public Storage shares 89,606—$3.8 million (2005)

Peter Ackerman, US **CB-** Rockport Capital (private), Director: FreshDirect (private), Founder: Crown Capital Group (private) **PE-** Principal: Drexel Burnham Lambert (Michael Milken's firm) **PC-** America Abroad Media, Unity08, Cato Institute, Director: Council on Foreign Relations, Director: Atlantic Council **E-** Colgate University (BA in Political Science), Tufts University–The Fletcher School (PhD) **F-** Drexel compensation $5 million (1989), Drexel compensation $165 million (1990)[203] (He had to pay back $73 million in a lawsuit settlement); donated $1.5 million to American Elect in 2010

Adrienne Arsht, US **CB**- Chair: Adrienne Arsht Center Foundation **PE**- Trans World Airlines, Morris, Nichols, Arsht & Tunnell, Chair: TotalBank **PC**- Executive Committee Atlantic Council, CFR, Aspen Institute, Center for National Policy, Center for the Study of the Presidency and Congress, Trustee: John F. Kennedy Center for the Performing Arts, Director: University of Miami **E**- Mount Holyoke College (BA in Economics and Political Science), Villanova University (JD) **F**- donated $30 million to the City of Miami's Performing Arts Center; from 1997 to 2007 was Chair of her family-owned bank, Totalbank, which sold for $300 million in 2007

Rafic Bizri, Lebanon **CB**- Scapetel Debtor (private), Hariri Foundation USA, President: Hariri Holding **PE**- Holiday Inn, Pointe Communications Corporation, Controller and Investor Representative: Mediterranean Investors Group, Financial Officer: Saudi Oger Ltd. **PC**- Director: Executive Committee Atlantic Council **E**- Virginia Commonwealth University (BA in Accounting and Finance) **F**- N/A

Thomas L. Blair, US **CB**- Americas Health Plan Inc., Founder: United Payors & United Providers **PE**- Catalyst Health Solutions, United Medical Bank, FSB, President and Chief Executive Officer: Americas Health Plan Inc., Principal: Jurgovan & Blair, Chairman: FedMed **PC**- Director: Atlantic Council **E**- University of Nevada School of Medicine **F**- United Payors shares 7.18 million—$193.8 million (2000)

R. Nicholas Burns, US **CB**- Vangent Holding Corporation (private), Veracity Worldwide (private), Cohen Group (private), Entegris, Professor: Harvard University **PE**- Under Secretary of State for Political Affairs, Ambassador to NATO, Ambassador to Greece, National Security Council, Senior Director of Russia, Ukraine, Eurasia Affairs, Special Assistant to President Clinton, Center for a New American Security **PC-** Executive Committee of the Atlantic Council, Trilateral Commission, America Abroad Media, Aspen Strategy Group, Ambassador: North Atlantic Council, Director: Council on Foreign Relations, Director: Future of Diplomacy Project under President George H.W. Bush **E-** Boston College (BA in History), H Nitze School of Advanced International Studies at Johns Hopkins University (MA in International Relations) **F-** Harvard salary approx. $200,000+ (2017), Entegris compensation $207,497 (2016), Entegris shares 46,139—$1.4 million (2016)

Richard R. Burt, US **CB-** New Germany Trust, Central & European Fund, European Equity Fund, Manager: McLarty Associates (private), Partner: McKinsey & Company (private $8 billion company) **PE-** Deutsche Bank, Kissinger McLarty Associates, UBS, Ambassador to Germany, Assistant Secretary of State for European and Canadian Affairs, Center for Strategic and International Studies, US Chief Negotiator: Strategic Arms Reduction Talks, Director of Politico-Military Affairs and Assistant Director: International Institute for Strategic Studies (IISS), Director: International Game Technology **PC-** America Abroad Media, Executive Committee of the Atlantic Council, Council on Foreign Relations, Center for the National Interest **E-** Cornell University (BA in Government), US Naval War College, Fletcher School of Law and Diplomacy (MA in International Relations) **F-** New Germany Fund shares $59,484 (2017), Central & European Fund shares $20,886 (2017), European Equity Fund shares $13,311 (2017), Fund compensation (for all 3) $38,629 (2017), Weirton Steel compensation $120,000 (2002), UBS compensation $108,000 (2001)

Ralph D. Crosby Jr., US **CB**- American Electric Power Company, EADS North America (private), Airbus Se, Serco Group plc (private) **PE**- Northrop Grumman Corporation, Chair and CEO: Ducommun **PC**- Executive Committee of the Atlantic Council **E**- US Military Academy at West Point (BA in Engineering), Harvard University (Public Administration degree), University of Geneva (MA in International Affairs), Graduate Institute of International and Development Studies (MA in International Relations) **F**- American Power compensation $293,803 (2017), American Power shares 41,094—$3.14 million (2017), Airbus Se compensation $152,100 (2017), Northrop Grumman shares 47,825—$2.67 million (1998), Northrop Grumman compensation $498,000 (2002)

Paula J. Dobriansky, US **CB**- Senior Fellow: Harvard University **PE**- Under Secretary of State, Democracy and Global Affairs, Albright Stonebridge Group, Head of the Delegation on US Climate Change Policy, United States Information Agency, Deputy Assistant Secretary of State for Human Rights and Humanitarian Affairs, Duoyuan Printing, Global Head of Government & Regulatory Affairs: Thomson Reuters **PC**- Partnership for a Secure America, Center for a New American Security, Trilateral Commission, Leadership Council, Foundation for Defense of Democracies, Executive Committee of the Atlantic Council, European and Soviet Affairs at the National Security Council, International Advisory Council at APCO Worldwide, Smith-Richardson Foundation, IRI's International Advisory Council, Freedom House, Project for a New American

Century, US Water Partnership, Former Senior Vice President: Council on Foreign Relations, Director: Georgetown University's School of Foreign Service, National Security Chair: US Naval Academy, Trustee: American University of Afghanistan, Chair: Bush Center's Women's Initiative Policy Advisory Council **E**- Georgetown University School of Foreign Service (BSFS in International Politics), Harvard University (MA, PhD in Soviet Political/Military Affairs) **F**- Harvard compensation approx. $200,000 (2017)

Richard Edelman, US **CB**- President and CEO: Edelman (private PR Marketing company) **PC**- Ad Council, Atlantic Council Executive Committee, Council on Foreign Relations, World Economic Forum, Children's Aid Society, National September 11 Memorial & Museum, International Business Leaders Forum, Jerusalem Foundation, Aspen Institute, National Committee on US China Relations, Committee Encouraging Corporate Philanthropy, Conference Board: Chicago Climate Exchange **E**- Phillips Exeter Academy, Harvard (BA, MBA) **F**- Edelman Co., founded in 1952 by Edelman's father, is currently worth hundreds of millions of dollars[204]

Stuart E. Eizenstat, US **CB**- International Advisory Board of Coca-Cola, BT Americas (private), GML Ltd. (private), Trustee: BlackRock Funds **PE**- Deputy Secretary of the Treasury, Under Secretary of State for Economics, Business and Agriculture, Ambassador to the European Union, Covington & Burling llp, Chief Domestic Policy Advisor to President Carter **PC**- Brookings Institution, Council on Foreign Relations, Zeta Beta Tau, Atlantic Council Executive Committee, European–American Business Council **E**- University of North Carolina, Chapel Hill

(BA), Harvard Law School (JD) **F**- BlackRock compensation $340,000 (2016), BlackRock shares $100,000 minimum (2017); awarded the Government of Israel's Courage Conscience Award, Germany's Knights Commander's Cross, and France's Legion of Honor

Alan H. Fleischmann, US **CB**- Albright Stonebridge Group (private), LATCORP, Latin American Trade Corporation, Director: ImagineNations Group (private), Vice President: Private Trade Finance Company **PE**- Policy Aide to German Chancellor Willy Brandt, JPMorgan Chase, Chief of Staff: Lt. Governor Kathleen Kennedy Townsend, Staff: House Committee on Foreign Affairs **PC**- Export-Import Bank of the United States, Council on Foreign Relations, Executive Committee of the Atlantic Council, World Economic Forum, Jane Goodall Institute, Trustee: Carnegie Hall **E**- American University (BA, BS), Johns Hopkins University (MA in Advanced International Studies) **F**- N/A

Ronald M. Freeman, US **CB**- Senior Advisor: Doughty Hanson & Co. European Real Estate Fund II (private), Director: CJSC Sberbank CIB (Russia) **PE**- Salomon Brothers, European Bank for Reconstruction and Development, McKinsey & Company, Baker & McKenzie llp, Volga Gas plc, Imagine Group Holdings, PLIVA Pharmaceuticals, CoTec Ventures Ltd., MMC Norilsk Nickel and Troika Dialog, Sberbank of Russia OJSC, Frontiers Capital Partners llp, Orange Polska Spolka Akcyjna, CEO: Citigroup Global Markets Ltd. (United Kingdom), CEO: Lipper & Company lp **PC**- Executive Committee of the Atlantic Council, World Economic Forum, Columbia University Law School International Institute, Development Committee at Mansfield College **E**- Université de Grenoble Alpes (Certificate d'Études),

Lehigh University (BA), Columbia University School of Law (LLB) **F**- N/A

Robert S. Gelbard, US **CB**- Kreab Gavin Anderon, SNR Denton **PE**- Pt Capital llc, PT Toba Bara Sejahtra Tbk, Institute for Defense Analyses, Valeant Pharmaceuticals International, Pacific Architects and Engineers Incorporated, US Ambassador to Indonesia and East Timor, Special Representative to the President and the Secretary of State for the Balkans, Member of the Obama–Biden Presidential National Security Transition Team, US Assistant Secretary of State, International Narcotics, Law Enforcement Affairs, Washington Global Partners llc, Boards of Advisors of PAE, Atlas International Investments, Imaging Automation **PC**- President's Council of Economic Advisors, Executive Committee of the Atlantic Council, International Institute for Security and Cooperation, University of Notre Dame's Center for Civil and Human Rights, Senior Defense Advisory Board, American Academy of Diplomacy, US–Serbia Business Council, Trustee: Colby College **E**- Colby College (BA in History), Harvard University (MPA in Economics) **F**- N/A

Sherri W. Goodman, US **CB**- Woodrow Wilson International Center **PE**- Deputy Undersecretary of Defense (Environmental Security), Goodwin Procter, RAND, SAIC, CEO: Consortium for Ocean Leadership, VP: CNA Analysis & Solutions, Staff: Senate Armed Services Committee **PC**- Military Advisory Board for CNA's National Security and the Threat of Climate Change project, Executive Committee of the Atlantic Council, National Academy of Sciences' Energy & Environmental Systems Board, Woods Hole Oceanographic Institution, Council on Foreign Relations **E**- Amherst College (BA), John F. Kennedy

School of Government at Harvard University (MA in Public Policy), Harvard Law School (JD) **F**- N/A

C. Boyden Gray, US **CB**- C. Boyden Gray & Associates, Washington, DC (private) **PE**- Wilmer, Cutler & Pickering, Counsel to the Vice President (Bush in the Reagan administration), White House Counsel to President George H.W. Bush, Ambassador to the European Union, Counsel to the Presidential Task Force on Regulatory Relief, Marine Corps Reserve, Clerk for Earl Warren, US Supreme Court, Adjunct Professor: Antonin Scalia Law School and NYU Law **PC**- Executive Committee of the Atlantic Council, Federalist Society, Council on Foreign Relations, Reason Foundation, Trust for the National Mall, European Institute, Freedom Works (Libertarian advocacy group), America Abroad Media **E**- Harvard University (BA), University of North Carolina at Chapel Hill (JD) **F**- heir to the R.J. Reynolds Tobacco Company fortune:[205] $200 million+ (2007)[206]

Stephen Hadley, US **CB**- RiceHadleyGates llc (private), Raytheon Co. **PE**- Assistant to the President for National Security Affairs, White House Foreign Policy Advisor to President George W. Bush, Assistant Secretary of Defense for International Security Policy for Secretary of Defense Dick Cheney, Shea and Gardner Law, Director: National Security Council **PC**- US Institute of Peace, RAND's Center for Middle East, Yale University's Kissinger Papers Advisory Board, Executive Committee of the Atlantic Council, John Hopkins University's Applied Physics Laboratory, US State Department's Foreign Affairs Policy Board, Department of Defense Policy Board, National Security Advisory Panel to the Director of Central Intelligence, Director:

Council on Foreign Relations, Officer: US Navy **E**- Cornell University (BA), Yale Law School (JD) **F**- Raytheon compensation $289,542 (2016), Raytheon shares 10,838—$2.03 million

Karl V. Hopkins, US **CB**- Partner and Global Security Officer: Dentons (world's largest law firm) **PC**- Board of Governors of the Middle East Institute, National Association of Corporate Directors, Business Executives for National Security, International Security Managers Association, ASIS International, InfraGard, Association of International Petroleum Negotiators, London Court of International Arbitration, Chancellor's Board of Texas A&M University, Executive Committee of the Atlantic Council, Chair: Atlantic Council's Security Committee **E**- Texas A&M University (BA, MA), Southwestern University School of Law (JD) **F**- N/A; ASIS International: "ASIS International is the leading organization for security professionals worldwide"[207]

Mary L. Howell, US **CB**- Esterline Technologies Corp., Vectrus, CEO: Howell Strategy Group **PE**- Executive Vice President: Textron **PC**- FM Global, Executive Committee of the Atlantic Council **E**- University of Massachusetts at Amherst (BA) **F**- Textron compensation $682,500 (2017), Textron shares 132,378—$3.1 million (2007), Vectrus compensation $150,009 (2016), Vectrus shares 3,097—$101,333 (2016), Esterline compensation $198,750 (2016), Esterline approx. shares 7,800—$571,740 (2016)

Jon M. Huntsman Jr., US **CB**- CEO: Huntsman Corporation (chemicals) **PE**- Governor of Utah, US Ambassador to China, US Ambassador to Singapore, Staff Assistant to President Ronald Reagan, Deputy US Trade Representative (under

George W. Bush), Deputy Assistant Secretary of Commerce, Mormon Missionary to China **PC-** Huntsman Cancer Institute, Chair: Executive Committee of the Atlantic Council **E-** University of Pennsylvania (BA in International Politics) **F-** net worth $1 billion; Ambassador to Russia appointed by President Trump: July 18, 2017

Wolfgang Friedrich Ischinger, Germany **CB-** Investcorp Bank BSC (private) **PE-** Staff for Secretary General of the UN, German Ambassador to the UK, German Ambassador to the US, Supreme Group B.V., Relations & Public Policy, Allianz SE, Chair: Euro-Atlantic Security Initiative, Professor for Security Policy and Diplomatic Practice: Hertie School of Governance **PC-** Stockholm International Peace Research Institute, European Council on Foreign Affairs, Global Zero Commission, European Leadership Network, World Economic Forum, Chair: Munich Security Conference, Trustee: International Crisis Group **E-** University of Bonn (Law degree), University of Geneva (Law degree), Tuffs University, Fletcher School of Law and Diplomacy (MA) **F-** N/A

James L. Jones Jr., US **CB-** Critical Signal Technologies (private), President: Jones Group International **PE-** Ivacare Corp., Chevron, The Boeing Company, General Dynamics Corporation, US Marine Corps Commandant **PC-** National Security Advisor to President Obama, East-West Communication Institute, President: US Chamber of Commerce's Institute for 21st Century Energy, Trustee: Center for Strategic and International Studies, Senior Fellow: Bipartisan Policy Center, Executive Committee Chair: Scowcroft Center of the Atlantic Council **E-** Georgetown University School of Foreign Service (BA) **F-**

US Marines Corps pension approx. $200,000+ (2017), Ivacare Corp. compensation $140,443 (2015), Ivacare Corp. shares 28,292—$4.5 million (2015), Boeing compensation $108,116 (2008), Boeing shares 1,250—$97,500 (2008)

Frederick Kempe, US **CB**- CEO: Atlantic Council (since 2006), Columnist: Bloomberg News and Reuters **PE**- Journalist and Editor: Wall Street Journal (for 30 years) **PC**- Council on Foreign Relations **E**- University of Utah (Journalism degree), Columbia University School of Journalism (MA) **F**- net worth $13 million as of 2017 (networthpost.com)

Zalmay M. Khalilzad, Afghanistan & US **CB**- Gryphon Capital Partners, President: Khalilzad Associates llc **PE**- Ambassador to the United Nations for the G.W. Bush administration, Ambassador to Afghanistan, Ambassador to Iraq, Rand Center for Middle-Eastern Studies, Analyst: IHS Cambridge Energy Research Associates, Professor: Columbia University **PC**- Council on Foreign Relations, America Abroad Media, National Endowment for Democracy, Project for a New American Century, American University of Iraq, American University of Afghanistan, Director: Executive Committee of the Atlantic Council **E**- American University Beirut (BA, MA), University of Chicago (PhD), George Washington University (MPA) **F**- net worth $990,000 as of 2017 (net-worth.com)

Richard L. Lawson, US **CB**- Chair: Energy, Environment and Security Group Ltd. **PE**- US Army General Deputy Commander of US European Command, Military Assistant to President Reagan, Chief of Staff of NATO, CEO: National Mining Association **PC**- US Energy Association, Washington Institute of

Foreign Affairs, World Energy Council, International Committee on Coal Research, Vice-Chair: Executive Committee of the Atlantic Council **E**- University of Iowa (BS in Chemical Engineering), George Washington University (MPA), National War College at Fort Lesley J. McNair, Washington, DC **F**- US Army pension approx. $200,000 (2017)

Jan M. Lodal, US **CB**- Chair: Lodal & Company **PE**- American Management Systems, Deputy Assistant to Henry Kissinger, Director of NATO for the Secretary of Defense (under the Johnson administration), CEO: Intelus, Staff: National Security Council **PC**- Aspen Strategy Group, Curtis Institute of Music, American Boychoir School, Council on Foreign Relations, International Institute of Strategic Studies, Executive Committee of the Atlantic Council, Federation of American Scientists, President: Group Health Association **E**- Rice University (BA) **F**- Lodal compensation $250,000 (2017); net worth $500,000+ (mylife.com)

George Lund, US **CB**- One America Bank (private), Blue Hackle Ltd. (British Private Security Company), Chair: Equilar Atlas (private), Chair and CEO: Torch Hill Investment Partners (private) **PE**- Ebcore Capital, CEO: Bank First **PC**- Executive Committee of the Atlantic Council **E**- Southern Methodist University (BA) **F**- N/A

Brian C. McK. Henderson, US (Native American) **CB**- Henderson International Advisors llc, BMC Bank of Africa, Chair: Espírito Santo Financial Group **PE**- Merrill Lynch, Chase Manhattan Bank **PC**- Harvard Project on American Indian Economic Development, National Museum of the American

Indian (Smithsonian), Fort Apache Heritage Foundation, Manhattan School of Music, Vice-Chair: Executive Committee of the Atlantic Council, Advisor: John F. Kennedy School of Government at Harvard University, School of Foreign Service at Georgetown University **E-** Georgetown University School of Foreign Service (BA), University of Barcelona, University of Edinburgh **F-** N/A

Judith A. Miller, US **CB-** General Counsel: Bechtel National, Partner: Williams & Connolly llp in Washington, DC **PE-** General Counsel for the US Department of Defense, Clerk for Justice Potter Stewart of the US Supreme Court **PC-** Executive Committee of the Atlantic Council, Defense Science Board of the US Department of Defense, Council on Foreign Relations, Markle Task Force on National Security in the Information Age, Trustee: Beloit College **E-** Beloit College (BA), Yale Law School (JD) **F-** N/A

Alexander V. Mirtchev, US **CB-** President: Krull Corp., Senior Scholar: Woodrow Wilson International Center **PE-** Law Offices of Stewart & Stewart, Sovereign Wealth Fund Samruk-Kazyna **PC-** Senior Fellow: Russian & Bulgarian Academy of Sciences of Ukraine, Russian Academy of Natural Sciences, Washington & Jefferson College's Center for Energy Policy and Management, Executive Committee of the Atlantic Council, Chair: Royal United Services Institute for Defense and Security Studies International **E-** George Washington University (International Law degree), London School of Economics, Boston University, Harvard Business School, St. Kliment Ohridski University (PhD) **F-** N/A

Virginia A. Mulberger, US **CB**- Director: The Scowcroft Group **PE**- White House Special Assistant to the President (George W. Bush administration), National Security Council, DGA International, US Air Force Intelligence and Legislative Affairs, Deputy Director: Air Force Senate Liaison **PC**- Council on Foreign Relations, International Institute for Strategic Studies, Vice-Chair: Executive Committee of the Atlantic Council, Advisor: Bush School of Texas A&M University **E**- Georgetown University (MA in National Security Studies) **F**- N/A

Ana Palacio, Spain **CB**- Consejo de Estado del Reino de España (Council of State), Palacio y Asociados, Albright Stonebridge Group, PharmaMar, Investcorp, Adjunct Professor: Georgetown University **PE**- European Parliament, Minister for Foreign Affairs Spain, Spanish Parliament, Areva, VP: World Bank **PC**- European Council on Foreign Relations, Institute for Strategic Dialogue, Madrid Chamber of Commerce, European Leadership Network, World Economic Forum, Executive Committee of the Atlantic Council, Carnegie Corporation of NY, Aspen Institute, Hague Institute for Internationalization of Law **E**- Lycée Français (BA in Mathematics) **F**- PharmaMar shares 18,900—$59,724 (2016)

W. DeVier Pierson, US **CB**- Hunton & Williams llp **PE**- White House Counsel under the Johnson administration **PC**- Executive Committee of the Atlantic Council, Trustee Emeritus: University of Oklahoma Foundation **E**- University of Oklahoma (BA, JD) **F**- N/A

Walter B. Slocombe, US **CB**- Senior Counsel: Caplin & Drysdale **PE**- US Under Secretary of Defense (George W. Bush administration), Senior Advisor for National Defense in the Coalition Provisional Authority for Iraq, National Security Council Staff, Clerk to the Honorable Abe Fortas of the US Supreme Court **PC**- Commission on the Intelligence Capabilities of the United States Regarding Weapons of Mass Destruction, Council on Foreign Relations, Executive Committee of the Atlantic Council **E**- Princeton University (BA), Oxford (Rhodes Scholar), Harvard Law (LLB) **F**- N/A

Paula Stern, US **CB**- Avon Products, Chair: Stern Group **PE**- Hasbro, Avaya, Chair: US International Trade Commission, Scholar: Brookings Institution **PC**- Committee for Economic Development, Council on Foreign Relations, Inter-American Dialogue, Carnegie Endowment of International Peace, Bretton Woods Committee, Global Subsidies Initiative of the International Institute for Sustainable Development, Advisor: US Export-Import Bank **E**- Goucher College (BA), Harvard University (MA in Regional Studies), Tufts University (MA, PhD in International Relations) **F**- Avon compensation $30,000 (2016, for part of first year), Avon shares pending (2017)

John Studzinski, US & UK **CB**- The Blackstone Group (private) **PE**- Morgan Stanley, HSBC, AIG **PC**- Genesis Foundation, World Economic Forum, Chair: Talitha Kum, Royal College of Art, Council on Foreign Relations, Institute for Public Policy Research, Peter G. Peterson Institute for International Economics, Chair: Human Rights Watch, Chair: Arise Foundation, Vice Chair: Executive Committee of the Atlantic Council, Trustee: Take Foundation, Trustee: J Paul Getty Trust, Trustee: Bowdoin College **E**- Bowdoin College (BA in Sociology and Biology), University of Chicago (MBA) **F**- N/A (lots); awarded the Commander of the Order of the British Empire, as well as the Knight of the Order of St. Gregory and Knight of the Order of St. Sylvester from Pope John Paul II

Ellen O. Tauscher, US **CB**- BAE Systems (private), SeaWorld Entertainment, Southern California Edison, eHealth, Caldwell & Berkowitz PC, Advisor: Baker Donelson Bearman **PE**- Invacare, California Member of Congress, Under-Secretary for State Arms Control and International Security Affairs (Obama administration), Bache Halsey Stuart Shields, Bear Stearns & Co., Drexel Burnham Lambert, Aurora Flight Sciences Corporation, Tauscher Foundation **PC**- Nuclear Threat Initiative, Council on Foreign Relations, Executive Committee of the Atlantic Council, National Endowment for Democracy, National Comprehensive Cancer Network Foundation, Governor: Lawrence Livermore National Security llc, Los Alamos National Security llc **E**- Seton Hall University (BA) **F**- SeaWorld compensation $189,987 (2015), SeaWorld shares 28,072—$368,585 (2015), Southern California Edison compensation $253,133 (2016), Southern California Edison shares 4,798—$120,093 (2016), Invacare compensation $121,859 (2013), Invacare shares 7,135—$121,295 (2013), eHealth compensation $329,256 (2016), eHealth shares 31,838—$573,720 (2016)

These 35 Atlantic Council Executive Committee members are a key power elite nongovernmental group that combines financial capitalists with high-level security experts and establishment insiders. Nineteen of the Executive Committee members specialize in global security issues, many with decades of involvement. Fourteen have worked with or managed major capital investment companies. And nineteen have held high-level positions in the US government, several under multiple administrations and both parties. Collectively, they supervise the building of the parameters of policy and recommendations for change that people in governments, military, and politics perceive as acceptable directions for action. The NATO–US military command structure and administrators in governments and their intelligence agencies all pay attention to the Atlantic Council's reports. Protecting global capitalism and the TCC's ability to securely and safely invest worldwide is their primary agenda.

PRIVATE MILITARY COMPANIES IN SERVICE TO THE GLOBAL POWER ELITE AND TCC

When the empire is slow to perform or faced with political resistance, private security firms and private military companies increasingly fulfill the TCC and Global Power Elite demands for the protections of their assets. These protection services include personal security for TCC executives and their families, protection of safe residential and work zones, tactical military advice and training of national police and armed forces, intelligence gathering on democracy movements and opposition groups, weapons acquisitions and weapon systems management, and strike forces for military actions and assassinations.[208] The expanding crisis of desperate masses/refugees, alienated work forces, and environmental exhaustion means an unlimited opportunity for Private Military Companies (PMCs) to engage in protection services for the Global Power Elite and the TCC.[209]

PMCs—known less formally as mercenaries—have been an important part of armed conflicts since at least the Roman

Empire. However, a newer form of PMC has been emerging in the past few decades, one that involves the investment of private capital into the security business of protecting the TCC interests and global capitalism. It's estimated that at least $200 billion is spent on private security globally, with higher annual expenditures anticipated. The industry currently employs some fifteen million people worldwide. Many of these companies are offering a range of services, from guarding banks and private buildings to armed security and outright warfare.[210]

The Iraq War opened the opportunity for a rapid increase of PMCs. The United States spent billions annually on security, with some 150 PMCs in the Iraq and Afghanistan war zones.[211] By 2008, there were more PMC contractors than actual US government troops in Iraq.[212] In 2010–11, the Department of Defense (DoD) had 90,339 contractor personnel in Afghanistan and 64,250 in Iraq. From 2005 to 2010, the DoD spent $146 billion on PMCs in the Afghan–Iraqi war theater. The majority of the private contracting was for base support and logistics; however, 18 percent of the private contractors in Iraq—roughly 10,000 people—were listed as working in security. A third of these security contracts involved US citizens, 15 percent were locals, and the balance were third-party nationals.[213] Many of the PMCs in Middle East wars were opportunistic organizations that withdrew as the war scaled down. However, not only have the largest PMCs maintained their presence in the Middle East today, they have also expanded their services to other countries and private corporations worldwide.

Actual expenditures by the US government for PMCs remain high as the United States scales down its troop presence in the Middle East region.[214] Some of the largest and most famous firms have merged and/or reconfigured in order to hide negative reputations. They are increasingly integrated in ways that expand their abilities to offer security and safety to the TCC while generating profits. According to the American political scientist P.W. Singer, "The newest wave of private military agents are commercial enterprises first and foremost. They are hierarchically organized and registered businesses that trade and compete openly (for the most part) and are vertically integrated into the wider global marketplace."[215]

Blackwater (part of the Constellis Holdings)

Blackwater is probably the best-known private security company in the world. Started in 1997 by Erik Prince, an ex–Navy SEAL (Sea, Air, and Land teams), the company was established to provide top-level training for the United States military and law enforcement. Their training center was 6,000 acres of swampland on the border of North Carolina and Virginia. Blackwater was awarded its first government contract after the bombing of the USS Cole in October 2000. It opened another training center in 2001 with indoor and outdoor shooting ranges, urban city reproductions, a manmade lake, and several driving tracks.

In early 2002, Blackwater USA established a branch specifically devoted to fulfilling security contracts. One of its first big contracts was to provide twenty men with top-secret security clearances to protect the Central Intelligence Agency (CIA) headquarters in Kabul, Afghanistan, which had been tasked with hunting down Osama bin Laden.[216]

Soon thereafter, Blackwater had a firm footing in America's business overseas, especially in Iraq and Afghanistan. In addition to governmental business, Blackwater has also been the recipient of numerous private contracts, most of which have been kept secret. In the aftermath of Hurricane Katrina, 200 Blackwater employees deployed to the devastated areas. There are conflicting reports as to their actual business in the areas affected by Katrina. Blackwater insisted they were there to provide humanitarian aid, free of charge, while others note that many Blackwater employees were under contract to protect government buildings. Either way, Blackwater was an undeniable presence in Katrina's aftermath.[217]

In May 2006 the US government awarded Blackwater, DynCorp, and Triple Canopy contracts to provide diplomatic security in Iraq, establishing a new precedent by engaging such a large number of hired guns overseas for this purpose.[218]

Perhaps the most notorious event involving Blackwater took place at Nisour Square in Baghdad on September 16, 2007, when Blackwater employees killed seventeen Iraqi civilians. In October 2014 a US federal district court found that the deaths were not a battlefield tragedy, but the result of criminal acts. The court convicted four of the Blackwater guards on charges of murder, manslaughter, and use of a machine gun. All of the guards convicted faced at least several decades, and potentially life, in prison.[219] However, a federal appeals court ruled in August 2017 that three of the men needed to be resentenced and a fourth retried, throwing out their lengthy prison sentences. The three-judge panel declared the contractors' sentences "grossly disproportionate to their culpability for using government-issued weapons in a war zone."[220]

Following the Nisour Square incident, Blackwater began a process of restructuring its public image. In October 2007 Blackwater USA changed its name to Blackwater Worldwide, altered its company logo, and started shifting resources away from security contracting. In 2009 Blackwater Worldwide changed its name yet again to Xe Services llc, and also began another round of restructuring. Founder and CEO Erik Prince resigned as CEO and Joseph Yorio took over daily operations, while Prince continued as chairman of the board. In 2010 a private group of investors purchased Xe and renamed the company Academi. The new company instituted a new management system, created a compliance and governance program, and assembled a leadership team characterized by "deep experience with crisis management" and prior experience in senior government positions.[221]

Constellis Holdings came into existence in June 2014 with the merger of Academi (Blackwater) and Triple Canopy. At the time, the conglomerate acquired numerous other prominent companies that were part of the former Constellis Group, including Strategic Social, Tidewater Global Services, and National Strategic Protective Services.[222]

While all of the Constellis Group companies, including Academi and Triple Canopy, remain officially separate, they are under the control of the larger umbrella of Constellis Holdings. The members of Academi's board of directors all serve on the corporate board of Constellis. With the merger, all of these companies are able to utilize each other's resources, most notably Academi's world-class training facility. Constellis is managed by an all-male board of directors that includes billionaire Red McCombs; John Ashcroft, the former attorney general; retired admiral Bobby Ray Inman; and Jack Quinn, a leading Democratic advisor who served as chief of staff to Vice President Al Gore and as counsel to President Clinton.

In 2016 two New York City private equity firms, Forté Capital Advisors (where Jason DeYonker is managing partner) and Manhattan Partners (where Dean C. Bosacki and Patrick McBride are managing partners), were the principal investors in Constellis.

Erik Prince has recently been in the news as an advisor to Donald Trump. Prince's sister, Betsy DeVos, is the Secretary of Education in the Trump administration.[223] Constellis's newest division is EP Aviation, an air force of helicopters providing services in Africa. The resources and manpower now consolidated as Constellis likely make it one of the most powerful PMC firms. Erik Prince now advocates for an "East India company approach" to Afghanistan, whereby the United States would subcontract with his companies to militarily manage and control the country.[224]

G4S

With roughly 625,000 employees in more than 120 countries spanning five continents, G4S is the second largest private-sector employer in the world. Some of its more important contractors are the governments of the United Kingdom, the United States, Israel, and Australia; in the private sector, it has worked with corporations such as Chrysler, Apple, and Bank of America.[225]

G4S's CEO: **Ashley Martin Almanza**, South Africa **CB-**CEO: G4S, G4S Secure Solution Israel, G4S Solutions Singapore, Noble Corporation plc **E-** London Business School (MBA) **F-** G4S shares 466,777—$1.7 million, Noble shares 59,916—$249,251 (2017)

G4S offers security guards, alarms, management and transportation of cash and valuables, prison management, and electronic monitoring of offenders in 120 countries worldwide.[226] G4S's annual revenue in 2014 was nearly $10.5 billion.[227]

Increasingly, G4S operates in "complex environments" and accepts jobs that national armies are not trained to do.[228]

In Nigeria, Chevron contracts with G4S for counterinsurgency operations that include fast-response mercenaries. G4S undertakes similar operations in South Sudan, and has provided surveillance equipment for checkpoints and prisons in Israel and security for Jewish settlements in Palestine.[229] *G4S* was one among several private *security* companies protecting construction of the Dakota Access Pipeline.[230]

As of July 2012, the Global Power Elite are heavily invested in G4S.[231] Nine of the Giants had direct investment holdings in G4S.[232]

In *Global Capitalism and the Crisis of Humanity*, William I. Robinson devotes a chapter to the policing of global capitalism in the twenty-first century. He describes Transnational Capitalist Class elites' responses to democracy movements, including their reliance on militarism, masculinization, racism, and scapegoating as ideological justifications for police state repression.[233]

Robinson hypothesizes that continuing concentration of capital and massive poverty will lead to nation-states facing legitimation crises that would require them to employ a vast host of coercive control mechanisms, including mass incarceration, various levels of martial law, and an increasing separation of classes into restrictive geographical zones.[234]

Private military contractors would likely play an essential role in the enforcement of this future neo-fascist capitalist world that Robinson foresees. Capital would be free to travel instantly and internationally to anywhere profits are possible, while nation-states would become little more than population containment zones with increasingly repressive labor controls.

For these reasons, many scholars have come to understand PMCs as a component of neoliberal imperialism that now supplements nation-states' police powers and could eventually substitute for them.[235]

The firms we reviewed offer the full range of PMC services. These larger firms are increasingly integrated within the world of transnational capital. PMC boards of directors and advisors—almost exclusively male—represent some of the most powerfully connected people in the world, with multiple sociopolitical links to governments, military, finance, and policy groups.[236]

The trend toward privatization of war is a serious threat to human rights, due process, and democratic transparency and accountability.[237] The US–NATO military empire sets the moral standards for denial of human rights by using pilotless drones to kill civilians without regard for international law. Labeling dead civilians as insurgents and terrorists after the fact, the military empire displays a complete lack of due process and human rights belying any standard of governmental moral legitimacy. This lack of moral legitimacy in turns sets standards for private military companies to operate with much the same malice in the shadow of the empire.

The globalization of PMC operations alongside transnational capital investment, international treaty agreements, and an increasing concentration of wealth in the TCC means that the repressive practices of private security companies abroad will inevitably come home to the United States, the European Union, and other developed nations.

The 99 percent of us without wealth and private police power face the looming threat of overt repression and complete loss of human rights and legal protections. We see signs of this daily with police killings (now close to one hundred per month in the United States), warrantless electronic spying, mass incarceration, random traffic checkpoints, airport security/no-fly lists, and Homeland Security compilations of databases on suspected resisters. Understanding that these repressive measures only make us and our families personally less safe, and that these measures are being installed primarily for the protection of the TCC Global Elite, is an important step to recognizing how power works in the world today.

CHAPTER 6

IDEOLOGISTS
CORPORATE MEDIA AND PUBLIC RELATIONS PROPAGANDA FIRMS— SELLING EMPIRE, WAR, AND CAPITALISM[238]

Global corporate media are owned and controlled by ideologists for the Global Power Elite. Corporate media today are highly concentrated and fully international. Their primary goal is the promotion of product sales and pro-capitalist propaganda through the psychological control of human desires, emotions, beliefs, fears, and values. Corporate media do this by manipulating the feelings and cognitions of human beings worldwide, and by promoting entertainment viewing as a distraction to global inequality. Corporate media receive anywhere from two thirds to 80 percent of their broadcast and print news content from public relations and propaganda (PRP) firms, meaning that nearly all content inside the global corporate media system today is pre-packaged, managed news, opinion, and entertainment.

The rapid consolidation of global media has reduced the total news sources for most of the world to only a handful of corporations. While many hundreds of regional media organizations still exist around the world, the largest corporate media entities dominate news and entertainment content worldwide.

The annual revenue from media is projected to hit $2.1 trillion in 2017, with US media earning $632 billion.[239]

Since the passage of the Telecommunications Act of 1996, a gold rush of media mergers and takeovers has been occurring in the United States. Six major media corporations, down from fifty in the early 1980s, now dominate the US news and information systems. Giant companies, such as iHeartMedia, own more than 1,200 radio stations. Ninety-eight percent of all cities have only one daily newspaper, and those newspapers are increasingly controlled by huge chains.[240]

The 24-hour news shows on MSNBC, Fox, and CNN are closely connected with various governmental and corporate sources of news. Maintenance of continuous news shows requires a constant feed and an ever-entertaining supply of stimulating events and breaking news bites. Advertisement for mass consumption drives the system, and pre-packaged sources of news are vital within this global news process. Ratings demand continued cooperation from multiple sources for ongoing weather reports, war stories, sports scores, business news, and regional headlines.

The preparations for and the reporting on ongoing wars and terrorism fits well into the ideological kaleidoscope of pre-planned news. Government and private public-relations specialists provide ongoing news feeds to the transnational media distribution systems. The result is an emerging macro-symbiotic relationship between news dispensers and news suppliers. Perfect examples of this relationship are the press pools organized by the Pentagon both in the Middle East and in Washington, DC, which give pre-scheduled reports on wars and terrorism to selected groups of news collectors (journalists) for distribution through their specific media organizations.

Embedded reporters working directly with military units in the field must maintain cooperative working relationships with unit commanders as they feed breaking news back to their transnational media distributors. Cooperative reporting is vital to continued access to government news sources. Therefore, rows of news story reviewers back at corporate media headquarters rewrite, soften, or spike news stories from the field that threaten the symbiotics of global news management and the ideological parameters of acceptable coverage.

Journalists who fail to recognize their role as cooperative news collectors will be disciplined in the field or barred from reporting, as in the celebrity cases of Geraldo Rivera and Peter Arnett at the time of the invasion of Iraq in 2003.

Symbiotic global news distribution is a conscious and deliberate attempt by the power elite to control news and information in society and promote a pro-capitalist ideology. The Homeland Security Act, Title II Section 201(d)(5), specifically asks the directorate to "develop a comprehensive national plan for securing the key resources and critical infrastructure of the United States, including . . . information technology and telecommunications systems (including satellites) . . . [and] emergency preparedness communications systems."

Global corporate media today are perhaps too vast to enforce complete control over all content 24 hours a day. However, NATO governments and power elites are seeking total information control and the elimination of any media challenges to capital's freedom to grow. "Transnational Media are instruments of and for the transnational capitalist class," writes Lee Artz in his book *Global Entertainment Media*.[241] The deep investments in media by the global Giants tells a story of influence at best and dominance at worst.

The top six transnational news and entertainment corporations and their TCC power elite executives are listed below.

Comcast Corporation

Comcast Corporation provides media and television broadcasting services. The company offers video streaming, television programming, high-speed internet, cable television, and communication services. Comcast serves customers worldwide. Their net revenue in 2016 was $80.4 billion. Their largest brands include NBC, Telemundo, and Universal Pictures. Comcast is primarily a family-owned business, with 33 percent of the control held by the Ralph Roberts family.

The global Giants are deeply invested in Comcast: BlackRock ($14.4 billion), Vanguard Group ($12.3 billion), State Street ($7.3 billion), Bank of America ($2.3 billion), Bank of NY Mellon ($2.16 billion), JPMorgan Chase ($2.1 billion), Capital Group ($2.1 billion), UBS ($1.4 billion), Goldman Sachs Group ($1.19 billion), Prudential Financial ($737 million), Morgan Stanley & Co. ($663 million), Allianz SE (PIMCO) ($568 million), Credit Suisse ($333 million), Barclays plc ($228 million), and Amundi/ Crédit Agricole ($195 million).

Comcast's CEO: **Brian L. Roberts**, US **CB**- CEO: Comcast Corporation (has worked with Comcast from 1981 to present) **PE**- Bank of NY Mellon **PC**- Business Roundtable, National Cable and Telecommunications Association, Simon Wiesenthal Center, Walter Kaitz Foundation, Director Emeritus: CableLabs **E**- University of Pennsylvania, Wharton School, All-American in squash: competed five times in the Maccabiah Games in Israel **F**- Comcast compensation $28.6 million (2016); net worth $1.8 billion

Disney

The Walt Disney Company is an entertainment conglomerate employing 195,000 people. Their revenue for 2016 was $55.6 billion. The company operates in four business segments: Media Networks, Parks and Resorts, Studio Entertainment, and Consumer Products and Interactive Media. The Media Networks segment includes cable and broadcast television networks, television production and distribution operations, domestic television stations, and radio networks and stations. The American Broadcasting Company (ABC), owned by Disney, has 243 owned and affiliate TV stations reaching 96 percent of American homes. ABC Radio is licensed to more than 500 radio stations. Disney owns ABC, ESPN, the Disney Channels, A&E Networks, Lucasfilm (producer of the *Star Wars* franchise), and Freeform. ABC broadcasts throughout North, South, and Central America, Asia, Europe, and the Middle East. They operate fourteen theme parks around the world.

Global Giants invested in Disney include Vanguard Group ($10.7 billion), BlackRock ($9.3 billion), State Street ($7.1 billion), Morgan Stanley & Co. ($2.7 billion), Bank of NY Mellon ($2.5 billion), Bank of America ($1.8 billion), JPMorgan Chase ($1.8 billion), UBS ($927 million), Goldman Sachs Group ($921 million), UBS ($669 million), Capital Group ($847 million [two groups]), Allianz SE (PIMCO) ($329 million), Credit Suisse ($322 million), Prudential Financial ($310 million), Barclays plc ($221 million), Amundi/Crédit Agricole ($158 million), and AXA Group ($78 million).

Disney's CEO: **Robert Iger**, US **CB**- Apple, CEO and Chair: Disney **PE**- President: ABC **PC**- September 11 Memorial &

Museum, Bloomberg Family Foundation, World Economic
Forum, Lincoln Center, Outward Bound Program, National
Campaign Against Youth Violence, Co-Chair: Hillary Clinton
for President 2016, Trump's Strategic Policy Forum (resigned
June 1, 2017 over Trump's position on the Paris Climate
Agreement), Trustee: Ithaca College E- Ithaca College (BS in
Communication/Radio and TV) F- Disney compensation $43.8
million (2016), Disney shares 1.47 million—$159 million (2017)

Time Warner

Time Warner is an American multinational mass media and
entertainment conglomerate headquartered in New York City.
Time Warner owns HBO, Warner Bros., Turner Broadcasting,
and Cinemax, and operates in 150 countries. Time Warner revenue for 2015 was $28.1 billion, and they employ 25,000 people.

Giants with holdings in Time Warner include Vanguard
Group ($4.5 billion), BlackRock ($4 billion), State Street ($2.7
billion), Goldman Sachs Group ($908 million), Capital Group
($907 million), Fidelity Investments (FMR) ($820 million),
Credit Suisse ($783 million), Bank of NY Mellon ($707 million),
JPMorgan Chase ($636 million), Morgan Stanley & Co. ($624
million), Bank of America ($517 million), UBS ($395 million),
Amundi/Crédit Agricole ($308 million), Barclays plc ($140 million), and Prudential Financial ($105 million).

(In June 2018, a federal judge approved AT&T's $85.4 billion
acquisition of Time Warner, following a challenge from the Justice Department in December 2017.)

Time Warner's CEO: **Jeff Bewkes**, US **CB**- Chair and CEO: Time
Warner **PE**- Citibank, CEO: HBO **PC**- Trustee: Yale University,

The Creative Coalition, Business Council, World Economic Forum, Council on Foreign Relations, Media.NYC.2020 **E-** Yale (BS), Stanford (MBA) **F-** net worth $12.7 million

21st Century Fox

21st Century Fox is a multinational mass media corporation with an operating revenue of $27.2 billion in 2016. It is the fourth largest media conglomerate behind Comcast, Disney, and Time Warner. 21st Century Fox owns 20th Century Fox Films, Fox Broadcasting Company, and Star TV (an Asian cable company based in Hong Kong). Fox holds a 73 percent share in *National Geographic* magazine and TV network. Rupert Murdoch has controlling interests in Fox and owns 800 news companies in fifty countries.

Giants with holdings in Fox include Vanguard Group ($997 million), BlackRock ($852 million), State Street ($588 million), Morgan Stanley & Co. ($569 million), Goldman Sachs Group ($207 million), JPMorgan Chase ($162 million), Bank of NY Mellon ($135 million), Fidelity Investments (FMR) ($96 million), UBS ($83 million), Prudential Financial ($70 million), Bank of America ($64 million), Credit Suisse ($17.9 million), and Barclays plc ($13.6 million).

21st Century Fox's CEO: **Rupert Murdoch**, US (former Australian citizen) **CB-** *Times News* (London), *Wall Street Journal*, *NY Post*, HarperCollins, Sky UK, *The Sun* (London), CEO and Chair: 21st Century Fox **PE-** Publisher: *The Australian*, *Daily Telegraph* **PC-** Council on Foreign Relations, Cato Institute, Australian Labor Party **E-** Oxford (BA, MA) **F-** net worth $13.1 billion (2017)

James Rupert Murdoch, US, UK, **CB**- CEO 21st Century Fox, Sky plc, Telsa, Yankee Global Enterprises LLC, **PE**- GlaxoSmith-Kline, CEO News Corp., Sky Italia, Sky Deutschland, Star TV, British Sky Publishing, News Datacom, BskyB, **PC**- Leadership Council of Climate Group, *Harvard Lampoon*, Dia Center for the Arts, Ghetto Film School, Center for a New American Security, **E**- Harvard, **F**- Fox Compensation $26 million 2016, Net worth $160 million

Bertelsmann

Bertelsmann is a privately-owned media, services, and education company that operates in nearly 50 countries. It includes the broadcaster RTL Group, the trade book publisher Penguin Random House, the Bertelsmann Printing Group, the Bertelsmann Education Group, and Bertelsmann Investments. The company has 116,000 employees and generated revenues of $20.2 billion in the 2016 financial year. RTL Group is Europe's leading entertainment network, with holdings in 60 television channels and 31 radio stations, as well as production companies throughout the world. The television portfolio of Europe's largest broadcaster includes RTL Television in Germany, M6 in France, RTL channels in the Netherlands, Belgium, Luxembourg, Croatia, and Hungary, Antena 3 in Spain, and various channels in Southeast Asia. In addition, with its Fremantle-Media subsidiary, RTL Group is one of the largest international companies outside the United States in the areas of production, licensing, and distribution of television content.[242]

Bertelsmann's CEO: **Thomas Rabe**, Luxembourg **CB**- Allianz SE, Symrise, Archivio Ricordi Spa, CEO: Bertelsmann **PE**-

Forrester, Norall & Sutton Law, Treuhand Agency (Berlin) (privatization of the assets of the former GDR), Neue Länder investment agency of the Association of German Banks, Cedel International, CFO: RTL Group **PC**- Edmond Israel Foundation **E**- University of Cologne (BA in Business, MBA, PhD in Economics) **F**- N/A

Bertelsmann's Chair: **Christoph Mohn,** Germany **CB**- Chair Bertelsmann **E**- University Munster (BA in Marketing) **F**- Christoph Mohn is the son of Bertelsmann matriarch **Liz Mohn** and her late husband, **Reinhard. Liz** (net worth $4.8 billion), **Christoph**, and sister **Brigitte Mohn** all sit on the Bertelsmann board, which controls all voting rights to the media group Holdings in Bertelsmann are not publicly listed.

Viacom and CBS

Viacom and CBS are both owned by National Amusements Inc., a privately-held corporation controlled by Sumner Redstone and Shari Redstone. Viacom operates 170 networks with 700 million subscribers in more than 160 countries. Viacom's annual revenue in 2016 was $12.4 billion. Viacom owns Paramount Pictures, MTV, BBC America, and Nickelodeon.

Columbia Broadcasting System (CBS) had an annual revenue of $13.8 billion in 2015. CBS has 240 owned or affiliated TV stations in the United States, and 116 radio stations, including nearly all of the all-news radio stations in San Francisco, Los Angeles, New York City, Boston, Dallas, St. Louis, and Detroit. CBS programming is also shown widely in Europe and Asia.

Global Giants invested in CBS include Capital Group ($1.74 billion), Vanguard Group ($1.39 billion), BlackRock ($1.28 billion), State Street ($861 million), JPMorgan Chase ($476 million), Bank of NY Mellon ($252 million), Morgan Stanley & Co. ($215 million), UBS ($168 million), Bank of America ($154 million), Goldman Sachs Group ($109 million), Allianz SE (PIMCO) ($102 million), Credit Suisse ($70.9 million), and Prudential Financial ($68.7 million).

National Amusements Inc.'s Owner: **Sumner Redstone**, US **CB**- Viacom, Paramount Pictures, Owner: National Amusements Inc. **PE**- US Department of Justice, US Military Intelligence in WWII **PC**- World Economic Forum **E**- Harvard (BA, JD) **F**- net worth $6.4 billion

Viacom's CEO: **Robert Bakish**, US **CB**- AVID Technologies, CEO: Viacom **PE**- Booz Allen Hamilton **PC**- World Economic Forum, Board of Overseers of Columbia University **E**- Columbia (BA, MBA) **F**- net worth $1.2 million

CBS's CEO: **Leslie Roy Moonves**, US **CB**- ZeniMax Media, CEO: CBS Corporation **PE**- CEO: Warner Brothers **E**- Bucknell University (BA) **F**- net worth $300 million

These six media firms control the lion's share of news around the world. They are the unofficial spokespersons for the Global Power Elite and the ideological protectors of concentrated global capital. Owned and controlled by multimillionaires with heavy investments from the global Giants, these companies are the foundation of capitalist ideological hegemony.

PROPAGANDA MODEL OF CORPORATE MEDIA
AND PUBLIC RELATIONS PROPAGANDA FIRMS

Public relations (PR) is defined by Edward Bernays, one of the primary founders of public relations in the United States, as information provided to the public to modify attitudes and actions toward various institutions.[243] In his 1952 book *Public Relations* Bernays claims that PR strives to create favorable opinions toward ideas, products, and persons, which can include both good will between people and increased sales of products. In the chapter entitled "The Engineering of Consent," Bernays writes that "it is impossible to overestimate the importance of engineering consent, it affects almost every aspect of our daily lives. When used for social purposes, it is among our most valuable contributions to the efficient functioning of society. But the techniques can be subverted: demagogues can utilize them for antidemocratic purposes as successfully as those who employ them for socially desirable ends."[244] Clearly, Bernays, in the shadow of World War II, saw the possibilities of the dark side of PR.[245]

The practice of public relations is commonly referred to as "helping an organization and its public adapt mutually to each other."[246] On the other hand, propaganda is defined as "the dissemination of ideas and information for the purpose of inducing or intensifying specific attitudes and actions."[247] Propaganda was widely used during World War II and the Cold War[248] by the CIA and other government agencies to advance US policies and war interests.[249]

The propaganda war film *The Green Berets*, featuring John Wayne, was released in 1968 at the height of the Vietnam War and demonstrated the relentlessness of Hollywood's production of propaganda movies in support of US military policies. The Department of Defense was concerned that *The Green Berets* would look so much like propaganda that they asked the producers to remove credit at the end thanking the Department of Defense and the Army for their generous assistance.[250] Pentagon and governmental involvement in Hollywood continues to this day. The recent film *Argo* is one example of continuing deliberate US government propaganda disseminated via Hollywood.[251] New research shows that military intelligence agencies have influenced more than 1,800 films and TV shows since 2005, making Hollywood a propaganda machine for the US national security state.[252]

The war on terror requires continuing ideological justifications aimed at the mass of people who instinctively favor peace. Public Relations and Propaganda (PRP) firms provide an ongoing rationalization for war by servicing government propaganda activities, military contractors, and pro-war Hollywood films, and marketing war toys, cartoons, and related products. The techniques for marketing brands are essentially the same as for marketing war. PRP firms provide support for military propaganda by creating visually stimulating, emotional ads featuring families with loving young children imperiled by terrorists and protected by official authorities, homeland security, police, or military. *America's Navy—the Shield* was one such ad on TV and YouTube, first aired during the 2014 Army–Navy football game.

Expanding levels of media propaganda coordinated by public relations firms are particularly well documented during the Iraq War.[253] The Rendon Group has been cited as one of the primary PR firms supporting the US propaganda efforts in Iraq. In the 1980s, the Rendon Group created public relations propaganda for the ousting of President Manuel Noriega in Panama. They shaped international support for the first Gulf War, and in the 1990s created the Iraqi National Congress. The Rendon Group also provided the images that shaped support for a permanent war on terror, including the toppling of the statue of Saddam Hussein, Private Jessica Lynch's heroic rescue, and dramatic tales of weapons of mass destruction. Pentagon documents show 35 contracts with Rendon between 2000 and 2004 worth a total of $50–100 million.[254]

Before the first Gulf War, a propaganda spectacle took place courtesy of WPP's Hill & Knowlton Strategies. They were hired by Citizens for a Free Kuwait, a front group Hill & Knowlton had established with Kuwaiti money to promote the first war on Iraq. Hill & Knowlton eventually received nearly $10.8 million for one of the largest and most effective public relations campaigns in history. Hill & Knowlton built a national outrage against Iraq through a public recounting of horrifying crimes supposedly perpetrated by Iraqi soldiers in Kuwait after they invaded. A young woman named Nayirah claimed in congressional testimony, and before a national TV audience, that she saw "Iraqi soldiers come into the [Kuwaiti] hospital with guns. They took the babies out of the incubators, and left the children to die on the cold floor."[255] What the public was not told is that Nayirah was the daughter of Kuwait's ambassador to the United States. The public also wasn't told that her performance was coordinated by the White House and choreographed by the US PRP firm Hill & Knowlton on behalf of the Kuwaiti government.[256]

David Altheide and Jennifer Grimes trace the history of how the Project for the New American Century, a neoconservative think tank, helped plan the propaganda campaign for the second Iraq War.[257] A recent journal article by David Guth reports on the history of the debate over propaganda and public diplomacy, focusing on the diversion stories and even outright lies employed by the George W. Bush administration to raise support for the Iraq War.[258]

By definition, propaganda and public relations are both trying to change the public's views, beliefs, and feelings about various issues, ideas, and products. Both propaganda and PR seek to change behaviors and ideas among the masses in support of the agendas of the institutions initiating the actions.

A number of researchers have asserted that propaganda and public relations are virtually identical.[259] According to Corporate Watch,

> powerful and pervasive public relations firms ensure that pro-corporate stories and perspectives dominate journalistic output. PR firms and other corporate lobbying agencies ensure that corporate-friendly messages are given preferential treatment within the corridors of power. The upshot is a climate in which market dominance over ever increasing aspects of our lives is often accepted as common-sense, rather than challenged as a cause of suffering and inequality.[260]

In addition, Ryszard Lawniczak believes that this pro-corporate perspective extends internationally, giving the public relations industry a global role in the political economy of marketing.[261] Public relations firms and governments have increasingly begun to overlap, especially since 9/11. In this regard, it makes perfect sense to study the transnational impacts of propaganda and public relations by combining the two terms into the term "Public Relations Propaganda" (PRP).

Edward S. Herman and Noam Chomsky's *Manufacturing Consent*, first published in 1988, claims that the media reflect the class values and concerns of their owners and advertisers because they are firmly embedded in the market system.[262] According to Herman and Chomsky, the media maintain a corporate class bias through five systemic filters: concentrated private ownership; a strict bottom-line profit orientation; over-reliance on governmental and corporate sources for news; a strong tendency to avoid offending the powerful; and an almost religious worship of the market economy, strongly opposing alternative beliefs and ideologies. These filters limit what becomes news in modern society and set parameters on acceptable coverage of daily events.

In a 2017 update on the Propaganda Model, Edward Herman wrote, just a few months before his recent passing, that "mainstream media locates their regular behavior and performance in the elite-dominated corporate structures and relationships, not in journalists' news-gathering practices or any supposed role as an independent watchdog serving the general public interest."[263] Herman goes on to say that the main development in mainstream media over the past 30 years has been the emergence of the internet, which undermined print news, resulting in a 60 percent drop in the newspaper workforce between 1990 and 2016 as well as a drop in advertisement revenue from $65 billion in 2000 to $18 billion in 2015. Alphabet (Google) has been the largest beneficiary of internet advertisement revenue, garnering more than $75 billion annually as of 2016. Herman writes that "these internet giants (Google and Facebook) are in the surveillance and marketing (spying and selling) business.... [T]hey use micro-technology to identify and sell to advertisers full dossiers on the personal habits, relationships, and tastes of vast numbers of people." We should note that governments, political campaigns, and intelligence agencies also are in the market for this trove of personal information.

Media consolidation and the expansion of public relations propaganda (PRP) firms inside news systems in the world today has resulted in a deliberate form of ideological news management. The corporate media are deeply interlocked with the military–industrial complex and policy elites in the American/European/Asian Transnational Corporate Class, and the media are increasingly dependent on various governmental and PRP sources of news. Twenty-four-hour news shows on MSNBC, Fox, and CNN maintain constant contact with the White House, Pentagon, and PRP companies representing both governments and private corporations.

The big three global PRP firms, WPP, Omnicom Group, and Interpublic Group, are key contributors to the total hegemony of capitalism in the world today. PRP firms and their corporate media partners serve corporations, governments, and nongovernmental organizations (NGOs) in an unrelenting ideological assault on the minds of masses throughout the world. Their messages encourage continued acquisition of material products and consumption, expanded desire for a life of luxury, fear of others—terrorists, criminals, and any peoples perceived as a threat—support of police states, acceptance of a permanent war on terrorism, and the notion that private corporations are an essential element of democracy. This is what Noam Chomsky called engineering opinion and parading enemies.[264]

The PRP industry continuously features products that are a danger to humanity. PRP firms offer brand enhancement worldwide for numerous tobacco, alcohol, junk food (sugary, salty, and fatty "treats"), and pharmaceutical products. As we examine the lists of clients for the big three PRP firms below, it is clear that unhealthy foods constitute some of the most heavily advertised products worldwide. It should be noted that the Giants are strongly invested in dangerous products as well. In 2017, 16 Giants invested a total of $49.8 billion in Philip Morris, the world's largest tobacco company: Vanguard Group ($11.8 billion), BlackRock ($9.7 billion), Capital Group ($8.1 billion), State Street ($6 billion), Bank of NY Mellon ($3.4 billion), Bank of America ($3.1 billion), Fidelity Investments (FMR) ($2.2 billion), Morgan Stanley & Co. ($1.8 billion), JPMorgan Chase ($1.7 billion), Goldman Sachs Group ($768 million), UBS ($317 million), Credit Suisse ($305 million), Prudential Financial ($267 million), Barclays plc ($197 million), Allianz SE (PIMCO) ($87 million), and AXA Group ($51 million).

The following data on the big three PRP firms was acquired with extensive research from the hundreds of websites they control. It is a consolidated view of the primary brands, agencies, and services offered by Omnicom Group, WPP, and Interpublic Group. Most of the financial Giants are invested in at least one, though often in all three, big PRP firms.

OMNICOM GROUP

Omnicom Group, based in New York City, had an annual revenue of $15.2 billion in 2017, with 74,000 employees in more than 200 agencies representing a group of subsidiaries, affiliates, and such quasi-independent agencies as BBDO Worldwide, DDB Worldwide, TBWA Worldwide, Integer, and Zimmerman & Partners, as well as FleishmanHillard, GSD&M, Merkley & Partners, and Rapp Worldwide, which fall under the Diversified

Agency Services division. Omnicom Group is represented at the Council on Foreign Relations in the United States.[265]

Omnicom Group has roots back to 1891, when George Batten opened the George Batten Co. in New York City. The following year, Batten hired William Johns as his assistant. Johns became the first president of the American Association of Advertising Agencies and, upon Batten's death in 1918, took the position as president of Batten Co. BDO came about when Bruce Barton, Roy Durstine, and Alex Osborn met at a United War Work fundraising effort. In 1928 BDO merged with the George Batten's Batten agency. The group was renamed Batten, Barton, Durstine & Osborn (BBDO). BBDO went on to expand around the world, merging with other PRP agencies and forming Omnicom Group in 1986. In 1991 Omnicom Group's revenue increased to $1.2 billion and has continued to progressively increase year after year. Presently, Omnicom Group is serving more than 5,000 brands among every sector of products and services, and the corporation has more than 1,500 agencies in more than 100 countries.

The global Giants invested in Omnicom Group include Black-Rock ($1.25 billion), Vanguard Group ($1.24 billion), State Street ($699 million), Bank of NY Mellon ($363 million), Goldman Sachs Group ($166 million), Bank of America ($104 million), UBS ($94 million), Morgan Stanley & Co. ($39 million), Prudential Financial ($36 million), Barclays plc ($32 million), Credit Suisse ($30 million), AXA Group ($15.5 million), and JPMorgan Chase ($13.4 million). The total annual investment in Omnicom Group by the global Giants is $4.06 billion.

Omnicom Group's CEO: **John Wren**, US **CB-** CEO: Omnicom Group **PE-** DDB Needham Worldwide, Arthur Anderson,

Macy's, Norton Simon Inc. **PC**- International Business Council of the World Economic Forum, Director: Lincoln Center, Trustee: St. Luke's–Roosevelt Hospital Center, Beth Israel Medical Center **E**- Adelphi University (BA, MBA) **F**- Omnicom Group compensation $23 million (2016); net worth $71 million (2017)

Omnicom Group's Major Clients

Governments and Government-Funded Organizations
Alberta, Barcelona, Brazil, British Columbia, Brooklyn, California Housing Finance Agency, California Lottery, Chicago, Dubai Department of Tourism and Commerce Marketing, Ecuador, Egypt, Georgia (country), Houston Airport System, Illinois State Lottery, Korea Tourism Organization, Library of Congress, Los Angeles, Mauritius, Mexico, Miami-Dade County, Montreal, New Orleans, New York Police Department, New York State Energy Research and Development Authority, Nicaragua, Nigeria, Peru, Portugal, Qatar, Republic of Congo, Royal Brunei Airlines, Spain, Toronto Transit Commission, Tourism New Zealand, UNICEF, United States Mint, Vienna, Washington State Department of Health, Veterans Affairs, Zurich

NGOs, Nonprofits, and Universities
Ad Council, Alcoa Foundation, Almond Board of California, American Academy of Actuaries, American Chiropractic Association, American International University, American Lung Association, American Petroleum Institute, American Public Transportation Association, American Red Cross, Argosy University, Big Brothers Big Sisters, Boy Scouts of America, California Endowment, California Raisin Marketing Board,

California Table Grape Commission, Campaign for Tobacco-Free Kids, Canadian Cancer Society, Canadian Nuclear Association, Canadian Tourism Commission/Destination Canada, Cancer Research UK, Centers for Disease Control and Prevention, Cincinnati Children's Hospital, College of the Holy Cross, Cornell University, Council on Foreign Relations (CFR), David and Lucile Packard Foundation, Democratic Governors Association, Doctors Without Borders, Ford Foundation, Howard Jarvis Taxpayers Association, Howard University, Impact Iran, International Pharmaceutical Federation, James Irvine Foundation, John F. Kennedy Center for the Performing Arts, Kaiser Foundation Health Plan/Kaiser Foundation Hospitals, Lupus Foundation of America, Montanans for Free and Fair Elections, Mount Sinai Medical Center, Munich Airport, National Association of Broadcasters, National Audubon Society, National Breast Cancer Foundation, National Catholic Health Council, National Hockey League, Pew Research Center, Robert Wood Johnson Foundation, Rockefeller Foundation, Rotary International, Ryukoku University, Salvation Army, San Francisco Bowl, Special Olympics, Sundance Institute, Sydney Opera House, Telecom Italia, Tony Awards, United Nations Foundation, University of California, Berkeley, University of Phoenix, University of Washington, Vancouver Convention Centre, World Bank, World Health Organization, YMCA

Major Corporations and Brands
3M, 7-Eleven, 7 Up, A&E Network, AAA, Adidas, Adobe, Aetna, AirAsia, Air France, Alaska Airlines, Albertsons, Alka-Seltzer, American Airlines, American Express, Amstel, Anheuser-Busch, Apple, Arby's, Argos, Arm & Hammer, Arthur Andersen, Aspen Pharmacare Holdings, AT&T, Bacardi, Bank of America,

Barnes & Noble, Bayer, Ben & Jerry's, Berkshire Hathaway, Best Buy, Best Western, BlackBerry, BlackRock, Blue Diamond Almonds, BMW, Bose, Bridgestone, British Airways, Burger King, Cadillac, Campbell's, Canadian Pacific Railway, Canon, Capital One, Captain Morgan, Carta Blanca (beer), Chase Bank, Cheetos, Chevrolet, Chrysler, Cîroc, Cisco, Citibank, Clorox, Coca-Cola, Colgate, Comcast, ConocoPhillips, Converse, Coppertone, Corning, Costco, CoverGirl, Crown Royal, CVS Pharmacy, De Nederlandsche Bank, Dick's Sporting Goods, DIRECTV, Dole, Downy, Dr Pepper, Dreyer's, Dunlop, Duracell, eBay, *The Economist*, Embassy Suites by Hilton, Equinox Fitness, ESPN, ExxonMobil, Facebook, FedEx, Ford, Fry's Electronics, G4S, Gatorade, Genentech, General Electric, General Mills, Gillette, Glad, Godiva, Goodyear, Google, Gucci, H&R Block, Häagen-Dazs, Hallmark, Hampton Inn, Harley-Davidson, HBO, Head & Shoulders, Heineken, Heinz, Hennessey, Hertz, Hilton, Holiday Inn, Horizon Organic, Hormel, Hovis Bakery, HP, Humana, Hyatt Hotels, Hyundai, IBM, IKEA, Ingersoll Rand, Instagram, Intel, Jack Daniel's, JCPenney, Jeep, Johnnie Walker, Johnson & Johnson, Kellogg's, Kia, Kimberly-Clark, Kleenex, Kmart, Kotex, Land Rover, Lay's, Levi's, Lexus, Lowe's, Macy's, Madison Square Garden, Major League Baseball, Marathon Oil, Marriott Hotels, Mars (chocolate bar), Marshalls, MasterCard, Maxwell House, Mazda, McDonald's, McGraw-Hill, Mercedes-Benz, Merck, Microsoft, MillerCoors, Mitsubishi, Monsanto, Morgan Stanley, Motorola, National Car Rental, NBC, Nestea, Nestlé, Netflix, Newcastle Brown Ale, Newman's Own, Nice 'N Easy, Nickelodeon, Nike, Nintendo, Nissan, Nokia, Novartis, Panasonic, Panda Express, PayPal, Peet's Coffee, Pepsi, PetSmart, Pfizer, PG&E, Philips, Pizza Hut, PlayStation, PNC Bank, Popeyes, Porsche, Prada, Procter &

Gamble, Quaker, RadioShack, Ritz Crackers, Rolex, Safeway, Saks Fifth Avenue, Sam's Club, Samsung, Sears, Sharp, Siemens, SiriusXM Radio, Smirnoff, Sol (beer), Sony, Southwest Airlines, Sprint, Staples, Starbucks, State Farm, Subaru, Subway, Sun Life, Tanqueray, Target, Telenet, Tesla, Teva, Thai Airways, Thomson Reuters, Thrifty Car Rental, Tide, Time Warner Cable, T-Mobile, TNT (TV network), Toshiba, Toyota, Toys"R"Us, Twitter, Uncle Ben's, Unilever, United Airlines, UPS, US Bank, Verizon, Virgin, Visa, Volkswagen, Walgreens, *Wall Street Journal*, Walmart, Walt Disney Company, WellPoint/Anthem, Wells Fargo, Wendy's, Western Union, Whirlpool, Whole Foods, Williams-Sonoma, Wrigley, Yahoo, YouTube, Zenith, Ziploc

WPP

WPP is a conglomerate of more than 125 of the world's leading PR and marketing firms, in fields that include advertising, media investment management, consumer insight, branding and identity, communications, direct digital promotion, and relationship marketing. WPP, a London-based conglomerate with an annual revenue of $21.1 billion as of 2017, employs around 190,000 people in 3,000 offices across 112 countries. WPP is a strategic partner with the World Economic Forum.

WPP was formed in 1985 when Martin Sorrell took control of a shell company, Wire & Plastic Products plc. It made its first acquisitions in 1986, buying ten marketing services companies by year-end. In 1987 WPP bought the J. Walter Thompson agency and, in 1989, the Ogilvy Group.[266] From 2000 to 2002, WPP acquired Young & Rubicam Group and Tempus Group plc, and continued to buy up stakes in a number of Chinese and other Asian businesses. The conglomerate continues to expands its reach through acquisitions, joint ventures, and partnerships, with investments in China, Brazil, Singapore, the United Kingdom, and the United States. Primary subsidiaries of WPP include Blanc & Otus, Burson-Marsteller, Cohn & Wolfe, Dewey Square Group, Finsbury, Grey Group, Hill & Knowlton, National Public Relations, and Ogilvy Public Relations.

While more than half of the 125 websites for WPP subsidiaries only mention a few of their clients, if any, many proudly boast about their largest clients. WPP represents several thousand brands worldwide. Our list below is but a sampling of those brands to give readers an idea of how far they've penetrated the media, governments, and the global capitalist market.

In 2017 WPP's top investor was Harding Loevner LP ($44.8 billion under management), at $1.6 billion. David Loevner, Harding Loevner LP's CEO and founder, was a managing director of Rockefeller & Co. ($16.9 billion in asset management). In 2017 Northern Trust in Chicago ($900 billion+ under management) was the second largest shareholder in WPP, at $1.29 billion. Financial Giants invested in WPP include Bank of America ($56 million), JPMorgan Chase ($214 million), Allianz SE (PIMCO) ($112 million), UBS ($61 million), Goldman Sachs Group ($54 million), Bank of New York Mellon ($18.6 million), and State Street ($3.4 million).

WPP's CEO: **Sir Martin Sorrell**, UK **CB**- CEO: WPP **PE**- Wire and Plastics, Products **PC**- Centre for International Business and Management (University of Cambridge), Council for Excellence in Management and Leadership (UK), World Economic Forum, Governor: London Business School, Director of Dean's Advisers: Harvard Business School, Chair: Media.

NYC.2020, Trustee: British Museum **E**- University of Cambridge (BA), Harvard Business School (MBA) **F**- net worth $595 million (2017); awarded the title of UK Knight Bachelor.

According to a CNBC Davos report from January 17, 2017,

> Sir Martin Sorrell, the boss of WPP, had expected the UK to remain in the European Union and also called Hillary Clinton to win the US election. But Sorrell admitted that his predictions were "a little bit wanting" and offered his thoughts on why the world, particularly the business community, got them wrong.
>
> "We all talk to one another in this bubble here in Davos, echo chamber in London, and it's true of the East Coast, West Coast liberals," Sorrell told CNBC in a TV interview at the World Economic Forum, adding that many people attending the event are "clearly out of touch."
>
> "In terms of their businesses, in terms of their regulation, in terms of intervention, I think most industries favored a more Republican route ... so it's a question about why were the pollsters wrong. Because nobody really told them the truth."
>
> Sorrell said he expects Trump's policies of infrastructure spending, tax reduction, and repatriation of cash overseas to be good for the US economy in the next two to three years. But the WPP boss warned about the low growth environment.
>
> "You're in a world of uncertainty, low growth, very little pricing power, because there's very little

inflation . . . and that eventually will bring a problem prior to the next presidential election," Sorrell told CNBC.[267]

WPP's Major Clients

Governments and Government-Funded Organizations
Australian Defense Force, BBC, BC Hydro, British Council, British Library, British Olympic Association, Citizens Information Board (Dublin), Disability Federation of Ireland, Dubai Food Festival, Dubai Shopping Festival, Failte Ireland, India Ministry of Tourism, Insolvency Services of Ireland, International Monetary Fund, Jordan, Kansas City Union Station, Lobbying (regulator of lobbying in Ireland), Minnesota State Lottery, NATO (OTAN), Natural History Museum (London), New Jersey State Lottery, Referendum Commission (Ireland), Rio 2016 Olympics, Royal Mail, Tennessee Department of Tourism, UNICEF, USPS, US Marine Corps, US State Department, Washington Lottery

NGOs, Nonprofits, and Universities
AARP, Amsterdam Gay Pride, Australian Museum, Bangor University, Bath Rugby, Beirut Digital District, British Lung Association, Campaign for Tobacco-Free Kids, Canadian Breast Cancer Foundation, Clinton Foundation, Danish Football Association, DeVry University, English Athletics, GB Rowing Team, Global Entrepreneurship Summit, International Olympic Committee, Irish Blood Transfusion Service, Irish Cancer Society, James Beard Foundation, Jewish Colorado, LTA British Tennis, Mobile World Congress, Museum of London,

National September 11 Memorial and Museum, National Standards Authority of Ireland, NFL, Obama for America, Open Connectivity Foundation, Population Services International (global health organization), The Prince's Trust, Psykiatrifonden (Danish mental health), Rotary Club, Royal Institution of Chartered Surveyors, Sons of Norway, Strayer University, Trinity College Dublin, University of Wales, World Economic Forum, World Rugby, Wounded Warrior Project, Youth Sports Trust (UK)

Major Corporations and Brands
3M, 7-Eleven, A&W Restaurants, Abbot Downing (Wells Fargo's bank for people with $50 million+), Absolut, Adidas, Adobe, *Advertising Age*, Aetna, Allegheny Health Network, Allegiance Health, Allstate, Amazon, American Express, American Swiss (jewelry), Amtrak, ANGA (America's Natural Gas Alliance), AOL, Argos, Ascot (horse races), Ask.com, AstraZeneca, Audi, Avis, Avon, AXA Life Invest, Bank of America, Bank of England, Bankers Life, Barclays, Baxter International, Bayer, Belvedere Vodka, Bentley, Berghaus, Best Buy, BG Group, Blinkbox (online movies), Blue Cross Blue Shield Association, BMW, Boeing, Bose, Boxfresh, British American Tobacco, British Gas, British Land, Britvic (soft drinks), Brown-Forman (whiskey), Budweiser, Bulleit Bourbon, Bupa (China health insurance), Cadillac, Campbell's, Canon, Capital One, Cargill, Carlsberg (beer), Carphone Warehouse, Castle Lite (beer), CBS, Chase Bank, Chivas Regal, Choice Hotels, Cirque du Soleil, Cisco, Citibank, Citroën, Club Orange, CNN, Coca-Cola, Colgate, Comcast, Commonwealth Bank, Converse, Crayola, Credit Suisse, Dailymotion, Danone (French foods), Darden Restaurants, Dasani, Datalex (online sales), Del Monte, Dell, Direct Energy (US gas and

electric), DirecTV, Discover, Disney, Downy, Ducati, Dunkin' Donuts, Dunlop, DuPont, ECCO (shoes), European Tour (golf), Eurostar, EVA Air (Taiwan airline), Evans Cycles (UK bikes), Facebook, Fanagans Funeral Directors, Fanta, Ferrari, Ferrero (chocolates and cookies), Fiat, Finansbank, Fine Gael, Finlandia Vodka, Florida Orange Juice Advertisements, *Forbes*, Ford, Gap, General Electric, General Mills, Genesis Luxury Cars, Geocon (engineering), Gillette, Ginsters (meat pasty), GlaxoSmithKline, Glenlivet, Golden Globes, Goodyear, Google, Grammy Awards, Grey Goose (vodka), GroupM (WPP's media investment group—$100 billion), Halls, Hasbro (toys), Hawaiian Airlines, Hawaiian Gardens Casino, Healthline Networks, Hearst, Heineken, Hennessy, Hershey's, Hertz, HIHO, Hobart (kitchen appliances), Holiday Inn, Hollywood Fashion Secrets, Home Depot, Honda, Honeywell, Hootsuite (social network management), Hotel Tonight, HSBC, Hyundai, IKEA, Imperial Tobacco, Infiniti, Intel, Intelligent Energy (energy tech), Interpublic Group, iProspect (digital media), Ipsen (global pharmaceutical group), *Irish Examiner*, Isuzu, J&B Scotch, Jack Daniel's, Jägermeister, Jaguar, Japan Tobacco International, Johnnie Walker, Johnson & Johnson, Kellogg's, Kentucky Fried Chicken, Kenwood, Khashoggi Holding, Kimberly-Clark, Kmart, Kraft, Kubota, L.L. Bean, Lady Speed Stick, Lamborghini, Levi's, LexisNexis, Lexus, Lincoln, L'Oréal, Lotus Cars, Lowe's, Lumber Liquidators, Luxgen (Taiwan auto), Macy's, MasterCard, Match.com, Mattel, Maxim, Mazda, McDonald's, Med 4 Home (respiratory), Merck, Microsoft, MillerCoors (beer), Mitsubishi, Mobile Marketer, Moccona (coffee), Mondelēz International (snacks), Monsanto, Motorola, MTM, Mundipharma International, NBC, Nedbank, Nestea, Nestlé, Netmarble (online games), Network Rail (UK), New York Life Insurance Company, Nextel, Nike, Nissan, Nobia (kitchenware), Nokia, Novant Health, Novartis, Nu Finish, Office Depot, Olay, Old Spice, Opel, Oracle, P&G, Panasonic, Penguin Random House, Pentland Group (global sports marketing), PepsiCo, Pernod Ricard, Peroni (beer), Pfizer, PGA Tour, Pond's (skin care), *Popular Science*, Porsche, Pringles, Prudential, Qudrah National Holding (Saudi investments), Quicken Loans, RBS, Red Bull, Reebok, Renault, Reverie, Revlon, Rite Aid, Roche Pharmaceuticals, Rockwell Automation, Rolls-Royce, Royal Exchange Theatre, Russian Standard Vodka, Safeway, Samsung, SAP, Saxo Bank, Scania, Schick, Schwan's (home groceries), ScoreSense (credit), Sears, Seattle Seahawks, Shell, Siemens, Silk (beverages), Smucker's, Snapfish (online photos), SnipSnap, Sony, Soreen, South African Airways, Southern Comfort, Speedo, Sprite, Standard Bank, Standard Life, Staples, Starbucks, Stoli Vodka, Stouffer's, Subway, Sunbites, Super 8 Motels, Swisscom, Symantec (cybersecurity), Tang, Target, Taste Inc., Tesco (UK/international groceries), The North Face, The Partners (brand strategy), *The Times*, Tidal (high fidelity music streams), *Time*, T-Mobile, Toyota, Travel Republic, Travelocity, Travelodge, UBS, Unilever, United Bankers' Bank, Universal, U.S. Bank, *USA Today*, Valspar, Vans, Vaseline, Verizon, Viacom, Vimeo, Visa, Vitaminwater, Volkswagen, Volvo, *Wall Street Journal*, Warner Brothers, *Washington Post*, Weight Watchers, Wells Fargo, Western Digital (hard drives), Wrigley, Wyeth, Xactly (cloud-based software), Xaxis (digital media), Xbox, Xfinity, Xoom (money transfer), Yahoo, YOU Technology (digital coupons), Zurich Insurance Group

INTERPUBLIC GROUP

Interpublic Group (IPG), based in New York City, made $7.9 billion in revenue in 2017, and employs 49,700 people in 88 agencies worldwide. IPG is represented on the Business Roundtable in the US. Thirteen of the global Giants are invested in IPG: Vanguard Group ($825 million), BlackRock ($727 million), State Street ($350 million), Goldman Sachs Group ($199.9 million), Bank of America ($172 million), Bank of NY Mellon ($116 million), Capital Group ($84.5 million) (four funds), Amundi/Crédit Agricole ($39 million), Morgan Stanley & Co. ($26.6 million), JPMorgan Chase ($12.9 million), Prudential Financial ($12.2 million), Allianz SE (PIMCO) ($9.7 million), and Barclays plc ($6.9 million).

Interpublic's CEO: **Michael I. Roth**, US **CB**- Pitney Bowes, Ryman Hospitality Properties, Chair and CEO: Interpublic Group **PE**- The MONY Group, Director: NY City Investment Fund Manager **PC**- Ad Council, Lincoln Center, Business Roundtable, The Partnership for New York City, Committee Encouraging Corporate Philanthropy, Director: Baruch College Fund **E**- City College of NY (BA), NYU (LLM), Boston University (JD) **F**- Interpublic Group compensation $17.9 million (2016), Interpublic Group shares 1.15 million—$23.2 million

Interpublic Group's Major Clients

Governments and Government-Funded Organizations
Boston 2024 Partnership (Olympics bid), California State Lottery, Copenhagen Airport, Covered California, Ministerio de Comercio Exterior y Turismo (Peru), Port of Corpus Christi, UNICEF, US Army

NGOs, Nonprofits, and Universities

Ad Council, American Red Cross, Bayer HealthCare, BJC HealthCare, Fuels America (renewables), Kaiser Foundation Health Plan/Kaiser Foundation Hospitals, National Cancer Institute, National Trauma Institute, NCAA Football, Open Space Institute, Peruvian Cancer Foundation, Pew Charitable Trusts, Society of Actuaries, St. John Ambulance, Tata (marathon runs), United for Peace and Justice, University of Alabama, University of Pittsburgh Medical Center, University of Southern Mississippi, University of Technology and Engineering (UTEC) (Peru)

Major Corporations and Brands

4C (social marketing), ABC, Acava (juices), Adelphic (advertising), ADmantX (online ads), Airbus Group, Amazon, American Standard, American Superconductor, AOL, Applebee's, Atlas Support (online rich media), Bang & Olufsen (high-end TVs), BBC America, Bertolucci (watches), Betty Crocker, Bisquick, BJ's Restaurants, BJC HealthCare, BMW, Boehringer Ingelheim (pharmaceutical), Brand Networks (social marketing), British Airways, Cadbury, Carrera Y Carrera (jewelry), Carrick Brain Centers, Chevrolet, Cisco, Clorox, Coca-Cola, Coffee-Mate, Columbia Records, Comfort Inn, comScore (media measurement), Cross Pixel (audience data), Crunch Chocolate, Daiichi Sankyo (global pharmaceuticals), Datonics (audience data), Denny's, Depomed (pharmaceuticals), Dr. Phil, Dynamic Glass, eBay, Electronic Arts (video games), Eli Lilly (pharmaceuticals), Entertainment Tonight, EQUS (golf), ESPN (Latin America), Expedia, Experian (credit reports), ExxonMobil, Eyeota (audience data), Facebook, Factual (data management), Genentech, General Mills,

General Motors, Gilead, GlaxoSmithKline, GOJO (online products), Hamburger Helper, Hot Pockets, Hyundai, IAG Cargo, iHeartRadio, IMS Health, Inside Edition, Intel, Janssen Pharmaceuticals, Johnson & Johnson, Juicy Juice, Kaiser Permanente, Kaspersky Labs (Russian software security), Kia Motors, Kohl's, Kwekkeboom (Dutch snacks), Lancel (luggage), LG Electronics, Linde North America (gas), LinkedIn, LNS Med, Luxury Finder (online sales), Machinima (online gaming), Marriott Hotels, MasterCard, McDonald's, Mercedes-Benz, Merrimack Pharmaceuticals, MGM Mirage Resort & Casino, Microsoft, Nature Valley, NBC, NCR, Nesquik, Nestlé, New York Sports Club, Nielsen, Nintendo, Noble Energy, Norse (cybersecurity), Ocean Spray, Oracle BlueKai, Ormat Nevada (geothermal), Patrón, Peer39, Pfizer, Pine-Sol, Purina, Roche, Rocket Fuel, Samsung, Sierra Trading Post (online clothing), Simple Mobile, Sony, St. Regis Hotels & Resorts, Stouffer's, Subaru, Tesco, The Insider (entertainment news), The Trade Desk, Tiffany & Co., Triad Retail Media, TubeMogul (software), Tumi (luggage), TurboTax, TVTY (online marketing), Twitter, Unilever, US Bank, VisualDNA (psychographic audience data), William Hill (online gambling), Yahoo, Zenith, Zippo

According to WPP's TNS group,

> the needs of citizens are changing rapidly. Government policies and social programs need to respond to these changing needs. And in an age of economic uncertainty there is increased pressure for accountability of expenditure—on governments, political parties and NGOs. TNS has the leading political and social research unit in the world. With over 500

dedicated social researchers in more than 40 countries, TNS Political & Social is uniquely placed to
conduct research on any social issue, in any environment. We assist decision makers in a wide range
of policy areas: health, education, social services,
environment, labor market, family policy, public
transport, road safety, justice, community integration—to name a few. We provide political parties
with strategic advice during elections and conduct social polling in many countries around the
world.[268]

On a webpage entitled "Understanding and Influencing
Washington," WPP's Glover Park Group (GPR) in Washington,
DC, reports:

No other firm is as effective at achieving winning
policy outcomes for its clients. We know the issues
inside and out. We have decades of experience in
government, from the halls of Congress to the upper
echelons of Democratic and Republican administrations. We fundamentally understand today's
decision-makers and what drives them.... GPG's
Government Affairs group helps clients develop
and execute legislative and regulatory strategies to
advance their goals in Washington at every level
and in every branch and agency of government.[269]

Without telling us the brands they promote, WPP's Sudler
and Hennessey claim on their website they have been proudly
pushing drugs for 75 years.[270]

Corporate media consolidation has provided the opportunity for PRP firms to emerge as orchestrators of global information and news. Corporate media news is taking an increasingly dependent, secondary position to PRP firms and government press events. The world today faces an ideological PRP media empire so powerful and complex that truth is mostly absent or reported in disconnected segments with little historical context. The result is managed news by government and PRP firms—often interlocked—including both the release of specific stories intended to build public support as well as the deliberate non-coverage of news stories that may undermine corporate capitalist goals.

PRP firms provide a variety of services to major corporations and institutions throughout the world. While brand enhancement and sales are undoubtedly among the key services, PRP companies offer clients a much wider range of options as well, including research and crisis management for corporations and governments, public information campaign control, web design and promotions, and corporate media placement. WPP's Hill & Knowlton proudly brag on their website that they service 50 percent of the Fortune Global 500 companies from their offices in 40 countries.[271] WPP's Hill & Knowlton and Omnicom's FleishmanHillard have been the key PRP firms working with Monsanto to protect its brand Roundup, which contains the herbicide glyphosate, recently declared "probably carcinogenic" by the World Health Organization. Roundup is the most widely used herbicide in the world, being sold in more than 130 countries. As countries begin to restrict its use, PRP firms gear up in full force to protect Monsanto's profits.[272]

WPP's Hill & Knowlton are also well known for their early involvement with the Council for Tobacco Research (CTR), originally set up in 1954 to counter *Reader's Digest*'s 1952 report linking tobacco smoking to cancer. CTR was described by the *Wall Street Journal* in 1993 as one of the "longest running misinformation campaigns in US business history."[273]

It was WPP's Burson-Marsteller that created the front group Global Climate Coalition (GCC) in 1989, a project which lasted until 2001.[274] The GCC was set up to help the oil and auto industries downplay the dangers of global warming. Initial members of the coalition included Amoco, American Petroleum Institute, Chevron, Chrysler, Exxon, Ford, General Motors, Shell, and Texaco. In addition, Burson-Marsteller created the front group Californians for Realistic Vehicle Standards in 1998 to oppose restrictions on car emissions.[275] PRP firms continue to this day to offer services to, or the creation of, front groups seeking to block public safety laws or progressive legislation that might interfere with corporate profits.

Global Counsel, a WPP advisory firm, provides political consultation to investors regarding risk, regulations, and policymaking in various regions throughout the world. In a recent report, Global Counsel described the results of the World Trade Organization's tenth meeting in Nairobi, Kenya, in December 2015: WTO agreements in 2015 were described as the "most significant package of reforms in trade of agricultural goods ever agreed." Declines in tariffs and expansion of free trade were key elements of the agreements.[276] In another report on their website, Global Counsel offers detailed information on private equity investment in Africa.

GOVERNMENT PRP CONTRACTING

The PRP industry holds significant power. The ease with which the American population accepted the invasion of Iraq was the outcome of a concerted effort involving the government, DoD contractors, PRP firms, and the transnational corporate media. Public relations and propaganda were pivotal in selling the 2003 Iraq War.[277] These institutions are the instigators and main beneficiaries of a permanent war on terror. Through connections to the PRP industry, important, well-funded segments of the power elite and the US national security state have the resources to articulate their propaganda repeatedly to the American people and the world, to the point that these messages become self-evident truths and conventional wisdom. Never mentioned in the lead-up to war is the fact that it will offer the financial Giants a profitable use of excess capital.

From 2007 to 2015 the federal government of the United States spent more than $4 billion for PRP services.[278] The United States employs 3,092 public relations officers in 139 agencies. An additional $2.2 billion goes to outside firms to perform PRP, polling, research, and market consulting.[279] A few of the top global PRP firms that reaped tens of millions of US dollars in 2014 alone include Laughlin Marinaccio & Owens ($87.98 million),[280] WPP's Young & Rubicam ($57.5 million), WPP's Ogilvy Public Relations Worldwide ($47.93 million), Omnicom Group's FleishmanHillard ($42.4 million), and Gallup ($42 million). WPP's Burson-Marsteller won a $4.6 million contract with the US Department of Homeland Security in 2005 to develop public awareness and education for a major emergency, disaster, or terrorist attack in Washington, DC.[281]

As Johan Carlisle writes in *CovertAction Quarterly*: "... Former CIA official Robert T. Crowley, the Agency's long-time liaison with corporations," acknowledged that "Hill & Knowlton's overseas offices ... were perfect 'cover' for the ever-expanding CIA. Unlike other cover jobs, being a public relations specialist did not require technical training for CIA officers."[282] Furthermore, the CIA, Crowley admitted, used its Hill & Knowlton connections to "put out press releases and make media contacts to further its positions... Hill & Knowlton employees at the small Washington office and elsewhere distributed this material through CIA assets working in the United States news media."[283]

The CIA invests in a PRP firm that monitors social media as part of the CIA's effort to access more "open source intelligence." The firm is known as Visible Technologies and has offices in New York City, Seattle, and Boston. A year after Visible Technologies was created in 2005 it developed a partnership with WPP, thereby linking a CIA PRP firm directly into the WPP network. Visible Technologies helps the CIA monitor information that gets overlooked in the massive number of online activities. The company is keeping track of influential internet posters and how foreigners view various news events. Although the CIA gathers information that is legally open for anyone to view, it is possible for the CIA to use the information for illegal political purposes, as with unauthorized domestic investigations into public figures. Visible Technologies can monitor more than half a million sites every day. These sites include any open social websites, such as Twitter or Flickr. Visible Technologies is already working for companies such as Microsoft and Verizon, keeping track of positive and negative feedback on their products.[284]

Omnicom Group's PRP firm Ketchum recently was hired by the Honduran government to whitewash its dismal human rights record after the US-backed military coup in 2009. Ketchum has been providing crisis management PRP services to Honduras since the assassination of renowned human rights movement leader Berta Cáceres. Ketchum also runs two front groups promoting the safety of GMOs paid for by Monsanto, DuPont, and other biotech firms.[285]

The consolidation of global capitalism and the emerging formation of an active Global Power Elite inside the Transnational Capitalist Class contributes to a growing dependence for PRP services. As capital consolidates there is an increasing need for new investment opportunities for the concentrated surplus capital, feeding the permanent need for continued growth and expansion. PRP firms provide market stimulation for growing sales through the creation of psychological demands for various goods among the world's masses. Even the 3.5 billion people living on less than $3 per day are encouraged to spend on feel-good products like Coke and cigarettes.

Corporate media consolidation has provided the opportunity for PRP firms to emerge as orchestrators of global information and news. The world today faces a PRP–military–industrial media empire so powerful and complex that, in the majority of news venues, basic truths about world events are concealed, skewed, or simply not reported at all. The result is ideological news managed by government and PRP firms, often interlocked; together, they release specific stories intended to build public support, and they deliberately deny coverage for news stories that may undermine capitalist goals.

PRP Firms in Service to the Global Power Elite

PRP firms and the major corporate media know that the core agenda for the global empire and the power elite is the protection of capital growth, insurance of debt collection, and the elimination of barriers and restrictions to the free movement of capital. Public relations propaganda firms and the transnational media play a vital role in the continuation of the Global Power Elite capitalist empire. The transnational media and the PRP industry are highly concentrated and fully global. Their primary goal is the promotion of capital growth through the hegemonic psychological control of human desires, emotions, beliefs, and values. PRP firms do this by manipulating the feelings and cognitions of human beings worldwide. With $35 billion in annual revenue, the big three PRP firms are increasingly important to the Global Power Elite and the Transnational Capitalist Class. The global Giants are deeply invested in both the PRP companies and the major corporate news companies. PRP firms are the ideological engine of capitalism both because of their massive influence on corporate media and their increasing embeddedness within government propaganda, up to and including psychological operations in support of permanent war.

Perhaps democracy movements can offer us some hope for the future. Awareness of the dark side of PRP and its unrestricted power to warp minds is an important first step toward freeing the people from the rule of Giants. Quebec was one of the first states to ban commercial advertising to children under the age of 13.[286] Three generations of people in Cuba have grown up without product advertising in their lives. A group of graduate students from the University of Havana simply laughed when I asked them six years ago if they ever wanted a "Happy Meal." It seemed absurd to them to even consider the idea. We, too, need to understand the absurdity of the PRP industry and move to restrict it from our lives, our cultures, and our world.

CHAPTER 7

FACING THE JUGGERNAUT
DEMOCRACY MOVEMENTS
AND RESISTANCE

According to a *Guardian* newspaper headline on December 26, 2017:"World's Richest 500 See Their Wealth Increase by $1tn This Year."[287]

In 2017 the Global Power Elites steered more than one trillion dollars into the personal coffers of the world's richest 500 people. Jeff Bezos (CEO of Amazon, and owner of the *Washington Post*) increased his net worth to $99.6 billion, making him the richest person in the world. Despite efforts by some of the richest, like Bill and Melinda Gates (of Microsoft), to increase philanthropic giving, wealth continues to concentrate under the current policies and practices of the Global Power Elite. The richest 1 percent increased their total wealth by 42.5 percent in 2008, and 50.1 percent in 2017.

In 2017 2.3 million new millionaires were created, bringing the total number of millionaires around the globe to more than 36 million. These millionaires represent 0.7 percent of the world's population controlling more than 47 percent of global wealth. At the same time, the world's bottom 70 percent only control 2.7 percent of the total wealth.[288]

As *The World Inequality Report 2018* states,

> Economic inequality is widespread and to some
> extent inevitable. It is our belief, however, that if
> rising inequality is not properly monitored and
> addressed, it can lead to various sorts of political,
> economic, and social catastrophes.... Economic
> inequality is largely driven by the unequal own-
> ership of capital, which can be either privately or
> publicly owned. We show that since 1980, very large
> transfers of public to private wealth occurred in
> nearly all countries, whether rich or emerging....
> Tackling global income and wealth inequality
> requires important shifts in national and global
> tax policies. Educational policies, corporate gov-
> ernance, and wage-setting policies need to be
> reassessed in many countries.[289]

Pope Francis, in a message to the World Economic Forum in
January 2014, stressed the importance

> the various political and economic sectors have
> in promoting an inclusive approach which takes
> into consideration the dignity of every human
> person and the common good. I am referring to
> a concern that ought to shape every political and
> economic decision, but which at times seems to be
> little more than an afterthought. Those working in
> these sectors have a precise responsibility towards
> others, particularly those who are most frail, weak
> and vulnerable. It is intolerable that thousands of

people continue to die every day from hunger, even
though substantial quantities of food are available,
and often simply wasted. Likewise, we cannot but
be moved by the many refugees seeking minimally
dignified living conditions, who not only fail to find
hospitality, but often, tragically, perish in moving
from place to place.[290]

There can be no doubt that continued concentration of
wealth cannot be economically sustained. Extreme inequality
and massive repression will only bring resistance and rebellion
by the world's masses. The danger is that the Global Power Elite
will fail to recognize the inevitability of economic and/or environmental collapse before making the necessary adjustments
to prevent millions of deaths and massive civil unrest. Without
significant corrective adjustments by the Global Power Elite,
mass social movements and rebellions, coupled with environmental collapse, will inevitably lead to global chaos and war.

The Global Power Elite identified in this book are the key
stewards of a major part of the world's financial wealth. This
wealth is being used for the economic colonialization and
privatization of the public commons in complete disregard
for human rights. Privatized wealth is able to buy ideologies,
governments, law enforcement, covert activities, wars—and,
ultimately, human beings. The direction that we are headed in is
toward the complete destruction of governmental democracies,
personal freedoms, privacy, and the economic survival of billions of humans around the world.

On October 11, 2011, 400 Occupy Wall Street protestors made
house calls on the Upper East Side in New York City. Dubbed
the "Millionaires March," the protester rang the doorbells at

several Global Power Elite homes. Included among the home visits were Rupert Murdoch (billionaire media mogul), Jamie Dimon (CEO of JPMorgan Chase), David Koch (billionaire industrialist), Howard Milstein (billionaire New York real estate developer), and John Paulson (billionaire hedge fund manager).[291] A statement from Occupy Wall Street declared, "We know where and how you live. We've crossed into your privileged space to let you know we find your wealth and power offensive."[292]

Ongoing resistance to neoliberal austerity policies, concentrations of wealth and power, police state abuses, and ideological propaganda are occurring worldwide. Movements of resistance include the Bolivarian Continental Movement in Latin and South America, Arab Spring protests in North Africa, Black Lives Matter in the United States, Indignant Citizens Movement ("Aganaktismenoi") in Greece, Indignados Movement (anti-austerity) in Spain, Anti-Globalization Movement in Seattle and worldwide, Zapatista Movement in Mexico, Naxalite Resistance in India, and labor rights movements in China. What these movements have in common is populistic resistance to declining economic opportunities mainly for young people and in many cases strong collective actions in response to state/police violence, economic frustrations, and ideological manipulations. Even the Brexit electoral results in Great Britain were rooted in mass dissatisfaction with declining economic opportunities for the 99 percent.

University of California, Berkeley, Public Policy Professor Robert Reich wrote in a 2011 article "Why We Must Occupy Democracy" that the disparity between the wealthy 1 percent and the unmoneyed 99 percent leads to increasing violence by the state toward Occupy demonstrators. Reich notes that the demonstrators are "assaulted, clubbed, dragged, [and] pepper-sprayed" when attempting to exercise their rights to free speech and assembly, and he adds, "If there's a single core message to the Occupy movement it's that the increasing concentration of income and wealth at the top endangers our democracy. With money comes political power." Reich believes that if democracy is to be saved as we witness even greater inequality in the distribution of wealth, Americans will have to get out there and make their voices heard. Reich explains that it is at exactly the times when one's voice is being muffled that one must speak loudest.[293]

Mass social movements like Occupy Wall Street will continue to emerge. The next Occupy/resistance movement will already have the 99 percent vs. 1 percent consciousness. Police state repression may delay the inevitable, but wealth concentration is unsustainable. Environmental and/or economic collapse under current conditions is inevitable.

The real question is, Will the Global Power Elites take action to restructure capital concentration before social movements topple their capitalist regime with massive civil unrest, noncooperation, and eventually violence? Or can nonviolent social movements stimulate a consciousness of needed change within the Global Power Elite that can lead to corrective actions and the redistribution of wealth to meet the common human needs of the world's people? These are fundamental questions for us all. Will our grandchildren and their grandchildren have a livable planet or will they witness the end of humankind?

The Davos crowd and the Global Power Elite are certainly aware of these concerns. The opening statement from the World Economic Forum's 2016–2017 annual report reads, "We are living at a time of unprecedented anxiety and polarization."[294]

The World Economic Forum proudly recognizes the importance of changing "mindsets" among their public–private global stakeholders for improved conditions with market connectivity and improved infrastructures. However, while the Davos crowd continues to applaud themselves, inequality expands and wealth consolidates, and the mindset for social change at Davos seems little more than wishful rhetoric.

It falls to the social movements in the world to help accelerate a change of mindset among the Global Power Elite. As these powerful and disruptive social movements continue to evolve, it becomes increasingly important for them to have a shared macro-understanding of why inequality, poverty, austerity, and concentrated wealth continues to occur, and who makes the decisions in continuation of this Juggernaut. These are timeless questions, and much has already been done to address the needed outcomes. We hope the specifics of this book contribute to social movement successes for radical deep-rooted change. The change that needs to come to insure trickle-down becomes a river that is real and adequate for all human needs is not billionaire philanthropy, where the power elite handpick their beneficiaries, but rather the restructuring of capitalism itself.

Seventy years ago, after World War II ended, people throughout the world were motivated to find ways to permanently prevent such terrible bloodshed from ever again taking place. As the United Nations was forming, a Nuclear Commission on the moral principles necessary for sustainable peace, made up of eighteen nations, met at Hunter College in New York City in 1946. They began what two years later would become the Universal Declaration of Human Rights, approved unanimously by the United Nations in December 1948. Eventually many nations sent representatives to work on the document, but the main stewards of the process were Carlos Romulo, journalist and Pulitzer Prize–winner from the Philippines, international law professor John Humphrey from Canada, women's rights activist Hansa Mehta of India, Chilean human rights activist Hernán Santa Cruz, Peng-chun Chang, Chinese philosopher, diplomat, and playwright, Nobel Peace Prize laureate René Cassin from France, Charles Malik, existentialist philosopher of Lebanon, and Eleanor Roosevelt, former first lady in the United States. They successfully, after two years of long hours, many debates, and discussions, brought forward a moral document which became a statement of principles for the natural human rights of all people in the world.[295]

The Universal Declaration of Human Rights is a document that social movements can easily adopt as a statement of moral principles for actions of resistance to wealth concentration and global inequality. It is equally important as a document of principles for the Global Power Elite to accept as a guide for corrective actions needed in the world today.

We think that the Universal Declaration of Human Rights is so important today that we are republishing it here in its entirety:

UNIVERSAL DECLARATION OF HUMAN RIGHTS

Preamble

Whereas recognition of the inherent dignity and of the equal and inalienable rights of all members of the human family is the foundation of freedom, justice and peace in the world,

Whereas disregard and contempt for human rights have resulted in barbarous acts which have outraged the conscience of mankind, and the advent of a world in which human beings shall enjoy freedom of speech and belief and freedom from fear and want has been proclaimed as the highest aspiration of the common people,

Whereas it is essential, if man[296] is not to be compelled to have recourse, as a last resort, to rebellion against tyranny and oppression, that human rights should be protected by the rule of law,

Whereas it is essential to promote the development of friendly relations between nations,

Whereas the peoples of the United Nations have in the Charter reaffirmed their faith in fundamental human rights, in the dignity and worth of the human person and in the equal rights of men and women and have determined to promote social progress and better standards of life in larger freedom,

Whereas Member States have pledged themselves to achieve, in co-operation with the United Nations, the promotion of universal respect for and observance of human rights and fundamental freedoms,

Whereas a common understanding of these rights and freedoms is of the greatest importance for the full realization of this pledge,

Now, therefore, The General Assembly proclaims this Universal Declaration of Human Rights as a common standard of achievement for all peoples and all nations, to the end that every individual and every organ of society, keeping this Declaration constantly in mind, shall strive by teaching and education to promote respect for these rights and freedoms and by progressive measures, national and international, to secure their universal and effective recognition and observance, both among the peoples of Member States themselves and among the peoples of territories under their jurisdiction.

Article 1
All human beings are born free and equal in dignity and rights. They are endowed with reason and conscience and should act towards one another in a spirit of brotherhood.

Article 2
Everyone is entitled to all the rights and freedoms set forth in this Declaration, without distinction of any kind, such as race, colour, sex, language, religion, political or other opinion, national or social origin, property, birth or other status. Furthermore, no distinction shall be made on the basis of the political, jurisdictional or international status of the country or territory to which a person belongs, whether it be independent, trust, non-self-governing or under any other limitation of sovereignty.

Article 3
Everyone has the right to life, liberty and security of person.

Article 4
No one shall be held in slavery or servitude; slavery and the slave trade shall be prohibited in all their forms.

Article 5
No one shall be subjected to torture or to cruel, inhuman or degrading treatment or punishment.

Article 6
Everyone has the right to recognition everywhere as a person before the law.

Article 7
All are equal before the law and are entitled without any discrimination to equal protection of the law. All are entitled to equal protection against any discrimination in violation of this Declaration and against any incitement to such discrimination.

Article 8
Everyone has the right to an effective remedy by the competent national tribunals for acts violating the fundamental rights granted him by the constitution or by law.

Article 9
No one shall be subjected to arbitrary arrest, detention or exile.

Article 10
Everyone is entitled in full equality to a fair and public hearing by an independent and impartial tribunal, in the determination of his rights and obligations and of any criminal charge against him.

Article 11
1. Everyone charged with a penal offence has the right to be presumed innocent until proved guilty according to law in a public trial at which he has had all the guarantees necessary for his defence.
2. No one shall be held guilty of any penal offence on account of any act or omission which did not constitute a penal offence, under national or international law, at the time when it was committed. Nor shall a heavier penalty be imposed than the one that was applicable at the time the penal offence was committed.

Article 12
No one shall be subjected to arbitrary interference with his privacy, family, home or correspondence, nor to attacks upon his honour and reputation. Everyone has the right to the protection of the law against such interference or attacks.

Article 13
1. Everyone has the right to freedom of movement and residence within the borders of each state.
2. Everyone has the right to leave any country, including his own, and to return to his country.

Article 14
1. Everyone has the right to seek and to enjoy in other countries asylum from persecution.
2. This right may not be invoked in the case of prosecutions genuinely arising from non-political crimes or from acts contrary to the purposes and principles of the United Nations.

Article 15
1. Everyone has the right to a nationality.
2. No one shall be arbitrarily deprived of his nationality nor be denied the right to change his nationality.

Article 16
1. Men and women of full age, without any limitation due to race, nationality or religion, have the right to marry and to found a family. They are entitled to equal rights as to marriage, during marriage and at its dissolution.
2. Marriage shall be entered into only with the free and full consent of the intending spouses.
3. The family is the natural and fundamental group unit of society and is entitled to protection by society and the State.

Article 17

1. Everyone has the right to own property alone as well as in association with others.

2. No one shall be arbitrarily deprived of his property.

Article 18

Everyone has the right to freedom of thought, conscience and religion; this right includes freedom to change his religion or belief, and freedom, either alone or in community with others and in public or private, to manifest his religion or belief in teaching, practice, worship and observance.

Article 19

Everyone has the right to freedom of opinion and expression; this right includes freedom to hold opinions without interference and to seek, receive and impart information and ideas through any media and regardless of frontiers.

Article 20

1. Everyone has the right to freedom of peaceful assembly and association.

2. No one may be compelled to belong to an association.

Article 21

1. Everyone has the right to take part in the government of his country, directly or through freely chosen representatives.

2. Everyone has the right of equal access to public service in his country.

3. The will of the people shall be the basis of the authority of government; this will shall be expressed in periodic and genuine elections which shall be by universal and equal suffrage and shall be held by secret vote or by equivalent free voting procedures.

Article 22

Everyone, as a member of society, has the right to social security and is entitled to realization, through national effort and international co-operation and in accordance with the organization and resources of each State, of the economic, social and cultural rights indispensable for his dignity and the free development of his personality.

Article 23

1. Everyone has the right to work, to free choice of employment, to just and favourable conditions of work and to protection against unemployment.

2. Everyone, without any discrimination, has the right to equal pay for equal work.

3. Everyone who works has the right to just and favourable remuneration ensuring for himself and his family an existence worthy of human dignity, and supplemented, if necessary, by other means of social protection.

4. Everyone has the right to form and to join trade unions for the protection of his interests.

Article 24
Everyone has the right to rest and leisure, including reasonable limitation of working hours and periodic holidays with pay.

Article 25
1. Everyone has the right to a standard of living adequate for the health and well-being of himself and of his family, including food, clothing, housing and medical care and necessary social services, and the right to security in the event of unemployment, sickness, disability, widowhood, old age or other lack of livelihood in circumstances beyond his control.
2. Motherhood and childhood are entitled to special care and assistance. All children, whether born in or out of wedlock, shall enjoy the same social protection.

Article 26
1. Everyone has the right to education. Education shall be free, at least in the elementary and fundamental stages. Elementary education shall be compulsory. Technical and professional education shall be made generally available and higher education shall be equally accessible to all on the basis of merit.
2. Education shall be directed to the full development of the human personality and to the strengthening of respect for human rights and fundamental freedoms. It shall promote understanding,

tolerance and friendship among all nations, racial or religious groups, and shall further the activities of the United Nations for the maintenance of peace. 3. Parents have a prior right to choose the kind of education that shall be given to their children.

Article 27
1. Everyone has the right freely to participate in the cultural life of the community, to enjoy the arts and to share in scientific advancement and its benefits.
2. Everyone has the right to the protection of the moral and material interests resulting from any scientific, literary or artistic production of which he is the author.

Article 28
Everyone is entitled to a social and international order in which the rights and freedoms set forth in this Declaration can be fully realized.

Article 29
1. Everyone has duties to the community in which alone the free and full development of his personality is possible.
2. In the exercise of his rights and freedoms, everyone shall be subject only to such limitations as are determined by law solely for the purpose of securing due recognition and respect for the rights and freedoms of others and of meeting the just requirements of morality, public order and the general welfare in a democratic society.

3. These rights and freedoms may in no case be exercised contrary to the purposes and principles of the United Nations.

Article 30
Nothing in this Declaration may be interpreted as implying for any State, group or person any right to engage in any activity or to perform any act aimed at the destruction of any of the rights and freedoms set forth herein.

Hundred and eighty-third plenary meeting, Resolution 217(A)(III) of the United Nations General Assembly,
December 10, 1948[297]

The Universal Declaration of Human Rights is a moral code and was deliberately not passed as international law or a treaty, allowing for civil society and social movements to use it as a foundational philosophy for activism, resistance, and social change.

Robert Reich's 2015 book *Saving Capitalism* offers some appropriate ending remarks for this book on the Giants and the Global Power Elite:

New Rules: "we need not be victims of the impersonal 'market forces' over which we have no control. The market is a human creation. It is based on rules that humans devise. The central question is who shapes those rules and for what purpose. Over the last three decades the rules have been shaped by large corporations, Wall Street, and very wealthy individuals in order to channel a large portion of the nation's total income and wealth to themselves.... The vast majority of the nation's citizens do have the power to alter the rule of the market to meet their needs. But to do so they must understand what is happening and where their interests lie, and they must join together."[298]

These remarks are not only appropriate for the United States, but are important for the entire world. The Global Power Elite manage, facilitate, and protect concentrated capital worldwide. This consolidation of wealth is the primary cause of world poverty, starvation, malnutrition, wars, and mass human suffering. Organizing resistance and challenging the Global Power Elite is the necessary agenda for democracy movements in all nations now and in the near future. Addressing top-down economic controls, monopolistic power, and the specifics of the Global Power Elite's activities will require challenging mobilizations in numerous regions. Using the Universal Declaration of Human Rights as a moral base will offer a united thread of consciousness seeking human betterment. Humankind deserves nothing less.

A LETTER TO THE GLOBAL POWER ELITE

Dear Global Power Elite,

We list some 389 of you by name in this book. You should be honored and proud of your station in the global power structure. Being listed in this volume means you are a key part of managing, supporting, and protecting a major portion of the world's wealth. You are personally wealthy, or certainly well off, highly educated, and have influence in multiple circles with access to vast financial resources and systems of power. Your engagement on the board of directors of one of the seventeen trillion-dollar money management firms, and/or your membership in such nongovernmental transnational policy planning groups as the Group of Thirty, Trilateral Commission, and Atlantic Council, makes you an active and influential participant in serving the interests of the wealthy 1 percent Transnational Capitalist Class.

There are many thousands of perhaps richer and even more individually powerful people in the world. We think that the 389 of you are collectively the financial and policy core of global capitalism and have the power, using your networks, to save the world from deadly inequality and pending economic or environmental chaos.

We don't have a prescription for changing the world. However, we think that addressing the world's needs in the framework of the Universal Declaration of Human Rights is a good place to start. We absolutely believe that continued capital concentration and neoliberal austerity policies only bring greater human misery to the vast majority of people on earth. Tens of thousands of people die daily from malnutrition or easily curable diseases. Wars, covert actions, externally-induced regime changes, propaganda media, and technological surveillance, all in the name of protecting the freedom to do business, is hurting humankind and will be stopped. You can easily begin that process by instituting a simple guiding principle of thinking of the future of your grandchildren and their grandchildren when making decisions on the use of world capital resources.

It is no longer acceptable for you to believe that you can manage capitalism to grow its way out of the gross inequalities we all now face. The environment cannot accept more pollution and waste, and civil unrest is everywhere inevitable at some point. Humanity needs you to step up and insure that trickle-down becomes a river of resources that reaches every child, every family, and all human beings. We urge you to use your power and make the needed changes for humanity's survival.

Sincerely,

Peter M. Phillips, Robin Anderson, Adam Armstrong, Philip Beard, Byron Belitsos, Khalil Bendib, Marty Bennett, Dennis Bernstein, Joseph Oliver Boyd-Barrett, Ben Boyington, Jacques Brodeur, Carol Brouillet, Kenn Burrows, Noel Byrne, Ernesto Carmona, Kathy Charmaz, Pao-yu Ching, Vesta Copestakes, Michael Costello, Christopher R. Cox, Geoff Davidian, James Dean, Michael Diamond, C. Peter Dougherty, Kristine S. Drawsky, Lotus Fong, Bruce Gagnon, Ann Garrison, Alex Glaros, Colin Godwin, Diana Grant, David Ray Griffin, Robert

Hackett, Debora Hammond, David Hartsough, Janet Hess, Nolan Higdon, Kevin Howley, Mickey Huff, Dahr Jamail, Paul Kaplan, Earl Katz, Bob Klose, VaLinda Kyrias, Pierre Labossiere, Susan Lamont, Elaine Leeder, Mary M. Lia, Cassandra Lista, Peter Ludes, Rick Luttmann, Wayne Madsen, Abby Martin, Concha Mateos, Miles Mendenhall, Andy Merrifield, Ralph Metzner, Mark Crispin Miller, Susan Moulton, Therese Mughannam, Mary Norman, Tim Ogburn, Jennie Orvino, Michael Parenti, Kevin Pena, Rosemary Powers, Susan Rahman, Paul Rea, Napoleon Reyes, William I. Robinson, Susan Rogers, Andy Lee Roth, David Rovics, Linda Sartor, T.M. Scruggs, Jon D. Shefner, Will Shonbrun, Laurence H. Shoup, William J. Simon, Gar Smith, Kimberly Barbosa Soeiro, Jordan Steger, Michael Sukhov, Chelsea Turner, Francisco Vázquez, Elaine Wellin, Laura Wells, Derrick West, Rob Williams, Chingling Wo, and Nicole Wolfe

ACKNOWLEDGMENTS

I want to first acknowledge Mary M. Lia, my wife and partner, who has unrelentingly supported me in the multiyear effort toward the completion of this book. The staff and board of Project Censored have been long-term supporters of my research on global elites. Thank you to Mickey Huff and Andy Roth for including versions of some of the chapters of *Giants* in earlier *Censored* yearbooks. A huge thank you to University of California sociologist Michael I. Robinson for his great introduction to this book.

My twenty years with Project Censored and Media Freedom Foundation (MFF) has been a training ground toward preparing to write *Giants*. The Project Censored Media Freedom Foundation board of directors has been continuously encouraging in this research. Thank you, MFF board members Nicholas Baham III, Ken Boyington, Kenn Burrows, Allison Butler, Mary Cardaras, Nolan Higdon, Mickey Huff, Chris Oscar, Susan Rahman, Andy Lee Roth, T. M. Scruggs, and Elaine Wellin. Thank you also to hundreds of faculty members and students for years of challenging global corporate media research leading to an understanding of how elite ideological hegemony works in the world today.

The Green Oaks Men's Group has been my personal weekly

support network for twenty-four years. Thank you, Bill Simon, Derrick West, Bob Klose, Peter Tracy, Noel Byrne, and Colin Godwin for regular advice and suggestions toward *Giants*. Other close friends have long advised me on this effort, including Tim Ogburn, Geoff Davidian, Diana Grant, Michael Sukhov, Will Shonbrun, and Rick Luttman. Appreciation also goes to Ernesto Carmona, chief correspondent of TeleSur Chile, for his Spanish translation of portions of this work and for years of translating the annual *Censored News*. Thank you also to the ninety friends and associates who cosigned the postscript letter to the Global Power Elite at the end of this book.

Undergraduate Sonoma State University (SSU) students participated in research for this book for the past several years. Thank you to Jordan Steger for significant research and editing of the databases and for creating the charts. Thank you to Kimberly Soeiro and Brady Osborne for writing portions of earlier chapters appearing in *Censored 2013* and *2014* that helped form sections in this volume. SSU student researchers for chapter 5 were Ray McClintock, Melissa Carneiro, and Jacob Crabtree. SSU student research assistants for chapter 6 included Ratonya Coffee, Robert Ramirez, Mary Schafer, and Nicole Tranchina. Research on the Global Power Elite biographies was conducted by SSU students Robert Carrillo, Kristy Dale, Sanam Lodhi, Damont Partida, and Jordan Steger during the spring of 2017. SSU researcher Brianna Earls assisted with publicity planning during the summer of 2018. Research done over ten years ago at SSU on power elites seeking global dominance after 9/11 was assisted by Bridget Thornton, Lew Brown, and Celeste Volger, and contributed to our understanding of the Global Power Elites today.

I especially appreciate support from Sonoma State University

School of Social Science, including John Wingard, dean of social science, Karen Leitsch, administrative manager, Julie Woods, operations analyst, and Viri Ruiz, operations coordinator.

The sociology department faculty and staff provide ongoing consultation and advice. Thank you, James Dean, department chair, and faculty members Kathy Charmez, Cindy Sterns, Melinda Milligan, Debora Paterniti, Juan Salinas, Suzel-Bozada-Deas, Roxanne Ezzet, Nicole Wolfe, Elaine Wellin, Jerry Krause, James Preston, Manisha Salinas, and Elaine Leeder. Sociology department staff Emily Kyle and Monique Morovat have been most helpful.

Thank you to the twenty scholars/journalists who read our early drafts, provided feedback, and wrote positive statements for the cover, including Noam Chomsky, Leslie Sklair, Abby Martin, William Carroll, Laurence H. Shoup, Mark Crispin Miller, Mickey Huff, Robin Anderson, Andy Lee Roth, Deepa Kumar, Marc Pilisuk, Michael Parenti, Robert Hackett, Loan K. Lee, David Cobb, Susan Rahman, Donna Brasset, Dennis Bernstein, Peter Ludes, and Rob Williams.

Great thanks to Seven Stories Press for their hard work in editing and arranging for the publication of *Giants: The Global Power Elite*. A special acknowledgement to publisher Dan Simon, whose belief in the importance of this work was unwavering. Thank you to Lauren Hooker, editor; Stewart Cauley, art director; Jon Gilbert, operations director; Noah Kumin, marketing; and Allison Paller and Ruth Weiner, publicists. We want to offer a high note of praise to copy editor Michael Tencer for his detailed and thorough corrections of the writings and data within *Giants*.

We must think of the future of the world in the context of our grandchildren and their grandchildren. My work is motivated by my love/concern for my own grandchildren, Katelyn Phillips, age thirteen, and Jake Phillips, age nine, who are coming of age in a world with serious problems. We are hopeful that by identifying the trillion-dollar Giants and their Global Power Elite managers, facilitators, defenders, and ideologists by name and network we will bring an awareness of inequality to both the 1 percent and the 99 percent that will encourage positive change in the world. It will require 100 percent cooperation and goodwill from activists everywhere. Let's expand this process by any and all means.

Thank you all,
Peter Phillips

NOTES

1. Evan Halper, "Climate Scientists See Alarming New Threat to California," *Los Angeles Times*, December 5, 2017, p. A1.

2. Portions of this chapter were published as Peter Phillips and Kimberly Soeiro, "The Global 1 Percent Ruling Class Exposed," in *Censored 2013: Dispatches from the Media Revolution*, eds. Mickey Huff and Andy Lee Roth with Project Censored (New York: Seven Stories Press, 2012), 235–58.

3. "62 People Own the Same as Half the World, Reveals Oxfam Davos Report," Oxfam International, January 18, 2016, https://oxf.am/2FKdKZR; and "Just 8 Men Own Same Wealth as Half the World," Oxfam International, January 16, 2017, https://oxf.am/2F-HHpCR.

4. Luisa Kroll and Kerry A. Dolan, "Forbes 2017 Billionaires List: Meet the Richest People on the Planet," *Forbes*, March 20, 2017, https://www.forbes.com/sites/kerry-adolan/2017/03/20/forbes-2017-billionaires-list-meet-the-richest-people-on-the-planet/#4a1fbf8f62ff.

5. See G. William Domhoff, *Who Rules America? The Triumph of the Corporate Rich*, 7th ed. (New York: McGraw Hill, 2014); and Peter Phillips, "A Relative Advantage: Sociology of the San Francisco Bohemian Club," Sonoma State University, 1994, https://library.sonoma.edu/specialcollections/bohemianclub/.

6. Early studies by Charles Beard, published as *An Economic Interpretation of the Constitution of the United States* (1913), established that economic elites formulated the US Constitution to serve their own special interests. Henry Klein, in a 1921 book entitled *Dynastic America and Those Who Own It*, argued that wealth in America had power never before known in the world and was centered in the top 2 percent of the population, which owned some 60 percent of the country. In 1937 Ferdinand Lundberg published *America's 60 Families*, which documented intermarrying, self-perpetuating families, for whom government was the "indispensable hand-maiden of private wealth." In 1945, C. Wright Mills determined that nine out of ten business elites from 1700 to 1729 came from well-to-do families ("The American Business Elite: A Collective Portrait," *Journal of Economic History 5* (December 1945), 20–44).

7   See Robert A. Brady, *Business as a System of Power* (New York: Columbia University Press, 1943); and Val Burris, "Elite Policy-Planning Networks in the United States," *Research in Politics and Society, Vol. 4: The Political Consequences of Social Networks*, eds. Gwen Moore and J. Allen Whitt (Greenwich, CT: JAI Press, 1992), 111–34, http://pages.uoregon.edu/vburris/policy.pdf.

8   C. Wright Mills, *The Power Elite* (New York: Oxford University Press, 1956).

9   See Michael Soref, "Social Class and a Division of Labor within the Corporate Elite," *Sociological Quarterly* 17 (Summer 1976), 360–68, and two works by Michael Useem: "The Social Organization of the American Business Elite and Participation of Corporation Directors in the Governance of American Institutions," *American Sociological Review* 44 (August 1979), 553–72, and *The Inner Circle* (New York: Oxford University Press, 1984).

10 Mills, *The Power Elite*, 284.

11 Thomas Koenig and Robert Gogel, "Interlocking Corporate Directorships as a Social Network," *American Journal of Economics and Sociology* 40 (January 1981), 37–50; and Peter Phillips, "The 1934–35 Red Threat and the Passage of the National Labor Relations Act," *Critical Sociology* 20, No. 2 (1994), 27–50.

12 For a discussion of principle people inside the higher-circle policy elites who pursue US military domination of the world as their key agenda, see Peter Phillips, Bridget Thornton, and Celeste Vogler, "The Global Dominance Group: 9/11 Pre-Warnings & Election Irregularities in Context," Project Censored, May 2, 2010, http://projectcensored.org/the-global-dominance-group/.

13 Leslie Sklair, *The Transnational Capitalist Class* (Oxford, UK: Blackwell, 2001).

14 Ibid., 4–7.

15 William I. Robinson, *A Theory of Global Capitalism: Production, Class, and State in a Transnational World* (Baltimore: Johns Hopkins University Press, 2004).

16 Ibid., 155–56.

17 William K. Carroll, *The Making of a Transnational Capitalist Class: Corporate Power in the 21st Century* (London/New York: Zed Books, 2010).

18 *Handbook of Transnational Governance: Institutions & Innovations*, eds. Thomas Hale and David Held (Cambridge, UK and Malden, MA: Polity Press, 2011).

19 David Rothkopf, *Superclass: The Global Power Elite and the World They are Making* (New York: Farrar, Straus and Giroux, 2008).

20 Peter Dale Scott, *American War Machine: Deep Politics, the CIA Global Drug Connection, and the Road to Afghanistan* (Lanham, MD: Rowman & Littlefield, 2010). See also *Censored* story #22, "Wachovia Bank Laundered Money for Latin American Drug Cartels," *Censored 2013: Dispatches from the Media Revolution*, eds. Mickey Huff and Andy Lee Roth with Project Censored (New York: Seven Stories Press, 2012), 66–68.

21 Kroll and Dolan, "Forbes 2017 Billionaires List."

22 David Rothkopf, "Superclass," Public Address at the Carnegie Endowment for International Peace, April 9, 2008. A video of the event, broadcast by C-SPAN2, is online at https://www.c-span.org/video/?204428-1/superclass.

23   "World Economic Forum 2017," ed. Stéphanie Thomson, World Economic Forum, January 20, 2017, https://www.weforum.org/agenda/2017/01/davos-populism-global-ization-social-divides/.

24   Phillips, "A Relative Advantage."

25   William I. Robinson, *Global Capitalism and the Crisis of Humanity* (New York: Cambridge University Press, 2014).

26   "Tyler Durden," "Half of the Population of the World is Dirt Poor—and the Global Elite Want to Keep It That Way," ZeroHedge, November 23, 2016, http://www.zero-hedge.com/news/2016-11-23/half-population-world-dirt-poor-and-global-elite-want-keep-it-way.

27   William I. Robinson, "Global Capitalism and the Restructuring of Education: The Transnational Capitalist Class' Quest to Suppress Critical Thinking," *Social Justice* 43, No. 3 (2016), 1–24.

28   Homi Kharas, "The Unprecedented Expansion of the Global Middle Class: An Update," Brookings Institution, February 28, 2017, https://www.brookings.edu/research/the-unprecedented-expansion-of-the-global-middle-class-2/.

29   Ann M. Simmons, "On World Hunger Day, a Look at Why So Many People Don't Get Enough Food," *Los Angeles Times*, May 28, 2017, http://www.latimes.com/world/la-fg-global-world-hunger-day-20170528-story.html.

30   Chasen Turk, "15 World Hunger Statistics," Borgen Project, March 15, 2017, https://borgenproject.org/15-world-hunger-statistics/.

31   Ibid.

32   "GRAIN in 2016: Highlights of Our Activities," GRAIN, March 16, 2017, https://www.grain.org/article/entries/5681-grain-in-2016-highlights-of-our-activities.

33   "SIPRI Military Expenditure Database," Stockholm International Peace Research Institute, [2017], https://www.sipri.org/databases/milex.

34   "Military Expenditure by Country, in Constant (2015) US$m., 1988–1996," Stockholm International Peace Research Institute, 2017, https://www.sipri.org/sites/default/files/Milex-constant-2015-USD.pdf.

35   Dwight D. Eisenhower, "The Chance for Peace," April 16, 1953, online at the American Presidency Project, http://www.presidency.ucsb.edu/ws/index.php?pid=9819&st=every+gun+that+is+made&st1=#axzz1ZRmq4yT4.

36   Richard Norton-Taylor, "Global Armed Conflicts Becoming More Deadly, Major Study Finds," *Guardian*, May 20, 2015, https://www.theguardian.com/world/2015/may/20/armed-conflict-deaths-increase-syria-iraq-afghanistan-yemen.

37   "UN Refugee Agency: Record 65.6 Million People Displaced Worldwide," BBC News, June 19, 2017, http://www.bbc.com/news/world-40321287.

38   Samuel Stebbins and Thomas C. Frohlich, "20 Companies Profiting the Most from War," MSN Money, May 31, 2017, https://www.msn.com/en-us/money/companies/20-companies-profiting-the-most-from-war/ar-AAmTAzm#page=1.

39   Jonathan Turley, "Big Money behind War: The Military–Industrial Complex," Al Jazeera, January 11, 2014, http://www.aljazeera.com/indepth/opinion/2014/01/big-money-behind-war-military-industrial-complex-20141473026736533.html.

40   David Ray Griffin, *Unprecedented: Can Civilization Survive the CO_2 Crisis?* (Atlanta: Clarity Press, 2015).

41   Tess Riley, "Just 100 Companies Responsible for 71% of Global Emissions, Study Says," *Guardian*, July 10, 2017, https://www.theguardian.com/sustainable-business/2017/jul/10/100-fossil-fuel-companies-investors-responsible-71-global-emissions-cdp-study-climate-change.

42   Kirsten Zickfeld and Tyler Herrington, "The Time Lag between a Carbon Dioxide Emission and Maximum Warming Increases with the Size of the Emission," *Environmental Research Letters* 10, No. 3, http://iopscience.iop.org/article/10.1088/1748-9326/10/3/031001.

43   Griffin, *Unprecedented*, 34–79.

44   Ibid., 80–107.

45   Ibid., 118–33.

46   "*The Lancet* Commission on Pollution and Health," *Lancet*, October 17, 2017, http://www.thelancet.com/commissions/pollution-and-health.

47   Griffin, *Unprecedented*, 134–50; Jake Johnson, "Warning of Sixth Mass Extinction, Scientists Implore Global Action," Common Dreams, July 11, 2017, https://www.commondreams.org/news/2017/07/11/warning-sixth-mass-extinction-scientists-implore-global-action.

48   Todd Millay, "Climate Change Investing Heats Up," *Forbes*, December 19, 2016, https://www.forbes.com/sites/toddmillay/2016/12/19/climate-change-investing-heats-up/#f16c903213c8; and Barry Ritholtz, "Profit for Global Warming or Get Left Behind," Bloomberg View, February 24, 2014, https://www.bloomberg.com/view/articles/2014-02-24/profit-from-global-warming-or-get-left-behind.

49   Mark Nuttall, "Zero-Tolerance, Uranium and Greenland's Mining Future," *The Polar Journal* 3, No. 2 (December 18, 2013), http://www.tandfonline.com/doi/abs/10.1080/2154896X.2013.868089.

50   Water for All campaign, "Top 10 Reasons to Oppose Water Privatization," Public Citizen, undated, https://www.citizen.org/sites/default/files/top10-reasonstoopposewaterprivatization.pdf.

51   Portions of this chapter were published as Peter Phillips and Brady Osborne, "Exposing the Financial Core of the Transnational Capitalist Class," in *Censored 2014: Fearless Speech in Fateful Times*, eds. Mickey Huff and Andy Lee Roth with Project Censored (New York: Seven Stories Press, 2013), 313–30.

52   Stefania Vitali, James B. Glattfelder, and Stefano Battiston, "The Network of Global Corporate Control," *PLoS ONE* 6, No. 10 (October 26, 2011), http://www.plosone.org/article/info%3Adoi%2F10.1371%2Fjournal.pone.0025995; see also Censored story #6, "Small Network of Corporations Run the Global Economy," *Censored 2013: Dispatches from the Media Revolution*, eds. Mickey Huff and Andy Lee Roth with Project Censored (New York: Seven Stories Press, 2012): 69–70.

53   More details on this University of Zurich study, and the list of the top 25 of the 147 super-connected companies, is printed in full in *Censored 2013: Dispatches from the Media Revolution*, eds. Mickey Huff and Andy Lee Roth with Project Censored (New York: Seven Stories Press, 2012), 247–86.

54 "BlackRock Reports Full Year 2017 Diluted EPS of $30.23, or $22.60 as Adjusted," BlackRock, January 12, 2018, http://ir.blackrock.com/file/Index?KeyFile=391744442; PNC Financial Services Group from Pittsburgh holds 20.8 percent of BlackRock common shares; "BlackRock Reports Full Year 2017 Diluted EPS of $30.23, or $22.60 as Adjusted," BlackRock, January 12, 2018, http://ir.blackrock.com/file/Index?Key-File=391744442; PNC Financial Services Group from Pittsburgh holds 20.8 percent of BlackRock common shares.

55 Vitali, *et al.*, "Network of Global Corporate Control."

56 "Top Asset Management Firms," Banks around the World, 2016, updated January 10, 2018, http://www.relbanks.com/rankings/largest-asset-managers.

57 "BlackRock, Schedule 14A, 2015," US Securities and Exchange Commission, Washington, DC, 2015, https://www.sec.gov/Archives/edgar/data/1364742/000119312515135243/d891582ddef14a.htm.

58 Methods Note: Data for this chart was taken from Nasdaq.com for the Institutional Portfolios for each of the Giants. Full listings of all invested assets is only partially available for several of the Giants. There is enough information available to demonstrate sociologically the interlocking capital between the Giants.

59 Honor Whiteman, "How Coca-Cola Affects Your Body When You Drink It," Medical News Today, August 15, 2015, https://www.medicalnewstoday.com/articles/297600.php.

60 Sandra Laville, "Coca-Cola Increased Its Production of Plastic Bottles by a Billion Last Year, Says Greenpeace," *Guardian*, October 2, 2017, https://www.theguardian.com/environment/2017/oct/02/coca-cola-increased-its-production-of-plastic-bottles-by-a-billion-last-year-say-greenpeace.

61 Teresa Carey, "3 Eye-Opening Science-Based New Year's Resolutions That Could Help Everyone," PBS, December 29, 2017, https://www.pbs.org/newshour/science/3-eye-opening-science-based-new-years-resolutions-that-could-help-everyone.

62 See the Censored news cluster by Andy Lee Roth, "Iceland, the Power of Peaceful Revolution, and the Commons," in *Censored 2014: Fearless Speech in Fateful Times*, eds. Mickey Huff and Andy Lee Roth with Project Censored (New York: Seven Stories Press, 2013), 143–54, for coverage of Iceland as a notable exception to the international trend of banks not being held accountable for systemic misconduct.

63 Dylan Murphy, "Money Laundering and the Drug Trade: The Role of the Banks," Global Research, May 13, 2013, http://www.globalresearch.ca/money-laundering-and-the-drug-trade-the-role-of-the-banks/5334205.

64 Ibid.

65 Nomi Prins, All the Presidents' Bankers: The Hidden Alliances That Drive American Power (New York: Nation Books, 2014), 395.

66 Kylie MacLellan, compiler, and Matthew Tostevin, editor, "Factbox: Banks Drawn into Libor Rate-Fixing Scandal," Reuters, July 11, 2012, http://www.reuters.com/article/2012/07/11/us-banking-libor-panel-idUSBRE86A0P020120711.

67 "Barclays Fined for Attempts to Manipulate Libor Rates," BBC News, June 27, 2012, http://www.bbc.co.uk/news/business-18612279.

68   "CFTC Orders the Royal Bank of Scotland to Pay $85 Million Penalty for Attempted Manipulation of US Dollar ISDAFIX Benchmark Swap Rates," Press Release 7527-17, US Commodity Futures Trading Commission, February 3, 2017, http://www.cftc.gov/PressRoom/PressReleases/pr7527-17.

69   Matthew Leising, Lindsay Fortado, and Jim Brunsden, "Meet ISDAfix, the Libor Scandal's Sequel," *Bloomberg Businessweek*, April 18, 2013, http://www.businessweek.com/articles/2013-04-18/meet-isdafix-the-libor-scandals-sequel; and Matt Taibbi, "Everything is Rigged: The Biggest Price-Fixing Scandal Ever," *Rolling Stone*, April 25, 2013, http://www.rollingstone.com/politics/news/everything-is-rigged-the-biggest-financial-scandal-yet-20130425.

70   Matthew Leising, "Rate Benchmark Scandal Hits $570 Million in Fines as RBS Settles," Bloomberg, February 3, 2017, https://www.bloomberg.com/news/articles/2017-02-03/rbs-pays-85-million-to-settle-cftc-s-isdafix-manipulation-case.

71   Dan Margolies and Ross Kerber, "Vanguard Sued Again for 'Illegal Gambling' Investments," Reuters, April 8, 2010, http://www.reuters.com/article/2010/04/08/vanguard-lawsuit-idUSN0818833420100408.

72   Taibbi, "Everything is Rigged."

73   Sam Sacks, "Big League Drop Off in Banking Fines under Trump," District Sentinel, August 7, 2017, https://www.districtsentinel.com/big-league-drop-off-banking-fines-trump/.

74   Jill Treanor, "Barclays Bank and Former Bosses to Stand Trial in January 2019," *Guardian*, July 17, 2017, https://www.theguardian.com/business/2017/jul/17/barclays-bank-and-former-bosses-to-stand-trial-in-january-2019.

75   Yasha Levine, "Exposed: The Billionaire-Backed Group Strong-Arming Parents into Destroying Their Kids' Public Schools," AlterNet, April 26, 2013, http://www.alternet.org/education/exposed-billionaire-backed-group-strong-arming-parents-destroying-their-kids-public. On efforts to privatize public education, see also, Adam Bessie, "GERM Warfare: How to Reclaim the Education Debate from Corporate Occupation," in *Censored 2013: Dispatches from the Media Revolution*, eds. Mickey Huff and Andy Lee Roth with Project Censored (New York: Seven Stories Press, 2012), 271–96.

76   Phillips and Osborne, "Exposing the Financial Core."

77   Suzanna Andrews, "Larry Fink's $12 Trillion Shadow," *Vanity Fair*, March 2, 2010, http://www.vanityfair.com/news/2010/04/fink-201004.

78   Landon Thomas Jr., "At BlackRock, a Wall Street Rock Star's $5 Trillion Comeback," *New York Times*, September 15, 2016, https://www.nytimes.com/2016/09/18/business/dealbook/at-blackrock-shaping-the-shifts-in-power.html.

79   Michael J. de la Merced, "BlackRock to Acquire Stake in Barclays Unit," *New York Times*, June 11, 2009, http://www.nytimes.com/2009/06/12/business/global/12barclays.html.

80   Andrews, "Larry Fink's $12 Trillion Shadow."

81   Yves Smith, "Social Security Privatizer Larry Fink of Giant Asset Manager BlackRock is a Clinton Treasury Secretary in Waiting," Naked Capitalism, March 3, 2016, http://www.nakedcapitalism.com/2016/03/social-security-privatizer-larry-fink-of-giant-asset-manager-blackrock-is-clintons-treasury-secretary-in-waiting.html; David Dayen,

"Larry Fink and His BlackRock Team Poised to Take Over Hillary Clinton's Treasury Department," *Intercept*, March 2, 2016, https://theintercept.com/2016/03/02/larry-fink-and-his-blackrock-team-poised-to-take-over-hillary-clintons-treasury-department/.

82   Bloomberg News, "CalPERS Drops BlackRock as Manager of Apartment Portfolio," *Los Angeles Times*, October 4, 2010, http://articles.latimes.com/2010/oct/04/business/la-fi-calpers-blackrock-20101004.

83   Andrews, "Larry Fink's $12 Trillion Shadow."

84   Berkeley Lovelace Jr., "BlackRock Earnings Beat the Street; iShares ETFs Post Record Inflow," CNBC, April 19, 2017, http://www.cnbc.com/2017/04/19/blackrock-reports-2017-first-quarter-earnings-before-the-bell.html.

85   Zach Carter, "Wall Street is Even More Craven Than We Thought," Huffington Post, February 5, 2017, http://www.huffingtonpost.com/entry/jamie-dimon-donald-trump_us_589670cce4b09bd304bbb417.

86   Thomas, "At BlackRock, a Wall Street Rock Star's $5 Trillion Comeback."

87   "Laurence D. Fink" bio, Council on Foreign Relations, undated, https://www.cfr.org/experts/laurence-d-fink.

88   Laurence D. Fink and Maria Bartiromo, "CEO Speaker Series: It's a New World: So What Should we Do?" Council on Foreign Relations, February 29, 2012, https://www.cfr.org/event/ceo-speaker-series-its-new-world-so-what-should-we-do-laurence-d-fink-chairman-and-ceo.

89   "Laurence D. Fink Net Worth," The Richest, undated, http://www.therichest.com/celebnetworth/celebrity-business/men/laurence-d-fink-net-worth/.

90   "JPMorgan Chase & Co. Annual Report 2016," JPMorgan Chase & Co., April 4, 2017, https://www.jpmorganchase.com/corporate/annual-report/2016/.

91   Monica Langley, *Tearing Down the Walls: How Sandy Weill Fought His Way to the Top of the Financial World . . . and Then Nearly Lost It All* (New York: Simon & Schuster, 2003), 50.

92   Justin Walton, "Jamie Dimon's Success Story: Net Worth, Education & Top Quotes," Investopedia, April 4, 2016, http://www.investopedia.com/articles/investing/040416/jamie-dimons-success-story-net-worth-education-top-quotes-c-jpm.asp.

93   Patricia Crisafulli, *The House of Dimon: How JPMorgan's Jamie Dimon Rose to the Top of the Financial World* (Hoboken, NJ: John Wiley & Sons, 2009).

94   Ibid.

95   Ibid.; and Walton, "Jamie Dimon's Success Story."

96   "Jamie Dimon Net Worth," Celebrity Net Worth, undated, http://www.celebritynetworth.com/richest-businessmen/ceos/jamie-dimon-net-worth/.

97   Nick Allen, "President Barack Obama Has $1 Million Account with JPMorgan, Personal Wealth of up to $10 Million," *Telegraph*, May 16, 2012, http://www.telegraph.co.uk/news/worldnews/northamerica/usa/9268807/President-Barack-Obama-has-1-million-account-with-JPMorgan-personal-wealth-of-up-to-10-million.html.

98   Tracy Kitten, "JPMorgan Chase Fines Exceed $2 Billion," BankInfoSecurity, January 7, 2014, http://www.bankinfosecurity.com/chase-a-6356.

99   Anthony Noto, "JPMorgan Chase Pays Fine for Discriminating Against Minority Borrowers," New York Business Journal, January 18, 2017, http://www.bizjournals. com/newyork/news/2017/01/18/jpmorgan-chase-pays-fine-for-discriminating.html.

100   Philip Mattera, "JPMorgan Chase: Corporate Rap Sheet," Corporate Research Project, February 3, 2017, http://www.corp-research.org/jpmorganchase.

101   Ibid.

102   "CNBC Transcript: JPMorgan Chase Chairman & CEO Jamie Dimon Speaks with CNBC from the World Economic Forum in Davos Today," CNBC, January 18, 2017, http://www.cnbc.com/2017/01/18/cnbc-exclusive-cnbc-transcript-jpmorgan-chase-chairman-ceo-jamie-dimon-speaks-with-cnbc-from-the-world-economic-forum-in-davos-today.html.

103   "The Trilateral Commission: North American Group 2008," American Free Press, May 12, 2008, http://www.americanfreepress.net/html/trilateral_commission_attend-ee.html.

104   Andrew Gavin Marshall, "Meet the Elites Inside the $4 Trillion Global Powerhouse Bank of JP Morgan Chase," AlterNet, July 4, 2013, http://www.alternet.org/economy/ jp-morgan-chase-bank-4-trillion-global-powerhouse-meet-elites-charge.

105   Paul M. Barrett, "I, Banker," New York Times, October 29, 2009, http://www.nytimes. com/2009/11/01/books/review/Barrett-t.html.

106   Marshall, "Meet the Elites Inside the $4 Trillion Global Powerhouse Bank."

107   "Dodd–Frank Wall Street Reform and Consumer Protection Act," Investopedia, undated, http://www.investopedia.com/terms/d/dodd-frank-financial-regulatory-re-form-bill.asp.

108   Dealbook, "How Obama and Dimon Drifted Apart," New York Times, June 17, 2010, https://dealbook.nytimes.com/2010/06/17/how-obama-and-dimon-drifted-apart/.

109   Bonnie Kavoussi, "Jamie Dimon: 'It's a Free. Fucking. Country.'" Huffington Post, August 13, 2012, http://www.huffingtonpost.com/2012/08/13/jamie-dimon-free-fuck-ing-country_n_1772433.html.

110   "JPMorgan Chase & Co. Annual Report 2016."

111   "Barclaycard," Barclays, undated, https://www.home.barclays/about-barclays/history/ barclaycard.html.

112   "Barclays PLC Common Stock Historical Stock Prices," Nasdaq, updated March 12, 2018, http://www.nasdaq.com/symbol/bcs/historical.

113   "Welcome to Dumfries Academy," Dumfries Academy, undated, http://www.dum-friesacademy.org.

114   "About Us," Aviva, undated, https://www.aviva.com/about-us/.

115   "About FirstGroup," FirstGroup, undated, http://www.firstgroupplc.com/about-first-group.

116   "About," Westfield Corporation, undated, https://www.westfieldcorp.com/about.

117   Lynsey Barber, "Davos 2016: Who's Who at the World Economic Forum (and Who's Notably Absent)—From Leonardo DiCaprio to Travis Kalanick and George Osborne," City A.M., January 17, 2016, http://www.cityam.com/232514/davos-2016-whos-who-at-the-world-economic-forum-and-whos-notably-absent-from-leonar-do-dicaprio-to-travis-kalanick-and-george-osborne.

118 *The International Who's Who 2004* (London: Europa Publications, 2003), 1053.

119 Will Martin, "Barclays Boss: Bonuses Just Make Bankers 'Cut Corners,'" Business Insider, October 23, 2015, http://www.businessinsider.com/barclays-john-mcfarlane-attacks-bankings-bonus-culture-2015-10.

120 "John McFarlane, Chairman," Barclays, undated, https://www.home.barclays/about-barclays/leadership-team/john-mcfarlane.html.

121 Ruth Sunderland, "Bureaucracy-Bashing Barclays Chairman John McFarlane on Ousting Former Boss Antony Jenkins," This is Money, July 9, 2015, http://www.thisismoney.co.uk/money/news/article-3155239/CITY-INTERVIEW-Bureaucracy-bashing-Barclays-chairman-John-McFarlane-ousting-former-boss-Antony-Jenkins.html.

122 Martin Arnold, "City Grandees to Stay in the Chair at Barclays and Standard Life," *Financial Times*, March 8, 2017, https://www.ft.com/content/226b3a6a-0409-11e7-ace0-1ce02efodef9?mhq5j=e3.

123 Anjuli Davies and Andrew MacAskill, "Election Means 'New Game' of Brexit Negotiations for the City," Reuters, June 15, 2017, http://uk.reuters.com/article/uk-britain-eu-banks-idUKKBN1960RS.

124 "Executive Profile: James E. Staley," Bloomberg, undated, https://www.bloomberg.com/research/stocks/private/person.asp?personId=9377612&privcapId=323899.

125 "Barclays PLC: James E. Staley Appointed as Group Chief Executive," Barclays, October 28, 2015, https://newsroom.barclays.com/r/3249/barclays_plc__james_e__staley_appointed_as_group_chief.

126 Data for these listings came primarily from company webpages, annual proxy reports, Bloomberg.com, *Forbes*, and other corporate media reports.

127 Tim Geithner, "Remarks by Treasury Secretary Tim Geithner to the International Monetary Conference," US Department of the Treasury, June 6, 2011, https://www.treasury.gov/press-center/press-releases/Pages/tg1202.aspx.

128 Andrew Gavin Marshall, "It's Time to Expose Global Banking Elites at the International Monetary Conference," Occupy.com, May 6, 2014, http://www.occupy.com/article/its-time-expose-global-banking-elites-international-monetary-conference#sthash.B3RWJN0K.dpbs.

129 Andrew Gavin Marshall, "EXCLUSIVE: Leaked Documents from Secretive Meeting of Global Bankers at the 2013 International Monetary Conference (IMC)," AndrewGavinMarshall.com, March 6, 2014, https://andrewgavinmarshall.com/2014/03/06/exclusive-leaked-documents-from-secretive-meeting-of-global-bankers-at-the-2013-international-monetary-conference-imc/.

130 Jacob Pramuk, "Trump to Meet 'Frequently' with Blackstone's Schwarzman, Other Business Titans to Discuss Policy," CNBC, December 2, 2016, http://www.cnbc.com/2016/12/02/trump-to-meet-frequently-with-blackstones-schwarzman-other-business-titans-to-discuss-policy.html.

131 "Press Release—President-Elect Donald J. Trump Announces Travis Kalanick of Uber, Elon Musk of SpaceX and Tesla, and Indra Nooyi of PepsiCo to Join President's Strategic and Policy Forum," online at the American Presidency Project, December 14, 2016, http://www.presidency.ucsb.edu/ws/index.php?pid=119785.

132   Bob Bryan, "Warren Buffett, Jamie Dimon, and 11 Other US Corporate Titans Want Common Sense to Replace America's Worst Business Practices," Business Insider, July 21, 2016, http://www.businessinsider.com/buffett-dimon-titans-corporate-governance-letter-2016-7.

133   Sam Sacks, "Trump's Economic Council Implodes as White House Defends Fash," District Sentinel, August 16, 2017, https://www.districtsentinel.com/trumps-economic-council-implodes-white-house-defends-fash/.

134   David Gelles, Landon Thomas Jr., Andrew Ross Sorkin, and Kate Kelly, "Inside the C.E.O. Rebellion Against Trump's Advisory Councils," *New York Times*, August 16, 2017, https://www.nytimes.com/2017/08/16/business/trumps-council-ceos.html.

135   Matt Turner, "Here's the Memo Larry Fink, the Head of the World's Largest Investor, Just Sent to Staff about Trump's Council," Business Insider, August 16, 2017, http://www.businessinsider.com/larry-fink-blackrock-memo-trumps-council-2017-8.

136   "JPMorgan CEO Dimon's Memo on Trump to Employees," Fox Business, August 16, 2017, http://www.foxbusiness.com/markets/2017/08/16/jpmorgan-ceo-dimons-memo-on-trump-to-employees.html.

137   Clifford L. Staples, "The Business Roundtable and the Transnational Capitalist Class," in *Financial Elites and Transnational Business: Who Rules the World?*, eds. Georgina Murray and John Scott (Cheltenham, UK: Edward Elgar Publishing, 2012), 100–23.

138   See the Group of Thirty website, http://www.group30.org.

139   Andrew Gavin Marshall, "Global Power Project: The Group of Thirty and Its Methods of Financial Governance," Occupy.com, December 4, 2013, http://www.occupy.com/article/global-power-project-group-thirty-and-its-methods-financial-governance#sthash.4E6KwRTe.dpbs.

140   "Group of Thirty," Charity Navigator, June 1, 2017, https://www.charitynavigator.org/index.cfm?bay=search.summary&orgid=6009.

141   Ibid.

142   Abdlatif Al-Hamad and Philip Verleger Jr., "Oil and the Global Economy," Group of Thirty, October 2016, http://group30.org/publications/detail/678.

143   Data for these listings came primarily from company webpages, annual proxy reports, Bloomberg.com, *Forbes*, and other corporate media reports.

144   Kenneth Rogoff, "Giddy Markets and Grim Politics," Project Syndicate, January 8, 2018, https://www.project-syndicate.org/commentary/economic-growth-amid-political-uncertainty-by-kenneth-rogoff-2018-01.

145   "About," CFA Institute, undated, https://www.cfainstitute.org/pages/index.aspx.

146   Ibid.

147   Katrin Bennhold, "A Gathering of the Global Elite, Through a Woman's Eyes," *New York Times*, January 20, 2017, https://www.nytimes.com/2017/01/20/business/dealbook/world-economic-forum-davos-women-gender-inequality.html.

148   "Our Mission," World Economic Forum, undated, https://www.weforum.org/about/world-economic-forum.

149   "Annual Report 2015–2016," World Economic Forum, 2016, http://www3.weforum.org/docs/WEF_Annual_Report_2015-2016.pdf, 33.

150 Lewis Lapham, *The Agony of Mammon: The Imperial Global Economy Explains Itself to the Membership in Davos, Switzerland* (New York: Verso, 1998).

151 "Bilderberg Meeting 2017," Bilderberg Meetings, May 31, 2017, http://www.bilderberg-meetings.org/press-release.html.

152 Laurence H. Shoup, *Wall Street's Think Tank: The Council on Foreign Relations and the Empire of Neoliberal Geopolitics, 1976–2014* (New York: Monthly Review Press, 2015).

153 Ibid., 66.

154 "Who We Are: Global Board of Advisors," Council on Foreign Relations, undated, http://www.cfr.org/about/people/global_board_of_advisors.html.

155 Shoup, *Wall Street's Think Tank*, 162.

156 Ibid., 135.

157 Information for this section came from the Trilateral Commission website, http://trilateral.org/.

158 Hisanao Takase, "The Transnational Capitalist Class, the Trilateral Commission and the Case of Japan: Rhetorics and Realities," *Socialist Studies/Études socialistes* 10, No. 1 (Summer 2014), 86–110, https://www.socialiststudies.com/index.php/sss/article/download/23489/17374.

159 Paula J. Dobriansky, Andrzej Olechowski, Yukio Satoh, and Igor Yurgens, *Engaging Russia: A Return to Containment?* (Washington, DC: The Trilateral Commission, 2014). Synopsis at http://trilateral.org/file.showdirectory&list=Triangle-Papers.

160 *Seeking Opportunities in Crisis: Trilateral Cooperation in Meeting Global Challenges* (Washington, DC: The Trilateral Commission, 2009), http://trilateral.org/file/47.

161 *Tokyo 2000: The Annual Meeting of the Trilateral Commission* (Washington, DC: The Trilateral Commission, 2000), http://trilateral.org/file/67.

162 "IRELAND'S RICHEST 100; Fabulous Fortunes Shine on Nation's Wealthy, Famous," *Mirror* (London), March 22, 1999, reprinted at The Free Library, https://www.thefreelibrary.com/IRELAND%27S+RICHEST+100%3b+Fabulous+fortunes+shine+on+nation%27s+wealthy%2c...-a060401415.

163 Aleksei Gunter, "Estonia's Millionaires Club Grows," *Baltic Times*, April 11, 2002, https://www.baltictimes.com/news/articles/6238/.

164 Note that Net Worth Post consistently underreports real net worth.

165 "Top 10 Richest Politicians in Indonesia 2018," Viaset 1, undated, http://viasat1.net/top-10-richest-politicians-in-indonesia-2017/7/.

166 Portions of this chapter appeared as Peter Phillips, Ray McClintock, Melissa Carneiro, and Jacob Crabtree, "Twenty-First-Century Fascism: Private Military Companies in Service to the Transnational Capitalist Class," in *Censored 2016: Media Freedom on the Line*, eds. Mickey Huff and Andy Lee Roth with Project Censored (New York/Oakland: Seven Stories Press, 2015), 255–76.

167 David Vine, "Where in the World is the U.S. Military?" Politico, July/August 2015, http://www.politico.com/magazine/story/2015/06/us-military-bases-around-the-world-119321.

168 Nick Turse, "A Secret War in 135 Countries," TomDispatch, September 24, 2015, http://www.tomdispatch.com/blog/176048/; and Nick Turse, "The Stealth Expansion of a

Secret U.S. Drone Base in Africa," *Intercept*, October 21, 2015, https://theintercept.com/2015/10/21/stealth-expansion-of-secret-us-drone-base-in-africa/.

169 Donald C. Bolduc, Richard V. Puglisi, and Randall Kaailau, "The Gray Zone in Africa," *Small Wars Journal*, May 29, 2017, http://smallwarsjournal.com/jrnl/art/the-gray-zone-in-africa.

170 Manuel Perez-Rivas, "Bush Vows to Rid the World of 'Evil-Doers,'" CNN, September 16, 2001, http://edition.cnn.com/2001/US/09/16/gen.bush.terrorism/.

171 "Text: President Bush Addresses the Nation," *Washington Post*, September 20, 2001, http://www.washingtonpost.com/wp-srv/nation/specials/attacked/transcripts/bushaddress_092001.html.

172 Rothkopf, "Superclass," Public Address.

173 "Defence Against Terrorism Programme of Work (DAT POW)," North Atlantic Treaty Organization (NATO–OTAN), April 9, 2015, http://www.nato.int/cps/en/SID-EBFFE857-6607109D/natolive/topics_50313.htm.

174 "Summit Declaration on Defence Capabilities: Toward NATO Forces 2020," North Atlantic Treaty Organization (NATO–OTAN), May 20, 2012, http://www.nato.int/cps/en/SID-1CE3D0B6-393C986D/natolive/official_texts_87594.htm.

175 Glen Segell, "NATO's Policy in Africa: Initiated in Sudan, Continued in Libya," *Strategic Insights* 10, No. 3 (Winter 2011), 28–38, republished online at the Homeland Security Digital Library, https://www.hsdl.org/?view&did=792810.

176 Jonathan Masters, "The North Atlantic Treaty Organization (NATO)," Council on Foreign Relations, May 15, 2017, https://www.cfr.org/backgrounder/north-atlantic-treaty-organization-nato.

177 Johannes Stern, "NATO Expands Military Spending and Sends Thousands of Troops to Afghanistan," World Socialist Web Site, June 30, 2017, https://www.wsws.org/en/articles/2017/06/30/nato-j30.html.

178 Johannes Stern, "EU Establishes Military Headquarters," World Socialist Web Site, March 10, 2017, https://www.wsws.org/en/articles/2017/03/10/eujc-m10.html.

179 "Operations," Supreme Headquarters Allied Powers Europe (SHAPE) of the North Atlantic Treaty Organization (NATO–OTAN), undated, https://shape.nato.int/operations.

180 "NATO's Relations with Central Asia," North Atlantic Treaty Organization (NATO–OTAN), February 22, 2016, https://www.nato.int/cps/en/natohq/topics_107957.htm.

181 Michael R. Gordon, "The Anatomy of a Misunderstanding," *New York Times*, May 25, 1997, http://www.nytimes.com/1997/05/25/weekinreview/the-anatomy-of-a-misunderstanding.html.

182 For an expanded analysis of the history of US "global dominance," see Peter Phillips, Bridget Thornton, and Celeste Vogler, "The Global Dominance Group: 9/11 Pre-Warnings & Election Irregularities in Context," Project Censored, May 2, 2010, http://projectcensored.org/the-global-dominance-group/; and Peter Phillips, Bridget Thornton, and Lew Brown, "The Global Dominance Group and U.S. Corporate Media," *Censored 2007: 30th Anniversary Edition*, eds. Peter Phillips and Project Censored (New York/London/Melbourne/Toronto: Seven Stories Press, 2006), 303–33.

183   William I. Robinson and Jerry Harris, "Towards a Global Ruling Class? Globalization and the Transnational Capitalist Class," *Science & Society* 64, No. 1 (Spring 2000), 11–54.

184   John Pilger, *The New Rulers of the World, Updated Edition* (London/New York: Verso, 2003).

185   *The Global Economic Crisis: The Great Depression of the XXI Century*, eds. Michel Chossudovsky and Andrew Gavin Marshall (Montréal: Global Research Publishers, 2010).

186   Dennis Loo, *Globalization and the Demolition of Society* (Glendale, CA: Larkmead Press, 2011).

187   Andrew Kolin, *State Power and Democracy: Before and During the Presidency of George W. Bush* (New York: Palgrave MacMillan, 2011), 141.

188   Loo, *Globalization and the Demolition of Society*, 357.

189   Dana Priest and William M. Arkin, *Top Secret America: The Rise of the New American Security State* (New York: Little, Brown and Company, 2011).

190   Robert D. Blackwill, "Defending Vital U.S. Interests: Policy Prescriptions for Trump," *Foreign Policy*, January 25, 2017, http://foreignpolicy.com/2017/01/25/defending-vital-u-s-interests-policy-prescriptions-for-trump/.

191   "2016 Index of U.S. Military Strength: Threats to U.S. Vital Interests," The Heritage Foundation, 2016, http://index.heritage.org/military/2016/assessments/threats/.

192   Peter Dale Scott, *The American Deep State: Wall Street, Big Oil, and the Attack on U.S. Democracy* (London: Rowman & Littlefield, 2015).

193   Priest and Arkin, *Top Secret America*, 52.

194   Scott, *The American Deep State*, 30.

195   "History Since 1961," Atlantic Council, undated, http://www.atlanticcouncil.org/about/history.

196   "The Atlantic Council of the United States," Charity Navigator, June 1, 2017, https://www.charitynavigator.org/index.cfm?bay=search.summary&orgid=5395.

197   "Updated List of Atlantic Council Donors," Think Tank Watch, November 11, 2015, http://www.thinktankwatch.com/2015/11/the-donors-of-atlantic-council.html.

198   David Barno and Nora Bensahel, *The Future of the Army: Today, Tomorrow, and the Day After Tomorrow* (Washington, DC: Atlantic Council/Brent Scowcroft Center on International Security, September 2016), http://www.atlanticcouncil.org/publications/reports/the-future-of-the-army.

199   Madeleine K. Albright and Stephen J. Hadley, *Middle East Strategy Task Force: Final Report of the Co-Chairs* (Washington, DC: Atlantic Council, November 2016), http://mest.atlanticcouncil.org/final-report/.

200   Ibid., 54.

201   Note: While 28 countries are represented on the Atlantic Council, the 35 members of the Extended Executive Committee are predominately US citizens (28). This seems to reflect the heavy role the US plays as the worldwide protector of the Global Power Elite's investment capital.

202   Data for these listings came primarily from company webpages, annual proxy reports, Bloomberg.com, *Forbes*, and other corporate media reports.

203 Kurt Eichenwald, "Drexel Suit to Recover Bonus Pay," *New York Times*, February 12, 1992, http://www.nytimes.com/1992/02/12/business/drexel-suit-to-recover-bonus-pay.html.

204 Emily Smith, "PR Mogul Richard Edelman Splitting from Wife of 28 Years," Page Six, March 31, 2015, https://pagesix.com/2015/03/31/pr-mogul-richard-edelman-splitting-from-wife-of-28-years/.

205 Lisa Graves, "Which Millionaire Fat Cats are Backing the American Action Network's Ads Attacking Sen. Feingold?" PR Watch, September 2, 2010, https://www.prwatch.org/news/2010/09/9407/which-millionaire-fat-cats-are-backing-american-action-networks-ads-attacking-sen-.

206 "The 2007 Wealth List," *Washington Life Magazine*, June 1, 2007, http://washington-life.com/2007/06/01/the-2007-wealth-list/2/.

207 "About ASIS," ASIS International, undated, https://www.asisonline.org/footer-pages/about-asis/.

208 Graves, "Which Millionaire Fat Cats"; Christian Davenport, "Companies Can Spend Millions on Security Measures to Keep Executives Safe," *Washington Post*, June 6, 2014, http://www.washingtonpost.com/business/economy/companies-can-spend-millions-on-security-measures-to-keep-executives-safe/2014/06/06/5f500350-e802-11e3-afc6-a1dd9407abcf_story.html; and John Whitehead, "Private Police: Mercenaries for the American Police State," OpEd News, March 4, 2015, http://www.opednews.com/articles/Private-Police-Mercenarie-by-John-Whitehead-Police-Abuse-Of-Power_Police-Brutality_Police-Coverup_Police-State-150304-539.html.

209 Luke McKenna and Robert Johnson, "A Look at the World's Most Powerful Mercenary Armies," Business Insider, February 26, 2012, http://www.businessinsider.com/bi-mercenary-armies-2012-2.

210 William Langewiesche, "The Chaos Company," *Vanity Fair*, March 18, 2014, www.vanityfair.com/news/business/2014/04/g4s-global-security-company.

211 Shawn Engbrecht, *America's Covert Warriors: Inside the World of Private Military Contractors* (Dulles, VA: Potomac Books, 2011), 18.

212 Steve Fainaru, *Big Boy Rules: America's Mercenaries Fighting in Iraq* (Boston: Da Capo Press, 2008), 24.

213 Moshe Schwartz and Joyprada Swain, "Department of Defense Contractors in Afghanistan and Iraq: Background and Analysis," Congressional Research Service, May 13, 2011, https://www.fas.org/sgp/crs/natsec/R40764.pdf.

214 David Francis, "U.S. Troops Replaced by an Outsourced Army in Afghanistan," Fiscal Times, May 10, 2013, http://www.thefiscaltimes.com/Articles/2013/05/10/US-Troops-Replaced-by-an-Outsourced-Army-in-Afghanistan.

215 P.W. Singer, *Corporate Warriors: The Rise of the Privatized Military Industry* (New Delhi: Manas Publications, 2005), 45.

216 Jeremy Scahill, *Blackwater: The Rise of the World's Most Powerful Mercenary Army* (New York: Nation Books, 2007), 45.

217 James Ridgeway, "The Secret History of Hurricane Katrina," *Mother Jones*, August 28, 2009, http://www.motherjones.com/environment/2009/08/secret-history-hurricane-katrina.

218 "Iraq has become the largest single gathering of private armed men in recent history." Quoted from Robert Young Pelton, *Licensed to Kill: Hired Guns in the War on Terror* (New York: Crown Publishers, 2006), 343.

219 Spenser S. Hsu, Victoria St. Martin, and Keith L. Alexander, "Four Blackwater Guards Found Guilty in 2007 Iraq Shootings of 31 Unarmed Civilians," *Washington Post*, October 22, 2014, http://www.washingtonpost.com/world/national-security/verdict-expected-in-blackwater-shooting-case/2014/10/22/5a488258-59fc-11e4-bd61-346aee-66ba29_story.html; and Matt Apuzzo, "Blackwater Guards Found Guilty in 2007 Iraq Killings," *New York Times*, October 22, 2014, http://www.nytimes.com/2014/10/23/us/blackwater-verdict.html.

220 Jessica Corbett, "Court Throws Out Blackwater Guards' Sentences for 2007 Baghdad Massacre," Common Dreams, August 4, 2017, https://www.commondreams.org/news/2017/08/04/court-throws-out-blackwater-guards-sentences-2007-baghdad-massacre.

221 Spencer Ackerman, "Blackwater 3.0: Rebranded 'Academi' Wants Back in Iraq," *Wired*, December 12, 2011, http://www.wired.com/2011/12/blackwater-rebrand-academi/; and "Blackwater Name Change: Private Security Firm Switches Name Again to Academi from Xe," Huffington Post, December 12, 2011, http://www.huffingtonpost.com/2011/12/12/blackwater-name-change-private-security-firm-academi_n_1143789.html.

222 "Company Overview of Constellis Group Inc.," Bloomberg, 2015, updated March 14, 2018, http://www.bloomberg.com/research/stocks/private/snapshot.asp?privcapId=237562172.

223 Jeremy Scahill, "Blackwater Founder Erik Prince, the Brother of Betsy DeVos, is Secretly Advising Trump," *Democracy Now!*, January 18, 2017, https://www.democracynow.org/2017/1/18/scahill_blackwater_founder_erik_prince_the.

224 Jake Johnson, "'Literal Colonialism': Blackwater Founder Calls for 'American Viceroy' to Rule Afghanistan," Common Dreams, June 2, 2017, https://www.commondreams.org/news/2017/06/02/literal-colonialism-blackwater-founder-calls-american-viceroy-rule-afghanistan.

225 "The Largest Company You've Never Heard of: G4S and the London Olympics," *International Business Times*, August 6, 2012, http://www.ibtimes.com/largest-company-youve-never-heard-g4s-london-olympics-739232.

226 McKenna and Johnson, "A Look at the World's Most Powerful Mercenary Armies."

227 "G4S plc (GFS: London Stock Exchange)," Bloomberg, updated March 14, 2018, http://www.bloomberg.com/research/stocks/financials/financials.asp?ticker=GFS:L-N&dataset=incomeStatement&period=A&currency=US%20Dollar.

228 Langewiesche, "The Chaos Company."

229 Ibid.

230 "G4S Admits It Guards Dakota Pipeline as Protesters Get Attacked," Telesur, September 6, 2016, http://www.telesurtv.net/english/news/G4S-Admits-it-Guards-Dakota-Pipeline-as-Protesters-Get-Attacked-20160906-0036.html.

231 Corporate Watch's list of major corporate investors in G4S includes, but is not limited to, BlackRock, Prudential, UBS, Vanguard, Barclays, State Street, Allianz,

JPMorgan Chase, Credit Suisse, and FMR. See "G4S Company Profile," under the subheading "G4S: Finances & Investors," Corporate Watch, September 10, 2012, http://www.corporatewatch.org/company-profiles/g4s-finances-investors. Although Bank of America is not listed as an investor, it is a G4S client.

232   Phillips and Osborne, "Exposing the Financial Core."

233   Robinson, *Global Capitalism and the Crisis of Humanity*, "Policing Global Capitalism," 158–213.

234   Ibid., 163–65.

235   See, for example, Richard Godfrey, et al., "The Private Military Industry and Neoliberal Imperialism: Mapping the Terrain," *Organization* 21, No. 1 (January 3, 2013), 106–25.

236   In 1956, C. Wright Mills coined the term "interlocking directorate" to refer to "the community of interest, the unification of outlook and policy, that prevails among the propertied class." See Mills, *The Power Elite*, 123; for a contemporary application of Mills's concept, see Phillips and Soeiro, "The Global 1 Percent Ruling Class Exposed," http://projectcensored.org/the-global-1-exposing-the-transnational-ruling-class/.

237   Laura A. Dickinson, *Outsourcing War and Peace: Preserving Public Values in a World of Privatized Foreign Affairs* (New Haven, CT: Yale University Press, 2011).

238   Portions of this chapter appeared as Peter Phillips, with Ratonya Coffee, Robert Ramirez, Mary Schafer, and Nicole Tranchina, "Selling Empire, War, and Capitalism: Public Relations Propaganda Firms in Service to the Transnational Capitalist Class," in *Censored 2017: Fortieth Anniversary Edition*, eds. Mickey Huff and Andy Lee Roth with Project Censored (New York/Oakland: Seven Stories Press, 2016), 285–315.

239   "PWC's 2013 Entertainment Report," *Hollywood Reporter*, 2013, http://www.hollywoodreporter.com/sites/default/files/custom/Documents/PWC_chart_rev21012x-5711px.pdf.

240   Ben H. Bagdikian, *The New Media Monopoly* (Boston: Beacon Press, 2004).

241   Lee Artz, *Global Entertainment Media: A Critical Introduction* (Chichester, UK: John Wiley and Sons, 2015), 71.

242   "Bertelsmann at a Glance," Bertelsmann, undated, https://www.bertelsmann.com/company-profile/.

243   Edward L. Bernays, *Public Relations* (Norman, OK: University of Oklahoma Press, 1952), 1.

244   Ibid., 160.

245   Bernays wasn't beyond helping corporations illicitly attain power and profits. He helped United Fruit engineer the overthrow of the government of Guatemala in 1954 and aided American Tobacco in marketing smoking to women by touting cigarettes as great for weight loss and self-liberation. See: Larry Tye, *The Father of Spin: Edward L. Bernays & the Birth of Public Relations* (New York: Crown Publishers, 1998).

246   Fraser P. Seitel, *The Practice of Public Relations, Eighth Edition* (Upper Saddle River, NJ: Prentice Hall, 2001), 9.

247   *World Book Encyclopedia* (Chicago: World Book, 2015), s.v. "propaganda."

248 Nancy Hanover, "*The Mighty Wurlitzer: How the CIA Played America*," World Socialist Web Site, August 17, 2015, http://www.wsws.org/en/articles/2015/08/17/wur1-a17.html.

249 For an early history of state propaganda, see Jacquie L'Etang, "State Propaganda and Bureaucratic Intelligence: The Creation of Public Relations in 20th Century Britain," *Public Relations Review* 24, No. 4 (1998), 413–41.

250 David L. Robb, *Operation Hollywood: How the Pentagon Shapes and Censors the Movies* (New York: Prometheus Books, 2004).

251 Nima Shirazi, "Revisiting 'Argo,' Hollywood's CIA-Supported Propaganda Fable," AlterNet, April 12, 2016, http://www.alternet.org/grayzone-project/revisiting-argo-hollywoods-cia-supported-propaganda-fable.

252 Tom Secker and Matthew Alford, "Documents Expose How Hollywood Promotes War on Behalf of the Pentagon, CIA and NSA," July 4, 2017, INSURGE intelligence, https://medium.com/insurge-intelligence/exclusive-documents-expose-direct-us-military-intelligence-influence-on-1-800-movies-and-tv-shows-36433107c307.

253 Douglas Kellner, "Media Propaganda and Spectacle in the War on Iraq: A Critique of U.S. Broadcasting Networks," *Cultural Studies<=>Critical Methodologies* 4, No. 3 (August 2004), 329–38.

254 James Bamford, "The Man Who Sold the War," *Rolling Stone*, November 2005, republished online by Common Dreams, November 18, 2005, http://commondreams.org/headlines05/1118-10.htm.

255 Johan Carlisle, "Public Relationships: Hill & Knowlton, Robert Gray, and the CIA," *CovertAction Quarterly* 44 (Spring 1993), http://whatreallyhappened.com/RANCHO/LIE/HK/HK2.html.

256 Ibid.

257 David L. Altheide and Jennifer N. Grimes, "War Programming: The Propaganda Project and the Iraq War," *Sociological Quarterly* 46, No. 4 (Autumn 2005), 617–43; Two members of the Atlantic Council's expanded executive committee, Paula J. Dobriansky and Zalmay M. Khalilzad, were participants in the Project for a New American Century.

258 David W. Guth, "Black, White, and Shades of Gray: The Sixty-Year Debate Over Propaganda versus Public Diplomacy," *Journal of Promotion Management* 14, No. 3–4 (December 2008), 309–25.

259 Dave Gelders and Øyvind Ihlen, "Government Communication about Potential Policies: Public Relations, Propaganda or Both?" *Public Relations Review* 36, No. 1 (March 2010), 59–62.

260 "Media & PR Archive," Corporate Watch, undated, https://corporatewatch.org/categories/media-pr.

261 Ryszard Lawniczak, "Public Relations Role in a Global Competition 'to Sell' Alternative Political and Socio-Economic Models of Market Economy," *Public Relations Review* 33, No. 4 (November 2007), 377–86.

262 Edward S. Herman and Noam Chomsky, *Manufacturing Consent: The Political Economy of the Mass Media* (New York: Pantheon Books, 1988).

263 Edward S. Herman, "Still Manufacturing Consent: The Propaganda Model at Thirty," in *Censored 2018: Press Freedoms in a "Post-Truth" World*, eds. Andy Lee Roth and Mickey Huff with Project Censored (New York/Oakland/London: Seven Stories Press, 2017), 209–23.

264 Noam Chomsky, *Media Control, Second Edition* (New York: Seven Stories Press (Open Media Series), 2002).

265 Unless specifically cited, all data about the big three PRP firms was collected from the firms' websites, Bloomberg.com, and http://littlesis.org.

266 Corporate Watch UK did a profile on Ogilvy & Mather in July 2002. They charged Ogilvy & Mather with greenwashing for BP and Ford's corporate pollution. That report is online at https://corporatewatch.org/content/ogilvy-mather-worldwide-overview.

267 Arjun Kharpal, "Davos Elite Didn't Predict Brexit and Trump Because They're in a 'Bubble,' CEO of World's Largest Ad Agency Says," CNBC, January 17, 2017, https://www.cnbc.com/2017/01/17/davos-elite-in-bubble-so-didnt-predict-brexit-trump-wpp-martin-sorrell.html.

268 "Political and Social," Kantar TNS, undated, http://www.tnsglobal.com/what-we-do/political-and-social.

269 "Public Relations," GPG, undated, http://gpg.com/services/.

270 Homepage, Sudler and Hennessey, 2017, http://www.sudler.com/.

271 "About Us," Hill+Knowlton Strategies, undated, http://www.hkstrategies.com/about/.

272 Richard Gale and Gary Null, "Monsanto's Sealed Documents Reveal the Truth behind Roundup's Toxicological Dangers," Progressive Radio Network, September 11, 2015, http://prn.fm/monsantos-sealed-documents-reveal-the-truth-behind-round-ups-toxicological-dangers-richard-gale-and-gary-null/.

273 Sheldon Rampton and John Stauber, "ConsumerFreedom.org: Tobacco Money Takes on Activist Cash," *PR Watch* 9, No. 1 (2002), 7–8, https://www.prwatch.org/files/pdfs/prwatch/prwv9n1.pdf.

274 Laura Miller, "Global Climate Coalition Melts Down," *PR Watch*, February 27, 2002, http://www.prwatch.org/spin/2002/02/1061/global-climate-coalition-melts-down.

275 "PR Watch Launches the 'Impropaganda Review,'" *PR Watch* 9, No. 1 (2002), 8, https://www.prwatch.org/files/pdfs/prwatch/prwv9n1.pdf.

276 Stephen Adams and Daniel Capparelli, "Knowing When to Quit: Assessing the Nairobi WTO Ministerial," Global Counsel, January 12, 2016, https://www.global-counsel.co.uk/analysis/insight/knowing-when-quit-assessing-nairobi-wto-ministerial.

277 Ray Eldon Hiebert, "Public Relations and Propaganda in Framing the Iraq War: A Preliminary Review," *Public Relations Review* 29, No. 3 (September 2003): 243–55.

278 Megan R. Wilson, "Feds Shelling Out Billions to Public Relations Firms," The Hill, December 8, 2015, http://thehill.com/business-a-lobbying/business-a-lobbying/262387-feds-shelling-out-billions-to-public-relations-firms.

279 Adam Andrzejewski and Tom Coburn, "The Department of Self-Promotion: How Federal Agency PR Spending Advances Their Interests Rather Than the Public Interest, Fiscal Years 2007–2014: Oversight Study," Open the Books, November 2015,

http://www.openthebooks.com/openthebooks_oversight_report_-_the_department_of_self-promotion_federal_public_relations/.

280   Laughlin Marinaccio & Owens is a privately-owned PRP company based in Arlington, VA. Their clients include the US Department of Homeland Security, Coast Guard Reserve, Army National Guard, Air National Guard, Military Officers Association of America, American Psychological Association, Avis Budget Group, Advantage Rent A Car, Cruise Lines International Association, CRDF Global,* U.S. Edelman Financial Services, Evermay Wealth Management, First Virginia Community Bank, George Washington University, Johns Hopkins University, Marriott International, and Associated General Contractors of America.

281   US House of Representatives, Committee on Government Reform, Minority Staff Special Investigations Division, "Federal Public Relations Spending," January 2005, http://www.savetheinternet.com/sites/default/files/resources/pr_spending_doubles_under_bush.pdf.

282   Carlisle, "Public Relationships: Hill & Knowlton, Robert Gray, and the CIA."

283   Ibid.

284   Noah Shachtman, "U.S. Spies Buy Stake in Firm That Monitors Blogs, Tweets," *Wired*, October 19, 2009, http://www.wired.com/dangerroom/2009/10/exclusive-us-spies-buy-stake-in-twitter-blog-monitoring-firm/; and Noah Shachtman, interview by Amy Goodman and Juan González, "CIA Invests in Software Firm Monitoring Blogs, Twitter," *Democracy Now!*, October 22, 2009, http://www.democracynow.org/2009/10/22/cia_invests_in_software_firm_monitoring.

285   Sarah Lazare, "Meet the Corporate PR Firm Hired to Sell a Murderous Foreign Regime to the American Public," AlterNet, April 15, 2016, http://www.alternet.org/world/meet-corporate-pr-firm-hired-sell-murderous-foreign-regime-american-public.

286   "Quebec Law and Exceptions," Coalition Poids (Quebec Coalition on Weight-Related Problems), undated, http://www.cqpp.qc.ca/en/advertising-to-children/quebec-law.

287   Rupert Neate, "World's Richest 500 See Their Wealth Increase by $1tn This Year," *Guardian*, December 27, 2017, https://www.theguardian.com/inequality/2017/dec/27/worlds-richest-500-see-increased-their-wealth-by-1tn-this-year.

288   Ibid.

289   Facundo Alvaredo, et. al., *The World Inequality Report 2018* (Paris: World Inequality Lab, 2017), http://wir2018.wid.world.

---

* CRDF Global is an independent nonprofit organization that promotes international scientific and technical collaboration through grants, technical resources, training and services. CRDF Global is based in Arlington, VA, with offices in Moscow, Russia; Kyiv, Ukraine; Almaty, Kazakhstan; and Jordan. Funders include the Department of Defense, Homeland Security, USAID, US Department of Energy, SRI, Bechtel, UK Ministry of Defense, US State Department; the Ford, Carnegie, MacArthur, Soros, and Gates Foundations; and research institutes for Qatar, Saudi Arabia, and Kuwait. See "Who We Are," CRDF Global, undated, http://www.crdfglobal.org/about-us.

290   Pope Francis, "Message of Pope Francis to the Executive Chairman of the World Economic Forum on the Occasion of the Annual Meeting at Davos-Klosters (Switzerland)," The Holy See, January 17, 2014, https://w2.vatican.va/content/francesco/en/messages/pont-messages/2014/documents/papa-francesco_20140117_messaggio-wef-davos.html.

291   Cara Buckley, "Upper East Side Protest March Makes House Calls," *New York Times*, October 11, 2011, https://cityroom.blogs.nytimes.com/2011/10/11/upper-east-side-protest-march-makes-house-calls/.

292   Paul Street, *They Rule: The 1% vs. Democracy* (New York/Abingdon, UK: Routledge, 2014), 177.

293   Robert Reich, "The First Amendment Upside Down: Why We Must Occupy Democracy," Common Dreams, November 24, 2011, http://robertreich.org/post/13163087845.

294   "Annual Report 2016–2017," World Economic Forum, September 12, 2017, https://www.weforum.org/reports/annual-report-2016-2017.

295   Mary Ann Glendon, *A World Made New: Eleanor Roosevelt and the Universal Declaration of Human Rights* (New York: Random House, 2001).

296   The use of the term "man" was strongly debated in 1947. Eleanor Roosevelt felt that the term in the English language meant both men and women.

297   "Universal Declaration of Human Rights," included in the International Religious Freedom Report 2008, U.S. Department of State (reproducing the Declaration issued as Resolution 217(A)(III) of the United Nations General Assembly, December 10, 1948), https://www.state.gov/j/drl/rls/irf/2008/108544.htm.

298   Robert B. Reich, *Saving Capitalism: For the Many, Not the Few* (New York: Vintage Books, 2015).

INDEX

Manhattan Partners, 258

Manhattan School of Music, 249

Manufacturers Hanover Ltd., 117

Manufacturing Council, 157

Manulife Finance (Delaware), 85

Marathon Oil, 93, 283

Marine Corps Reserve, 244

Markle Task Force on National Security in the Information Age, 210

Marriott Hotels, 283, 293

Mars (chocolate bar), 283

Marsh & McLennan Companies, 83, 90 (See also: Marsh and McLennan Companies)

Marshall, Andrew Gavin, 151, 164

Marshalls, 283

Martineau, François, 65, 120

Martin Marietta, 111

Maryland National Bank, 88

Mascher, Christof, 64, 120

MasterCard, 111, 283, 289, 293 (See also: MasterCard Worldwide)

Match.com, 289

Mathieu, Michel, 64, 120-121

Mattel, 289

Maughan, Deryck Charles, 66, 121

Maurer, Peter, 219

Maus Frères SA, 147

Maxim, 289

Maxwell House, 283

May, Thomas J., 65, 121-122

Mayo Clinic, 103

Mazda, 207, 283 (See also: Mazda Motors America)

MBNA Corp., 88

McAdam, Lowell, 154

McAfee, 233

MCap Fund Advisors, 175

McBride, Patrick, 258

McCombs, Red, 257

McConnell Valdes llp, 91

McDonald's, 283

McFarlane, John, 66, 79-82, 122, 149

McGraw-Hill, 283

McK. Henderson, Brian C., 248-249

Mckinsey & Co., 85, 106, 136, 173, 239 (See also: McKinsey & Company, McKinsey Advisory Council)

McLarty Associates, 239

McLeodUSA, 87

McMillon, Doug, 152

McNabb, F. William, III, 69, 122, 154 (See also: McNabb, Bill)

McNerney, Jim, 152

Med 4 Home (respiratory), 289

MEDEF, 94, 116, 123 (See also: Medef)

Media.NYC.2020, 269

Mediaset, 209

Médica France SA, 101

Medicinema Enterprises Ltd., 92

Mediterranean Investors Group, 238

MedStar Health, 84

MedTech Innovation Partners AG, 101

Medtronic, 103

Meeschaert Rousselle, 116

Mehta, Hansa, 307

Menhaden Capital plc, 92

Menkul Degerler A.S., 106

Mercedes-Benz, 283, 293

Mercer, 90

Merck, 87, 283 (See also: Merck & Co.)

Merisant Company, 97

Merkel, Angela, 144

Merkley & Partners, 280

Merrill Lynch, 37, 39, 40, 41, 42, 43, 45, 46, 47, 48, 49, 50, 51, 65, 71, 85, 87, 88, 95, 119, 121, 124, 127, 133, 136, 140, 150, 171, 178, 187, 248

(See also: Bank of Merrill Lynch, Bank of America Merrill Lynch Preferred Capital Trust IV, Merrill Lynch & Co., Merrill Lynch Europe, Merrill Lynch International)

Merrimack Pharmaceuticals, 293

Metropolitan Investments, 237

Metropolitan Museum of Art, 106

Metrowerks Corporation, 146

Metzler Bank, 205

Mevion Medical Systems, 179, 213

Mexico Institute, 208

MGM Mirage Resort & Casino, 293

Microsoft, 39, 40, 41, 42, 43, 44, 45, 46, 47

Middle East Strategy Task Force, 235

Mildstorm Group, 125

Military Advisory Board for CNA's National Security and the Threat of Climate Change project, 243

Military Leadership Diversity Commission, 91

Milken, Michael, 237

Miller, Judith A., 249

MillerCoors (beer), 283, 289

Mills, C. Wright, 9, 16, 22-23

Mills, Cheryl, 66, 122-123

Milstein, Howard, 304

Ministerio de Comercio Exterior y Turismo (Peru), 291

Ministry of Finance, 210

Ministry of Industry, 92

Ministry of Justice, 88

Ministry of Labour, 92

Minnesota State Lottery, 287

Mirant Corporation, 90

Mirtchev, Alexander V., 249